Puzzled?!

An Introduction to Philosophizing

Puzzled?!

An Introduction to Philosophizing

RICHARD KENNETH ATKINS

Hackett Publishing Company, Inc.
Indianapolis/Cambridge

For further information, please address
 Hackett Publishing Company, Inc.
 P.O. Box 44937
 Indianapolis, Indiana 46244-0937

 www.hackettpublishing.com

Cover design by Božanka Kiprovska-Atkins
Interior design by Laura Clark
Composition by Aptara, Inc.

Library of Congress Cataloging-in-Publication Data
Atkins, Richard Kenneth.
 Puzzled?! : an introduction to philosophizing/Richard Kenneth Atkins.
  pages cm
 Includes bibliographical references and index.
 ISBN 978-1-62466-365-9 (pbk.)—ISBN 978-1-62466-366-6 (cloth)
 1. Philosophy—Introductions. I. Title.
 BD21.A87 2015
 100—dc23

                                                    2014034685

The paper used in this publication meets the minimum requirements of
American National Standard for Information Sciences—Permanence of
Paper for Printed Library Materials, ANSI Z39.48–1984.

                                    ∞

For Octavia and Augustin

All author proceeds from *Puzzled?!* are donated to the non-profit organization World Wide Hearing, about which readers can learn more at www.wwhearing.org.

CONTENTS

ACKNOWLEDGMENTS

In writing a book of this nature, it's hard to resist the temptation to thank everyone who has taught me anything about philosophy. And I do thank them, for this book is the outcome of many years of philosophical study and of many hours of philosophical conversation. There are two people, however, without whose assistance the very act of writing this book would never have come to pass. Foremost among them is my mother-in-law, who dutifully took care of my young children, prepared meals, and helped around the house while I sat hunched over my desk writing this. Without the time she afforded me to concentrate on this book—not to mention a number of other essays—I would have never been able to put fingertip to keyboard and see it to completion.

The second person is my wife. Without her support I wouldn't have even had a desk at which to write. Moreover, although she would be the first to admit that philosophy is not among her interests, she always listens politely when I start droning on about it. And she hasn't minded too much when I stare at her blankly while pondering a philosophical problem.

A number of other people have helped to bring this book into its current form. The ones I feel worst for are my former students at Fordham University, New York University, Iona College, and Gateway New York, all of whom suffered through my frequently blundering attempts to clearly explain the ideas contained herein. This book is a lot less blundering because of them.

Five people read various chapters of this book and rescued me from numerous errors. They are Eoin O'Connell, Greg Lynch, John T. F. Mumm, Brian Rak, and an anonymous reviewer for Hackett. I have greatly appreciated their feedback and this book has been much improved as a result. Of course, any mistakes found herein are my responsibility alone.

Lastly, I wish to thank Brian Rak, Laura Clark, and Hackett Publishing Company for supporting this project. Brian and Laura have been wonderful guides in bringing it to press, and I could not be more pleased.

PREFACE

This book is an introduction to philosophizing. It is intended for those who have no or little exposure to philosophical inquiry. It is designed to illustrate the practice of philosophizing by showing how many of the greatest minds in history have grappled with puzzling philosophical arguments.

I hope that you, dear reader, will get a sense of the complexity of philosophical puzzles and the creativity of philosophers in dealing with them. Philosophy is not just a bunch of theories cobbled together and mutually at odds. It is an attempt to deal with extremely challenging and subtle intellectual problems. Over the last two and a half millennia, philosophers have made slow but steady progress in addressing those problems, as I hope this book shows. To be certain, some of the proposals made have been dead ends, but that is part of intellectual progress. Sometimes you have to know what is wrong to figure out what is right.

I also hope that you will come to a basic understanding of the art and science of philosophizing. The word "philosophizing" is sometimes used in a pejorative way, but the person who uses the word pejoratively reveals far more about himself than about philosophy. Specifically, he reveals an aversion to clear, concise, and creative thought. There can be little doubt that philosophizing is a rigorous and exacting endeavor. As we shall see, much hinges on making important distinctions and grasping the linkages among different concepts. Yet philosophy isn't just about making distinctions. Philosophizing is also a creative endeavor. Philosophers create arguments. They develop novel concepts and theories. Philosophers ask us to see the world in a different light. They help us slough off the coil of habit and encourage us to think about the world anew.

INTRODUCTION

We're all passionate about something. For some of us it's music. For others it's movies. Or novels. Or history. Or religion, politics, public service, charity, art, or what have you. Whatever the case is for you, whatever you are passionate about, for me it has always been philosophy. Always, that is, since I was sixteen.

It was then that a nerdy, gangly, and, quite frankly, lonely boy wandered into a now-shuttered bookstore in Cedar Rapids, Iowa. He needed something to read. Tired of Michael Crichton and Stephen King novels, he considered picking up Homer's *Iliad*. Fortunately, he thought better of it. He wandered through the history aisle, but nothing caught his eye. Then, at the end of the aisle, he looked up and saw a book shining—no, gleaming—on the shelf. It was Plato's *Republic*, written around 380 BCE and considered one of the greatest books ever written.

That boy pulled it from the shelf, bought it, and eagerly began reading. He finished about the first hundred pages when, running home from school one day, it fell out of his partially zipped backpack.

Fortunately, an old man had seen it fall from the boy's backpack and into a bank of snow. Four months later, as that boy took the same path home from school, the old man hobbled out of his house. "Come here," he said. "I have something for you." Unwisely, the boy went inside. The striped, lime green wallpaper played havoc with his eyes. The kitchen reeked of unchanged cat litter. But there, on the table, was his book, safe, sound, and stinky.

Why it took the old man four months to return my book remains a mystery. But I assure you that from the moment I first started reading Plato's *Republic* I was hooked. You see, I had always thought I wanted to be an astrophysicist. I was stellar at math and science. By the time I was sixteen I had finished all the math and science classes they taught at my high school. So, I was sent to the local college.

I had started to doubt, however, that I really wanted to spend my time studying astrophysics. Math and science, I felt, gave me no freedom of thought. It was all about solving the problems. It was all about memorizing facts and formulae. Where was the creativity?

Where were the big, mind-blowing ideas? Where were the opportunities to make my own contributions? At that age, at that time, I simply didn't see them.

That's what fascinated me about philosophy. It was all about creativity. It was all about big, mind-blowing ideas. It was all about the opportunity to think through the issues for myself. To me, it was everything science wasn't.

But I want to let you in on a little secret. It's something almost no one else knows. And it's this: after studying philosophy nonstop for about fifteen years, I really, truly, deeply, passionately, and powerfully started to *hate* it. Sometimes that happens when you devote all of your time and energy to one thing. It happens to professional sports players. It happens to politicians. It happens to young lovers. And it happened to me.

That's when I decided to write this book. I wanted to get back to the very heart of philosophy. I wanted to get back to what made me fall in love with it in the first place. And what made me fall in love with philosophy was the fact that it was so *puzzling*. Puzzling, perplexing, mysterious and troubling, a thicket of ideas among which were hidden endless riches. That is what made me love philosophy in the first place. That is what would make me love it again. And that's when I hatched the idea for this book.

Philosophical Puzzles

My idea was simple. I would select three philosophical puzzles from each of the four major time periods—ancient, medieval, modern, and contemporary—of philosophizing. Each chapter would deal with an argument that has been perplexing since the moment it was first articulated, an argument that has preoccupied the greatest minds in human history. Then it would show how those great thinkers have tried to respond to the puzzle.

But what is a philosophical puzzle? *A philosophical puzzle is a valid philosophical argument with highly plausible premises but a surprising conclusion.* Here is a great example:

(1) If I know that I have two hands, then I know that I am not merely a brain kept alive in a vat of gelatinous goo and fed all of my experiences via electrodes.

(2) I don't know that I am not merely a brain in a vat.

(3) Therefore, I don't know that I have two hands.

Now that is an awesome puzzle! First of all, it is an *argument*. It's an argument because (1)–(3) are not just a list of claims. Rather, (1) and (2)—the premises—are supposed to give you a reason to accept the conclusion (3). That's what the "therefore" indicates: (3) *follows from* (1) and (2).

Second, the argument is valid. A valid argument is such that *if* you accept the premises (here (1) and (2)) then you *have* to accept the conclusion (here (3)). The premises *demonstrate* the conclusion. Here's another example of a valid argument:

(4) All horses are mammals.

(5) All mammals are animals.

(6) Therefore, all horses are animals.

It should be obvious to you that the premises of this argument—(4) and (5)—support or demonstrate the conclusion (6). *If* you accept (4) and (5), then you *have* to accept (6). Otherwise, you're illogical. You're irrational. You're downright crazy.

The argument in (1)–(3) is exactly the same. If you accept (1) and (2), then you have to accept (3). Otherwise, you're an illogical, irrational, crazy person. That, in a nutshell, is validity.

Third, it's a valid *philosophical* argument. Let me state off the bat that no one really knows what philosophy is, not even philosophers. I'm not going to lie to you about that. So it's hard to say what makes this a philosophical argument. What I can say is that the argument falls squarely in the purview of a science called epistemology, or the study (*-logy*) of knowledge (*epistēmē*, in Greek), which is regarded as an area of philosophical inquiry. Clearly, the argument deals with what we do and do not know. So, it is a philosophical argument. (For the rest of the puzzles in this book, you'll just have to trust me that they're philosophical.)

Fourth, notice that the premises are highly plausible. Let's begin with (1). If I have two hands, then I'm not just a brain in a vat. That should be obvious. If I were just a brain in a vat, then I would have no hands at all. I would be nothing more than a lump of white and grey matter.

Premise (2) is highly plausible as well. I don't know I'm not a brain in a vat. After all, brains can be stimulated—by electrical shocks, by pressure, by drugs—so as to cause hallucinations. So, it's at least possible that all of my experiences are nothing more than hallucinations, that all of my experiences are fed to me by way of carefully placed electrodes. I can't rule it out. So, I don't know I'm not a brain in a vat.

Clearly, then, both premises are highly plausible.

Fifth, the conclusion is surprising. I'm quite certain I have two hands. It's hard to think of anything that I am more certain of. After all, I'm looking at them right now. I'm using them to type on my computer. I use them to feed myself. I use them to drive my car. I *know* that I have two hands. The *problem* is that this argument proves otherwise. It *proves* I don't know I have two hands. And that is a surprising conclusion indeed!

Here we have a philosophical puzzle: the valid philosophical argument stated in (1)–(3) has highly plausible premises but a surprising conclusion. If we accept (1) and (2), then we have to accept (3). But accepting (3) seems like downright lunacy. The problem is that rejecting (1) or (2) seems equally loony. What are we to do?

Responding to a Philosophical Puzzle

Whenever we confront a philosophical puzzle we have two options. *Either* we can accept the conclusion *or* we can reject one of the premises. Importantly, we cannot simply reject the conclusion. Why? We cannot simply reject the conclusion because it logically follows from the premises. If you reject the conclusion, then you also have to reject one of the premises. If the conclusion is wrong, one of the premises must be wrong too.

The first option, accepting the conclusion of (1)–(3), is pretty straightforward. I don't know I have two hands. Of course, the argument could be run in any number of ways: I don't know I have eyes; I don't know whether I'm reading a book; I don't know whether I drive cars, etc. Accepting the conclusion would have some really significant consequences. It would mean I don't know much at all.

A second option is to reject premise (1). Premise (1) is an *if . . . then . . .* statement. Now this is very important: in order to reject an *if . . . then . . .* statement, we have to show that the *if . . .* part can be true while the *then . . .* part is false. That is the *only way* to reject an *if . . . then . . .* statement. (Actually, that last claim—like nearly every other claim in philosophy—is open for debate. However, the position currently prevailing is that the only way to reject an *if . . . then . . .* statement is to show that the *if . . .* part can be true while the *then . . .* part is false. And examining alternative views would take us too far afield.)

For example, suppose that I claim:

(7) If it is raining, then the uncovered ground is dry.

How do you prove (7) false? You prove (7) false by showing that while it is *true* that it is raining (the *if . . .* part) it is *false* that the uncovered ground is dry (the *then . . .* part). Accordingly, when it is raining (when the *if . . .* part is true), you go outside and show me that the uncovered ground is not dry (that the *then . . .* part is false). In like manner, if we reject (1), we need to show that it can be *true* that I know I have two hands but *false* that I know I'm not just a brain in a vat.

Here is a good place to pause and make a general statement about all of the premises of the puzzles in this book. All of the premises are of four general kinds.

(A) They are *simple sentences*, such as: material objects are in constant flux; or: God could not possibly be blameworthy.

(B) They are *conditionals*, such as: if there is gratuitous suffering, then God is blameworthy for not diminishing it; or: if all of our actions are determined, then we have no free will.

(C) They are *disjunctions*, such as: either you know such-and-such or you don't; or: either there is gratuitous suffering or humans cause evil.

(D) They are *conjunctions*, such as: humans cause evil and God exists; or: Santa Claus doesn't exist but he is bearded.

Now to reject such premises (supposing that we find them initially highly plausible) we have to do the following:

(A) For *simple sentences,* we need to show that the denial of it is true. For example: that material objects are *not* in constant flux; or: God could possibly be blameworthy.

(B) For *conditionals,* we need to show that the *if . . .* part can be true while the *then . . .* part is false. For example: that there can be gratuitous suffering but God is not blameworthy for failing to diminish it; or: that all of our actions are determined but we do have a free will.

(C) For *disjunctions,* we need to show that both disjuncts (the *either . . .* part is the first disjunct; the *or . . .* part is the second disjunct) are false. For example: you both do not know such-and-such and you do know it (which is clearly absurd); or: there is *not* gratuitous suffering and humans do *not* cause evil.

(D) For *conjunctions,* we need to show that just one of the conjuncts is false. For example: either humans do not cause evil or God does not exist; or: either Santa Claus does exist or he isn't bearded.

To repeat, if we want to reject premise (1), we need to show that I can know I have two hands and yet fail to know that I am not merely a brain in a vat. That's because (1) is a conditional. But can we reject (1)? After all, it's obvious that if I know that I have two hands then I'm not *merely* a brain in a vat.

Alternatively, we might reject premise (2). Premise (2) is a simple sentence. It states that I do not know that I am not a brain in a vat. So, to reject premise (2) we need to show that I do know that I am not a brain in a vat. But how do I know *that*?

Now which do you think is false? Do you reject (1)? Do you reject (2)? Or do you accept the conclusion? Here is your opportunity to make your own contribution to philosophy. And so I leave it to you to puzzle through what the best response is.

In sum and in conclusion, that is all this little book is: philosophical puzzles and how great thinkers have tried to respond to them. My hopes for you as you read this book are (i) that you can come to love philosophy as I have come to love it again, and (ii) that you can come to appreciate what it is philosophers do. And what is it that we do? We try to resolve philosophical puzzles, exploring their ins and outs, traveling their paths, and charting their terrain. And once you wander into these puzzles, once you travel into the forests of philosophy, you too will find yourself on an intellectual adventure, lost in a thicket of ideas where at every turn is a stinging nettle and with every prick comes a gleaming new insight.

Ancient Philosophy

The Flux

The Learner's Paradox

The Liar Paradox

PUZZLE ONE

The Flux

Upon those that step into the same rivers different and different waters flow. . . . They scatter and . . . gather . . . come together and flow away . . . approach and depart.
— *Heraclitus (c. 535–475 BCE)*

Since they [the early natural philosophers, such as Heraclitus] recognized that all material things are changeable and thought of them as being in continual flux, they concluded that we can have no certainty about the truth of things. For what is in continual flux cannot be known with certainty—it will have disappeared before the mind can discern it. Heraclitus said, "It is impossible to step into the same river," so Aristotle reports.
— *Thomas Aquinas (1225–1274 CE),*
Summa Theologiae, *Ia.84.1*

The Philosophers

Heraclitus

Some stories about the lives of philosophers are wonderful and bizarre. However, one of the best stories of all is about Heraclitus' death. Heraclitus had come down with dropsy. Dropsy is a medical condition that causes fluids to build up underneath the surface of the skin. It makes a person feel extremely thirsty. But drinking liquids only makes the sickness worse. That's because the person is introducing more fluid into his body, fluid that will build up under his skin.

Heraclitus wasn't a fool. He knew that if he drank more liquids he would die. He was, though, helplessly obscure and a lover of riddles. He went to the doctors to inquire as to whether they could cure him. He asked them, "Do you know how to make a drought out of rainy weather?" The rainy weather was his dropsy and the drought was to be the cure. Unfortunately, doctors in Heraclitus' time weren't very clever. They didn't understand the meaning of his little riddle.

Heraclitus had to take matters into his own hands. He observed that heat evaporates water. He hoped that if he placed himself in a hot environment it would evaporate the water under his skin. He decided to bury himself in a steaming hot pile of dung. As anyone nowadays might guess, his cure didn't work. He died, and his death became the stuff of philosophical legend.

In all likelihood, though, the whole story is legend too. Thinkers after Heraclitus probably made it up to disparage his works. The part of the story about burying himself in a pile of dung, for example, may well be inspired by Heraclitus' comment that corpses are more worthless than dung. The part of the story about dropsy may well be inspired by his belief that "it is death for souls to become water."

Thomas Aquinas

Thomas Aquinas is a medieval (rather than ancient) philosopher, but the quotation from him sums up what many philosophers took from Heraclitus. They thought Heraclitus to be claiming that because material objects are in constant flux we cannot know anything about them for certain.

Thomas—people in the Middle Ages didn't have last names; Thomas is his name and Aquinas refers to the town where he is from, Aquino in Sicily, Italy—is surely the most important and influential Catholic thinker from the medieval period. Although Thomas' views were quite radical for his time and engendered significant controversy, in 1879 Pope Leo XIII recommended the study of Thomas' philosophical writings for the development of Catholic theology. As a result, Thomas has become one of the most widely read and researched philosophers ever.

Perhaps the best story about Thomas' life is the one about his family kidnapping him. Thomas wanted to become a friar in the new upstart Dominican order. However, his family was far from pleased with his plans. They wanted him to join the older and more established Benedictine order of monks, especially since Thomas' uncle was a member.

To keep him from joining the Dominicans, Thomas' mother ordered his older brothers to kidnap him. His brothers complied. Thomas' family held him captive in their home for two years. They grew so desperate for Thomas to renounce his plans that his brothers hired a prostitute to seduce him. The prostitute failed at her task, but understandably so. When she entered the room, Thomas brandished a burning stick. She fled in terror.

His resolve strengthened, Thomas' mother decided that the best way to save face was to allow Thomas to "escape" through a window. That would be better than admitting defeat and permitting him to join the Dominicans. Thomas escaped, signed up for the Dominican order, and wrote some of the most important philosophical and theological works ever.

The Puzzle

Just what is our first philosophical puzzle? We can express it like this:

(1) All material objects are in constant flux.

(2) If a material object is in constant flux, then we cannot know anything about it for certain.

(3) Therefore, we cannot know anything about any material object for certain.

In the above argument, (1) and (2) are the premises and (3) is the conclusion. It is an argument because the premises (1) and (2) are supposed to give you a reason to believe the conclusion (3). The series (1)–(3) is not simply a list of claims. Rather, the premises (1) and (2) together constitute an *argument for* the conclusion (3).

Moreover, the argument is valid. A valid argument is an argument such that it is impossible for the premises to be true and yet for the conclusion to be false. In short, (3) logically follows from (1) and (2). If we accept (1) and (2), then we must also accept (3). Otherwise, we're being irrational.

The present argument has the most basic kind of valid argument form there is: *modus ponens*, the mode of positing. Whenever you see an argument with this structure (where S and S' are sentences) you can be sure the argument is valid:

If S, then S'.

S.

Therefore, S'.

As you can see, Heraclitus' argument has a surprising conclusion. The argument shows that we cannot know anything about any material objects for certain. Yet it seems that we *can* know things about material objects for certain. For example, you're certain you are right now reading this book. Moreover, you're a material object and so is this book. But because the argument is valid, if you accept the very plausible premises (1) and (2) from Heraclitus' argument, then you're forced to admit that you *cannot* be certain you are right now reading this book. Yet that sounds downright crazy! Equally crazy, if we accept Heraclitus' argument, we have to admit that absolutely no discoveries in the natural sciences—biology, chemistry, physics, etc.—are certain.

Valid arguments are, in many ways, what make philosophizing so fascinating and puzzling. Here's an argument with a weird and surprising conclusion, a conclusion that pretty much anyone would outright reject. However, the premises seem so very plausible. And that's the kicker: *if we accept the very plausible premises*, then we *have to* accept the very outlandish conclusion, too! That's pretty cool. And as we shall see, it can be disturbing.

The Premises

Premises are either true or false. They either correctly state the way the world is or they don't. For example, "Horses are animals" is true. Also, "Richard Atkins teaches in Boston" is true. In contrast, "Horses are goldfish" and "Richard Atkins was born in New Brunswick, New Jersey" are false.

If the premises of an argument are not true, then we can toss the argument in the wastebasket. We do not have to accept the argument's conclusion. Such an argument would not be sound. On the other hand, if an argument has a good form—if it's valid, as all of the puzzling arguments in this book are—and has true premises, then we must accept the conclusion. That's what makes an argument *sound*: it is valid and has true premises. Sound arguments are the gold standard of philosophizing.

(Note that a valid argument is such that *if the premises are true*, then the conclusion must also be true. It does not require the premises to be true in fact.)

As already stated above, the argument found in claims (1)–(3) is valid. But is the argument sound? To answer that question, we need to consider what can be said for and against premises (1) and (2). Let's do that now, starting with what can be said in their favor.

Premise (1)

The material world is the world around us. It's the world we can touch, see, taste, smell, and hear. It's the world made of mountains, rivers, clouds, and fire. It's the world of chairs, books, hats, televisions, houses, newspapers, caterpillars, computers, Venus flytraps, and many other such things. In other words, it's the world of material objects.

There might be an immaterial world too. For example, if God exists, God is not a material being (at least if some religions are correct). God is immaterial and so part of the immaterial "world." However, the argument at hand doesn't concern knowing things about *im*material objects for certain. It concerns knowing things about material objects for certain.

Saying that all material objects are in constant flux is just a fancy way of saying that they're always changing. That's the key idea from Heraclitus' quotation about a river. Rivers are always changing as new water flows through them. So, you cannot step into the very same river twice.

Heraclitus' observation is true not only for rivers but for every material thing in the entire world. Every material object is always changing. Your eyes, for example, are moving as you read this page. Hence, you are changing. Blood is circulating through your body.

Your skin is shedding cells. As you hold this book (or other reading device), the oils from your hands are slowly causing its decomposition. The book is reflecting different photons. The molecules of the book are moving rapidly. The electrons of all the atoms are whirring around their nuclei. Premise (1) is supported by modern biology, chemistry, and physics. It would be silly to deny it.

Of course, Heraclitus didn't know all of that stuff about biology, chemistry, and physics. He just looked around him and saw that things are always changing. The seasons change. Plants grow and wilt. Empires rise and fall. Temples are built and crumble. Cities are populated and then deserted. People live and die. One day we're happy and the next we're sad. In youth, we're strong, and in old age, weak.

In short, you can clearly see that all material objects are in constant flux. And that is why over 2,500 years ago Heraclitus thought (and still today many people think) premise (1) is true.

Premise (2)

Note that premise (2) doesn't state that if a material object is in constant flux, then we cannot know anything about it *at all*. Premise (2) is more modest. It states that if a material object is in constant flux, then we cannot know anything about it *for certain*. For example, you may very well know that you're holding a book right now even if it is in constant flux. All premise (2) states is that you don't know it *for certain*.

As Thomas Aquinas points out, premise (2) is true because as soon as we have thought about any material object it has already changed. Yet his point might be more obvious if we consider distant things that we can see. It takes eight minutes for the light that leaves the sun to reach the earth. That means that if we look up at the sun now we are actually seeing how the sun was eight minutes ago. We're not seeing how the sun in fact is at this very instant. The sun might have disappeared one minute ago. Since that is a possibility, you cannot know that the sun is still shining for certain.

Similarly, it takes 2.5 million years for light from the nearest galaxy, the Andromeda Galaxy, to reach our earth. So, if we look up in the night sky and spot the Andromeda Galaxy, we're seeing how it was 2.5 million years ago. We're not seeing how it in fact is now.

The Andromeda Galaxy may not even exist anymore! It might have disappeared 2 million years ago. If so, we won't learn that it disappeared for another 500,000 years.

Just as it takes time for light to travel from the sun or from the Andromeda Galaxy to the earth, it takes time for the light reflected off of this book to reach your eye. To be sure, that time is exceedingly small, but it's time nonetheless. The book as you are seeing it right now is slightly different from the book as it in fact is right now. The oils from your hands have caused the pages to decompose just a little bit. The molecules have moved. In fact, the book might have disappeared only a split second ago. Can you be certain it hasn't?

Here's another thought: There's a good chance somebody— a spouse, a friend, a parent, a guardian—in this world loves you. However, you also know that people fall in and out of love. So, how do you know that the person who presumably loves you still loves you right now? Maybe, in the last second, his or her feelings changed. Go ahead and ask that person whether he or she still loves you. Did you? Unfortunately, from the time your friend uttered "yes" or "no" and you heard it, his or her feelings may have already changed. Can you be certain they haven't?

Are you at home right now? If not, are you certain it's still there? Buildings sometimes burn down. When I was a child, I used to fear that the streets and sidewalks would change in such a way that if I followed my ordinary path home I might not find it. You know, as surely as I do, that cities sometimes redesign street layouts. Maybe they just did and your home is no longer where you think it is. Can you be certain it is?

On the other hand, if you're at home, maybe your favorite coffee shop has closed. Maybe your work place has moved. Maybe your friend has moved out of her apartment. Maybe your loved ones are on a space shuttle to Mars. Can you be certain they're not?

In short, things change. And the fact that things change means it is possible that what you now believe to be the case no longer is. And if it is possible that what you now believe to be the case no longer is, then you cannot know anything about material objects, which are constantly changing, for certain. After all, it's possible they've changed even in the split second it took you to think about them. And that is why premise (2) of Heraclitus' argument is so very plausible.

Possible Responses

If you're like me, then you find Heraclitus' argument to be puzzling. However, it's not immediately clear whether anything is wrong with it. We need to critically engage the argument. We need to inquire as to whether the premises of his argument really are true.

When it comes to critically engaging our puzzles we have two options: either accept the argument's conclusion or reject one of the premises. (There's a third option too. It's to show that the argument has a bad form, that it is invalid. But as I've already stated, all of our puzzles are valid arguments. So, that's not a live option here.) In what follows, let's explore our options: accepting the conclusion; rejecting premise (1); and rejecting premise (2).

Accept the Conclusion

One of the earliest and greatest philosophers ever accepts Heraclitus' argument but tries to strip it of its force. Plato (429–347 BCE) agrees that we cannot know anything about material objects for certain. Instead, he claims that all we can have are true beliefs about material objects.

In order to understand the distinction between true beliefs and certain knowledge, think about children. My daughter, for example, is only three years old. I have taught her that one plus one equals two. If I ask her, "What does one plus one equal?" she will say, "two." She has a true belief that one plus one equals two. However, it is implausible to suppose she knows it for certain. I'm pretty sure that she doesn't even know what "plus" means. If I ask her what three plus six equals, she looks at me quizzically. My daughter has a true belief about what one plus one equals. She does not have certain knowledge, though.

In like manner, you might have true beliefs that your house is still standing, that this book is in front of you, that the sun is shining, etc. However, Plato would say you couldn't know any of those things for certain. You cannot know those things for certain precisely because material objects are in constant flux, just as Heraclitus claimed. Plato would even make the stronger claim that we cannot know anything about material objects at all, regardless of any degree of certainty. That's because Plato thought that we could have knowledge only of unchanging objects.

Nonetheless, Plato didn't think accepting Heraclitus' conclusion was such a big deal. True belief, he noted, is still pretty good for getting around in the world. It's still useful. For example, whether you have a true belief about where your house is or whether you have certain knowledge about where your house is, you're going to get to your house. (Keep in mind that because your belief is true it accurately states the way the world is.) Whether you have a true belief that it's springtime or have certain knowledge that it's springtime, you're going to plant and tend to your garden.

Moreover, Plato argued that there are some things we can know for certain. Those things are Ideas. Ideas, he claimed, are not part of the material world. Rather, Plato thought there are two realms or worlds. One realm is the material world with its material, sensible objects. The other realm is the immaterial world, which is constituted of immaterial, intelligible objects. He calls those immaterial, intelligible objects *Forms* or *Ideas*.

Ideas are the immaterial, unchanging definitions of things. For example, the Idea Squareness is a closed, four-sided polygon with equal angles and equal sides. For Plato, mathematical objects like Squareness, Triangleness, Circularity, etc. are Ideas par excellence. Plato also thought there are Ideas of qualities (for example, Whiteness and Solidity), of virtues (Justice and Courageousness, among others), and of natural kinds (for example, Treeness and Humanness). (I should mention that it is a convention to capitalize terms like Humanness when one wishes to indicate they refer to Platonic Ideas.)

The Idea Squareness isn't the same thing as a material object that is square. Rather, material objects that are square—for example, a windowpane—imitate or participate in the Idea Squareness. According to Plato, that's what makes a windowpane square rather than circular. A windowpane is square because it imitates the Idea Squareness.

Plato theorizes that there are Ideas or Forms as a way of explaining how many different things can be identical in some respect. For example, a windowpane may be square. Also, tiles can be square, books can be square, tables can be square, and city blocks can be square. What explains the fact that all of those very different things (windowpanes, tiles, books, tables, and city blocks) nevertheless are similar with respect to being square? Plato's answer is that they are similar because they all imitate the same Idea: Squareness.

Nevertheless, since windowpanes are in constant flux, we can only have true beliefs that they're square. A windowpane might, after all, cease to be a square in the time it takes for you to think about it. In contrast, you can know, and know for certain, that Squareness is a closed, four-sided polygon with equal angles and equal sides. That's true by definition. That's an unchanging, immutable truth. Whereas windowpanes change, Ideas do not.

As noted, Plato thought Justice, Humanness, Solidity, etc., are Ideas. We can know all of those Ideas and know them for certain. We just have to figure out their correct definitions. That's still a lot of useful knowledge. It gets us pretty far in terms of mathematics, for example. Moreover and as already noted, we can still have true beliefs about material objects. And those true beliefs will still get us pretty far in terms of practical affairs.

Thus does Plato accept Heraclitus' argument while robbing it of its force. He admits that we cannot have certain knowledge of material objects. However, we can still have true beliefs about them. Also, we can have certain knowledge of the immaterial, unchanging Ideas.

What should we make of Plato's reply to Heraclitus' argument? Put bluntly, Plato's theory faces one really serious problem (and there are several others). Since Plato thought Ideas are existent things that are separate from material objects but agreed that material objects are in constant flux, he had to admit that we couldn't know anything about material objects themselves for certain. That's not a very good result if you care about physics, chemistry, and biology—sciences that try to arrive at certain knowledge about material objects. In short, Plato's view entails that the empirical sciences amount to no more than true belief. That, however, is an undesirable consequence indeed!

Reject Premise (1)

A second option is to deny premise (1). There are two strategies for rejecting premise (1). The first is to take the totally opposite view and claim that nothing is in flux at all. The second makes an important distinction regarding premise (1).

Strategy One: Parmenides and Zeno of Elea: The first strategy is to argue that premise (1) is false because nothing changes at all. As we've seen, making such a claim requires rejecting some very good scientific evidence, and that's not something we typically want to do. Nonetheless, two philosophers have rejected premise (1) by arguing that nothing changes at all, and theirs was the earliest response to Heraclitus' puzzling argument. Parmenides (c. 515–440 BCE) and his pupil Zeno of Elea (c. 490–430 BCE) argue that the world is not in constant flux. Rather, it is unchanging, immutable, continuous, and one. The change we see around us is only an illusion.

Before you write off this strategy as nonsense, consider this: You sometimes say that the sun moves. However, the sun does not move. The sun only appears to move. The sun is, in fact, perfectly still. (Actually, it orbits around the center of the galaxy, but we'll set that aside here.) Yet if the movement of the sun is an illusion, why is it not possible that all of the movement we observe is only an illusion?

Parmenides' argument against change begins by asking us to consider objects that could possibly be thought of. Whatever we think of—the moon, the stars, the seas, trees, hobbits, children, unicorns, or fleas—either exists or does not. The problem is that we can't think of something that doesn't exist. After all, if something doesn't exist, then it has no attributes. A non-existent thing is not red, it's not round, it's not heavy, and it's not located somewhere. It's nothing, *no thing*, at all. Yet if it has no attributes, how can it be thought of? Clearly, it cannot. For if you're thinking about something, then you're thinking of it in some way. You're thinking it is red or round or heavy, etc. But non-existent things are none of those. It follows that whatever we can possibly think of must exist.

Now we can ask whether those existent things come into being or not. That is to say, do they change? Do they *become*? For starters, it's fairly obvious that becoming requires change from not-being to being. If I'm not drunk and become drunk, then I change from not being drunk to being drunk. If I'm short and become tall, I must become what I was not. I must change from not being tall to being tall.

However, nothing can come from what is not. No beings can come from not-being. Consequently, nothing comes into being, nothing changes.

We can express Parmenides' argument in two parts, as follows:

Let O = Any object that could possibly be thought.

(4) Either O exists or O does not exist.

(5) If O does not exist, then O has no attributes.

(6) If O has no attributes, then it cannot be thought.

(7) O can be thought (for, by definition, it is an object that could possibly be thought).

(8) So, O exists.

(9) Either O comes into being (in other words, changes) or O does not.

(10) If O comes into being, then O must have come from what is not.

(11) Nothing can come from what is not.

(12) So, O does not come into being (in other words, it does not change).

If Parmenides is correct, then every object that could possibly be thought exists and is unchanging. Granted that the material world and the things in it are objects that could possibly be thought, it follows that the material world and its objects are unchanging. Premise (1) of Heraclitus' argument is false.

Many philosophers found Parmenides' theory highly implausible. They rejected his view out of hand. Of course the world is changing; just look around you! All of our experiences fly in the face of such a claim.

To defend his teacher, Zeno of Elea came up with several paradoxes to prove motion is only apparent. I'll mention just one of them, the paradox of Achilles and the Tortoise.

Imagine that the fastest runner ever, Achilles, is chasing a tortoise. Let's suppose that the tortoise is at a distance of one meter ahead of Achilles. For Achilles to get to the tortoise, he will have to travel one meter. But in that time, the tortoise will have moved a bit further, say a centimeter. So, Achilles will now have to travel that centimeter. But in the time Achilles travels that centimeter, the tortoise will have traveled a bit further yet, a millimeter. So, Achilles will now have to travel that millimeter. But in the time Achilles travels that millimeter, the tortoise will have traveled a bit further yet, and so on and so forth. So, Achilles will never reach the tortoise. He will always have to travel that extra distance, even if it's extremely small. Hence, while it appears that Achilles can catch the tortoise, he cannot. The appearance is but an illusion.

What's wrong with these arguments from Parmenides and Zeno of Elea? Surely something is, but we won't explore it here. You'll have to puzzle it out some other time. Nonetheless, here's a hint about the argument (9)–(12): Democritus (460–370 BCE) developed the theory of atomism—the ancient predecessor to our own contemporary theory of atoms—to explain how there can be change without something coming from nothing.

At any rate, if nothing is wrong with the arguments of Parmenides and Zeno of Elea, then we have a response to Heraclitus' argument. The first premise is false. Unfortunately, we're also left with a view just as puzzling: that nothing changes at all.

Strategy Two: Aristotle: A second strategy for rejecting Heraclitus' first premise originates with Aristotle (384–322 BCE). Aristotle demands some clarification with respect to premise (1). Notice that the first premise—all material objects are in constant flux—doesn't say anything about how or in what regard those objects are in flux. We can give at least two interpretations of (1), as follows:

(1a) All material objects are in flux in every respect at every moment.

(1b) All material objects are in flux in at least one respect at every moment.

Yet now we can see that premise (1a) is clearly false. Take me, for example. It's true that I am constantly changing in at least some respects. My blood circulates, my skin cells are shed, and my thoughts change. Nonetheless, from one moment to the next, I remain human, I remain alive, I remain blue-eyed, etc. I do not change in those respects, even though I change in other respects. So, (1a) is false. I am not changing in every respect at every moment.

Premise (1b), however, still seems very plausible given our current knowledge of physics, chemistry, and biology. If we plug (1b) into our original argument, we get this:

> (1b) All material objects are in flux in at least one respect at every moment.

> (2b) If a material object is in flux in at least one respect at every moment, then we cannot know anything about it for certain.

> (3b) Therefore, we cannot know anything about any material object for certain.

What should we say about (1b)–(3b)? To answer that question, we need to turn to our final option for responding to Heraclitus' argument: to reject premise (2).

Reject Premise (2)

Our next and final option is to reject premise (2) of Heraclitus' argument. We need to support the claim that it is false that if a material object is in constant flux, then we cannot know anything about it for certain.

In order to reject a highly plausible *if . . . then . . .* claim like premise (2), we need to show that the *if . . .* part (what philosophers call the *antecedent*) can be true while the *then . . .* part (what philosophers call the *consequent*) is false. In other words, we need to show that even if it's true material objects are in constant flux, it's false we cannot know anything about them for certain. Here we'll consider three strategies for doing precisely that.

Strategy One: Aristotle, Reprise: Let's pick up where we left off in the previous section. Aristotle, we saw, rejects version (1a) of premise (1). However, we still need to deal with (1b), which yields the following revised version of Heraclitus' argument:

> (1b) All material objects are in flux in at least one respect at every moment.

(2b) If a material object is in flux in at least one respect
at every moment, then we cannot know anything
about it for certain.

(3b) Therefore, we cannot know anything about any
material object for certain.

It should be pretty clear that premise (2b) is false. Even though
I am always changing in some respect (for example, my blood is
pumping through my body), it is false that we cannot know anything about me for certain. We can be certain that I am still alive.
We can also be certain that I am a human. Even though material
objects are in flux in at least one respect at every moment, we can
still know things about material objects for certain. Specifically, we
can have certain knowledge about material objects in their unchanging respects.

This line of response is very good, but it is not entirely satisfactory. We've rejected (2b) on the grounds that we can have
certain knowledge about material objects in their unchanging
respects. However, it is also the case that we can have certain
knowledge about material objects in their constantly changing
respects. For example, the location of the earth with respect to
the sun is constantly changing. Yet we can still know for certain
where the earth is with respect to the sun, where the earth has
been with respect to the sun, and even where the earth will be
with respect to the sun. How can we make sense of that sort of
certain knowledge, certain knowledge of the constantly changing
location of the earth with respect to the sun, for example? This
argument is still puzzling:

(1c) Some material objects are in constant flux in one
particular respect at every moment.

(2c) If a material object is in constant flux in one particular respect at every moment, then we cannot
know anything about the material object in that
constantly changing respect for certain.

(3c) Therefore, we cannot know anything about material objects in their constantly changing respects
for certain.

Strategy Two: The Scientific Revolution: Another strategy for rejecting premise (2) became prominent with the advent of the Scientific Revolution. The second strategy is to reject premise (2) by noting that although material objects are in constant flux, their change is governed by physical laws that we can know for certain. If every event, every change, is necessitated by prior events, conditions, and the laws of nature—a doctrine known as *determinism*—then "underneath" or "behind" the apparent constant flux are laws that order and make knowable what will happen in the flux.

With the mathematical advances of the Scientific Revolution (especially calculus) it became possible to give a mathematical account of the laws that govern the universe. Most notably, Isaac Newton (1643–1727 CE) formulated his three laws of motion and a theory of gravity. Those laws of motion and the theory of gravity make it possible for us to give an account of where the earth was, will be, and is with respect to the sun. So, we can have certain knowledge of material objects even in their constantly changing respects. Premise (2)—even premise (2c)—is false.

But is this a good response to Heraclitus' puzzling argument? There are four worries about it. First, as will be discussed later in Puzzle Nine, we might wonder whether committing ourselves to determinism leaves room for having a free will. Do we have a free will if every event is necessitated? When I walk across a room, that's a change in a material object (me). If the present reply to Heraclitus' puzzle is correct, then that change (me walking across a room) was necessitated by the laws of nature and prior events and conditions. I could not have done otherwise than I did. Yet if everything I do is necessitated, if I cannot do otherwise than I do, how can I have a free will?

Second, we might wonder whether the laws of the universe are themselves in flux. Are the laws of the universe unchanging? If not, then can we know the laws of the universe for certain?

Third, in order to know anything about material objects for certain using our formulae describing the laws of nature, we will have to plug some data into our formulae. But from where will we get these data? Presumably, the data will be based on observations. Yet if what we are observing is in constant flux, then how can we be certain that we are plugging the correct data into our formulae?

Our fourth worry will require yet another direction of response to our puzzle. Our current physical theories do a very impressive job of telling us the way the world is. But those physical theories also allow for peculiarities—or weird, chancy events—to occur. For example, I am certain that I cannot walk through a wall. If I try to do so I can be certain that I'll end up in pain. However, our current theories of quantum physics allow that it is a possibility—albeit an *extremely* remote possibility—that on some occasion I could walk through a wall. If all of the electrons line up and move just right, it's possible for me to walk through a wall. It's barely possible, but possible nonetheless. So, can I truly be certain that I cannot right now walk through the wall in front of me? I think I can be certain of it. But our very best physics indicates that it's possible for me to walk through walls after all.

Strategy Three: Degrees of Certainty: The comments in the last paragraph require us to adopt yet another line of response to Heraclitus' puzzle. This line of response owes its origins to the development of probability theory by Pierre-Simon Laplace (1749–1827 CE) and to the notion of subjective probability suggested by Frank Ramsey (1903–1930 CE).

We must begin with a fairly basic observation: certainty comes in degrees. It's not like an on/off switch but like a dimmer switch. We can be more or less certain of our beliefs. Our beliefs come in degrees of credence. For example, I can be certain that if I play the lottery I will not win. After all, my chances of winning the lottery are exceedingly small. To be sure, I cannot be absolutely, 100% certain that I will not win the lottery. I am only highly certain that I will not win. I am *almost* absolutely certain that I will not win. In contrast, if I flip a fair coin once I am but 50% certain it will land heads.

Probabilities may be objective or subjective. In the case of flipping a coin, the objective probability of a fair coin coming up heads when flipped is 50%. In like manner, my degree of belief that a flipped fair coin will land heads should be 50%. That (my proper degree of belief) is the subjective probability of the event happening.

When we know the objective probability of an event happening, our subjective probability—our degree of belief in it happening—should match the objective probability. In the coin case, there is a 50% chance of a flipped fair coin landing heads, so I should be

50% certain it will land heads. In the case of the lottery, there is a 1 in about 1.75×10^9 chance of me winning the lottery. Likewise, I should be $1/1.75 \times 10^9$ certain that I will win the lottery. In the case of the electrons lining up just right so I can walk through the wall in front of me, there is an extremely low probability of me walking through it. In fact, even if I had been trying to walk through the wall since the very beginning of the universe, it is highly unlikely I would have yet succeeded. Thus, I should have a very low degree of belief that I could right now walk through the wall in front of me.

Sometimes the objective probability of an event happening is already either 100% or 0%: it either happened or it didn't. That's the case with events in the past. Either an asteroid caused the extinction of the dinosaurs or it didn't. There isn't an objective probability to whether an asteroid caused the extinction of the dinosaurs or not; it's not like flipping a coin.

Nevertheless, we still say things like, "An asteroid probably caused the extinction of the dinosaurs." The probability here is only a subjective probability. However, the subjective probability does not rest merely on my opinion or your opinion. Rather, the subjective probability is determined by the evidence for or against the claim that an asteroid caused the extinction of the dinosaurs. It's the strength of the evidence that should determine how certain we are that an event happened.

Yet it is hard to quantify how strong the evidence is. Fortunately, Ramsey came up with a way to measure subjective probability for cases like whether an asteroid caused the extinction of the dinosaurs, where the subjective probability should be determined by the strength of the evidence. Ramsey argued that subjective probabilities could be measured by what odds a well-informed person is willing to take on an event happening. If a well-informed person is willing to take a high-stakes bet on the claim that an asteroid caused the extinction of the dinosaurs (for example, if the person is willing to bet all that he has on it), then we can be equally certain—certain in proportion to the bet—that an asteroid caused the extinction of the dinosaurs.

Now we can see that there are two ways of construing Heraclitus' original argument. The first construal is one about absolute certainty, where absolute certainty is understood as being 100% certain such that there are not even the remotest grounds for us to bet against the belief:

(1d) All material objects are in constant flux.

(2d) If a material object is in constant flux, then we cannot know anything about it with absolute, 100% certainty.

(3d) Therefore, we cannot know anything about any material object with absolute, 100% certainty.

(1d)–(3d) may well be a sound argument. We cannot know anything about material objects with 100% certainty. There is always a possibility that things have changed, and so there are no conditions under which we should assign a 100% degree of certainty to a belief about material objects.

That may sound surprising. It may seem as though you can be absolutely certain that you are reading a book right now. But in fact, you may be only highly certain that you are—99.999 . . . 999% certain. To see why, ask yourself this: Would you be willing to bet the lives of your loved ones on the claim that you are reading a book right now? I would guess not, and so you are not absolutely certain you are reading a book right now. In short, accepting the above argument just requires you to lower the level of certainty you have in your beliefs a smidgen. We can accept (1d)–(3d) but maintain it's not such a big deal after all.

The second construal of Heraclitus' argument is as an argument about high degrees of certainty or belief:

(1e) All material objects are in constant flux.

(2e) If a material object is in constant flux, then we cannot know anything about it with a high degree of certainty.

(3e) Therefore, we cannot know anything about any material object with a high degree of certainty.

But here (2e) is false. Some changes are gradual. Other changes are not substantial. Still other changes are objectively improbable.

As we noted with respect to our first strategy for rejecting premise (2), the things of the world aren't always changing in every respect. Such gradual, insubstantial, and improbable changes do not seriously damage the certainty of our beliefs.

For example, I'm well-informed enough to know my apartment building will eventually crumble to the ground. However, its rate of decay is exceedingly slow. In fact, it's so slow that I may be highly certain that my apartment building has not, right now, crumbled to the ground. True, I cannot be absolutely certain that it hasn't. But I may still be highly certain. I can be 99.999 . . . 999% certain. In like manner, this book will eventually decompose, your body will stop circulating blood, the sun will stop shining, etc. Nonetheless, you are well-informed enough such that you may still be highly certain that this book has not decomposed just yet, that your body is still circulating blood (I hope!), that the sun is still shining, etc.

It's important to note that this third strategy for rejecting premise (2) is compatible with the recognition that physical laws underlie changes in material objects, the second strategy for rejecting premise (2). However, the present view requires us to admit that we may never know the laws of the universe with absolute certainty and we may never be absolutely certain about the data we plug into our formulae. Also, I may be certain that I cannot right now walk through the wall in front of me, but I may not be absolutely, 100% certain that I cannot walk through the wall in front of me right now. I should only be 99.999 . . . 999% certain. And that degree of certainty reflects our current understanding, gleaned from quantum physics, of the objective probability that I can right now walk through the wall in front of me.

References

Aristotle. *Metaphysics*. In *The Complete Works of Aristotle*. Vol. 2. Trans. W. D. Ross. Ed. Jonathan Barnes. Princeton: Princeton UP, 1984.

Kirk, G. S., J. E. Raven, and M. Schofield. *The Presocratic Philosophers*. 2nd ed. Cambridge: Cambridge UP, 1983.

Laplace, Pierre-Simon. *A Philosophical Essay on Probabilities*. Trans. F. W. Truscott and F. L. Emory. New York: John Wiley and Sons, 1902.

Newton, Isaac. *The Principia: Mathematical Principles of Natural Philosophy.* Trans. I. Bernard Cohen and Anne Whitman. Berkeley: University of California Press, 1999.

Plato. *Meno.* In *Complete Works.* Trans. G. M. A. Grube. Eds. John M. Cooper and D. S. Hutchinson. Indianapolis: Hackett, 1997.

Plato. *Republic.* In *Complete Works.* Trans. G. M. A. Grube. Rev. C. D. C. Reeve. Eds. John M. Cooper and D. S. Hutchinson. Indianapolis: Hackett, 1997.

Ramsey, Frank. "Truth and Probability." In *The Foundations of Mathematics and Other Logical Essays.* London: Routledge and Kegan Paul, 1931.

Thomas Aquinas. *Summa Theologiae.* Vol. 12. Trans. Paul T. Durbin. London: Eyre and Spottiswoode Limited, 1968.

PUZZLE TWO

The Learner's Paradox

Meno: *How will you look for it, Socrates, when you do not know at all what it is? How will you aim to search for something you do not know at all? If you should meet with it, how will you know that this is the thing that you did not know?*

Socrates: *I know what you want to say, Meno. Do you realize what a debater's argument you are bringing up, that a man cannot search either for what he knows or for what he does not know, for he does not know what to look for.*

Meno: *Does that argument not seem sound to you, Socrates?*

—Plato *(429–347 BCE),* Meno

The Philosophers

The stories of Socrates (469–399 BCE) and Plato are intimately intertwined. First, nearly everything we know about Socrates we know because of Plato. Socrates himself never wrote any books. Second, Socrates was Plato's teacher. In ancient Greece, older men commonly took younger men under their wings. Socrates had many young men follow him around Athens. They wanted to learn from him. As we'll see momentarily, that became a big problem.

Sometimes these relationships between older and younger men turned sexual, as may have been the case with Parmenides and Zeno from our first puzzle. However, it's unlikely that the relationship between Socrates and Plato was also sexual. In another work of Plato's titled *Symposium* a student of Socrates named Alcibiades appears. Alcibiades drunkenly complains that Socrates refuses to have a sexual relationship with him. Socrates, it seems from the dialogue, may have been against such relationships on principle.

Both Socrates and Plato were extremely physically fit. Socrates served with distinction in military campaigns, most notably the

Battles at Potidaea (432 BCE) and Delium (424 BCE). In the Battle of Potidaea, Socrates saved the life of a young Alcibiades. In the Battle of Delium, a more mature Alcibiades saved the life of Socrates.

For his part, Plato was a renowned wrestler. In fact, "Plato" is a nickname meaning "broadbacked," a nickname indicative of Plato's wrestling prowess. His real name was Aristocles.

The Battle of Potidaea was a catalyst to the Peloponnesian War, the war between Athens and Sparta from 431 to 404 BCE, which Athens lost. Socrates served with distinction during that war. Another person who served with distinction was a general named Leon.

After Athens' defeat in the Peloponnesian War, a pro-Spartan oligarchy was established in Athens. The oligarchy consisted of thirty men, and they sought to secure their power. They are often called the Thirty Tyrants because they ruled ruthlessly. They severely limited the rights of Athenians, including the right to bear arms, the right to vote, and the right to trial by jury. Moreover, they sought to kill or to exile Athenians who posed a threat to their power. One such Athenian was Leon. Leon supported the establishment of a democracy. Also, because of his service during the war, the people liked him.

As a result of the ruthless rule of the Thirty Tyrants, Leon had fled to a town called Salamis. The Thirty hatched a plan to send five people to Salamis to capture Leon and bring him back to Athens. Their plan was to execute Leon unjustly. After all, he posed a threat to their power.

Socrates was one of the men recruited to kidnap Leon. However, he refused to participate. Discerning the Thirty's plan, Socrates declared he would not be part of a plot to execute a man unjustly. Under other circumstances Socrates' refusal would have surely resulted in his death. However, soon after they executed Leon the Thirty Tyrants were deposed and a democracy was established. Socrates was spared.

For his part, Plato had hoped the establishment of the Thirty would bring Athens back to virtue and glory after its defeat in the Peloponnesian War. In fact, the Thirty had asked Plato to join them. He took it into consideration. However, upon observing their oppressive and ruthless rule, he refused. Moreover, the Thirty's treatment of Socrates and their plan to unjustly execute Leon disgusted him.

So, instead of going into politics, Plato began to follow Socrates around Athens. He wanted to learn what Socrates had to say.

Socrates' own interest in learning and in philosophical puzzles began when he was thirty. Here's the story of its origins: In a little town called Delphi, a deep fissure had opened in the earth. According to legend, Apollo had slain the beast Python there and stuck its carcass into the opening. Python's rotting carcass emitted noxious fumes that rose up through it. In fact, noxious fumes still rise from that fissure. Today we know that the fumes are a toxic and hallucinogenic gas called ethylene. However, they did not know that in ancient Greece. Instead, they thought it was a sacred place. So they placed an old woman of great moral character on a stool spanning the fissure. She would rant and rave as a result of her hallucinations from inhaling the ethylene. That woman was known as the Oracle of Delphi, named Pythia.

People from all around would seek out Pythia for advice. The priests would translate Pythia's utterances into poetry. By "translate," I mean the priests would pretend that Pythia's rants and raves were meaningful and pass off their own poetic compositions as translations of Pythia's divine "inspiration."

Pythia, the Oracle of Delphi, offered some pretty sage advice. In fact, the Oracle became famous partly because the "translations" of the priests were vague or ambiguous. Much like modern-day astrology, their prophecies could be interpreted in multiple ways to fit whatever happened to occur.

Moving the story along, one day an impetuous fellow and friend of Socrates named Chaerephon asked Pythia a question. He wanted to know: Who's the wisest person of all? The Oracle said no one is wiser than Socrates.

When Socrates heard this story he didn't believe it. Socrates didn't think no one was wiser than himself. In fact, he thought he didn't know much of anything. Like a true philosopher Socrates decided to put the Oracle to the test. He went around asking people in Athens questions. Surely he would find people who knew more than he did. Surely he would find people who knew about truth, justice, beauty, and piety, topics about which Socrates pleaded ignorance.

He didn't. He asked politicians, teachers, and artists. He asked writers, actors, and laborers. This is what Socrates found: Those people weren't totally ignorant. Sailors knew how to sail. Actors knew how to act. Politicians knew about the laws. In short, politicians, actors, sailors, etc. knew exactly what one would expect them to know.

Where they erred is that in knowing a few things they supposed they knew a whole lot of things. The actor knew how to play a sailor but then assumed he knew how to sail. The sailor knew about plays but then supposed he knew how to act. The politician knew about the laws but then supposed he knew about justice too.

To make a long story short, Socrates was a gadfly. He stirred up trouble. He irritated people. He would go around Athens questioning people about the nature of truth, justice, beauty, piety, and the like. "What is it?" Socrates would ask. The person would try to answer. Socrates would show them that their answers were incorrect. The people were left perplexed, dumbfounded, like they'd been shocked by an electric eel. Laughter and ridicule would ensue. It was all very biting.

That all is precisely what happens in the dialogue from which our quotation is taken. Meno was a young man of great promise on his way to participate in a military campaign (in which, sadly, he would die). While passing through Athens, Meno asks Socrates whether virtue is teachable, whether it can be learned. Socrates says that he cannot answer the question until he knows what virtue *is*. After three failed attempts to define virtue, Meno gives up and presents the argument above, showing that no one can learn anything at all.

Of course, if Meno really thought that it's impossible to learn anything we might wonder why he even bothered to ask whether virtue is teachable!

Socrates did this—asking questions and embarrassing people—for nearly his whole adult life. And it cost him his life. Many a young man had decided to follow Socrates so as to learn from him. Plato and Alcibiades, I've already noted, were two such men. A third was the son of Anytus. Anytus was a leader in the democratic government newly established in Athens after the rule of the Thirty Tyrants. However, Socrates was sharply critical of that government, and Anytus worried Socrates was corrupting his son.

Socrates had also embarrassed and annoyed a man named Meletus. To get back at him, with the assistance of Anytus, Meletus brought trumped-up charges against Socrates. Those charges were for corrupting the youth, for teaching false gods, for making the weaker argument the stronger, and for investigating things above and below the earth.

At trial, Socrates was found guilty but by a slim margin. They might have let him off with a light sentence. After all, Socrates was 70 years old! But Socrates infuriated them. When it came time for sentencing he proposed that the Athenian people put him up in a palace with free meals for the rest of his life.

The jury decided not to. They sentenced poor Socrates to death instead. Although his friends urged him to escape from prison, Socrates refused on the grounds that it was unjust. A short while later, on the city's orders, he drank some hemlock, a poison. In ancient Athens, citizens sentenced to death were expected to take their own lives so as to spare the executioner the trouble.

Socrates died. His final words were to his friend Crito. He asked Crito to sacrifice a rooster to Asclepius, the god of medicine and healing. At last he would be cured of the injustice and ignorance that infects this earthly life.

According to one report, the Athenians felt pretty bad about all of this. Socrates didn't really deserve to die. To make up for it they banished Anytus and Meletus from Athens.

As his student, Plato attended Socrates' trial. Yet because of it, and because of his experience with the Thirty Tyrants, he came to think that every city and every constitution is corrupt through and through. He believed that no city would be a *kallipolis*, an excellent city, until the people who really care about things like truth, justice, beauty, piety, and the like ruled. So, Plato gave up his political ambitions. He established a school called the Academy—a school that would last hundreds of years—and took to educating Athens' youth. Also, he started writing. His writings, along with Aristotle's (384–322 BCE), are considered to be the most foundational works in philosophy.

The Puzzle

Our current puzzle is called the Learner's Paradox or Meno's Paradox. Here's how it can be expressed in an argument:

Let K = Anything that might possibly be known.

(1) Either I know K or I don't.

(2) If I know K, then I cannot learn it.

(3) If I don't know K, then I cannot learn it.

(4) So, I cannot learn K.

Here, (1)–(3) are the premises and (4) is the conclusion. Once again we have a valid argument with a surprising conclusion. If it's right, it follows that we cannot learn anything. But that seems crazy! I've learned lots and lots of things in the course of my life. This argument is paradoxical not the least because, if it's correct, then by accepting the conclusion I've just learned that I can't learn anything.

The Premises

Let's begin by considering why the premises are plausible.

Premise (1)

Nearly every philosopher agrees that (1) is true. Statements like "either S or not: S" (where S is any sentence, like "Cats are mammals" or "Some squares are circles") exhaust all of the possibilities. For example, either you're human or you're not. There are no other possibilities. Obviously, you're human. But if you're a horse, a plant, or a house, then you're not human. Either some people live in houses or no one does. There are no other possibilities. If even one person lives in a house, then some people live in houses. If no one lives in a house, then no one does. There are no other options. Either the South Rose Window in Notre-Dame de Paris is red or it's not. It's red. True, it is not entirely red, but parts of it are red. So, it is red. And finally, for any item of knowledge, either I know it or I don't. Those are the only two possibilities.

One important point: We can *know that* the sum of the squares of the sides of a right triangle equals the square of the hypotenuse (the Pythagorean theorem). We can also *know how* to draw a right triangle. There is a distinction between knowing that and knowing how. Knowing that is knowing some sentence or proposition. Knowing how is having an ability to accomplish some task. The Learner's Paradox is regarded as a paradox about knowledge that, not knowledge how.

Premise (2)

Premise (2) is highly plausible too. If I already know something how can I learn it? That seems silly. To learn is to gain knowledge. How can I gain knowledge I already have? In like manner, if I have a ten-dollar bill in my pocket I can't gain the *very same* ten-dollar bill. I already have it! If I already know that the sum of the squares of the sides of a right triangle is equal to the square of the hypotenuse I can't gain the very same item of knowledge again. I already know it!

Premise (3)

Imagine that I don't know where the fifth planet from the sun is in the night sky. When I look up at the night sky, how will I possibly know which light is the light of the fifth planet from the sun? How can I even aim to find it? I can look at each light shining in the night sky and wonder, "Is that it?" But since I don't know where the fifth planet from the sun is in the night sky, I won't know whether any of the lights I look at really is the fifth planet from the sun. If I don't know it, I don't know what I'm looking for. And if I don't know what I'm looking for, then I can't learn it. So, if I don't know it, I can't learn it. That's why premise (3) is plausible.

Here's another example. Imagine that a man is looking for his dog. However, he has never before seen his dog (maybe he's been away on a trip and his wife just bought it). If he doesn't know that his dog is a grey poodle, how will he know what to look for? He won't. If he doesn't know what to look for, he'll never find it. Imagine, then, that I start bringing him dogs. Will he ever learn which one is his? No. And so, since he doesn't already know that such-and-such is his dog, he can't learn it.

Possible Responses

Accept the Conclusion

Of course, one possible response is to accept the conclusion. We can accept that we cannot learn anything. However, that option is extremely strange, not least because, as already noted, the very act of accepting the conclusion suggests we can learn something. Moreover, if we cannot learn anything, we might wonder what the point of all our schooling has been.

Reject Premise (2)

It may seem like downright lunacy but three of the most important philosophers ever—Plato, Aristotle, and Descartes (1596–1650 CE)—reject premise (2). They think that we can know some claim and yet learn it. Let's see why.

Strategy One: The Theory of Recollection: Let's begin with Plato. Recall from Puzzle One that Plato thinks the only things we can know are Ideas. Ideas are immaterial entities that exist in another realm, the realm of Ideas.

Furthermore, Plato believes that the soul is immortal. Prior to our births our souls "live" in the realm of Ideas. While there, they hang out with the Ideas, drink a few beers, and shoot the breeze (or whatever it is souls and Ideas like to do together). As a result, our souls come to know all of the Ideas.

Then the worst possible event occurs. Our souls suffer the most miserable, horrible, regrettable fate they possibly could. What is this most lamentable event?

Our births.

According to Plato, when we are born our souls become encaged in our bodies. This encagement causes us to forget the Ideas. Our bodies impede our knowledge of the Ideas.

This might sound a little strange, but an analogy is helpful. Think about a helium balloon. It is the nature of a helium balloon to rise. Similarly, it is the nature of our souls to know the Ideas. However, if someone holds onto a helium balloon's string, she will keep it from rising. She will keep the balloon from doing what it does naturally.

Analogously, our bodies keep our souls from knowing. Our bodies are like the hand holding the helium balloon's string. Just as a hand holding a helium balloon's string keeps the balloon from doing what it naturally does (rise), so our bodies keep our souls from doing what they naturally do (know the Ideas).

What we lovers of wisdom, we philosophers, must do is try to recollect the Ideas. We must try to recollect the Ideas that we all *know* but our bodies *prevent us from bringing to mind*. We can do this through a process of question-and-answer called the Socratic *elenchus* or the Socratic method. That's the very method of asking questions that got Socrates in trouble.

This is why Plato thinks premise (2) is false. We do know all of the Ideas. However, we are impeded from accessing that knowledge. Through a process of question-and-answer we can recollect that knowledge. And that is all learning amounts to: recollection. Learning is not having knowledge "put" into our souls by a teacher. Rather, learning is simply recollecting what we already know.

That theory might sound interesting, but it is surely false. Thomas Aquinas (1225–1274 CE), whom we learned about in the previous puzzle, provides two strong objections to the theory in his *Summa Theologiae*.

First, he notes that Plato's theory presupposes a natural antagonism between the soul and the body. On Plato's theory, the soul and the body are naturally at odds. They are two different and opposed entities. However, nowadays we think that the body and soul—whatever the soul may be (indeed, some people think it is just a part of the body, the brain)—are closely related, closely intertwined. We'll talk about this more in Puzzle Nine.

Second, Thomas notes that if Plato's theory is true then a person blind from birth should still know the Ideas of color, since his soul was acquainted with those Ideas prior to being encaged in a body. But people blind from birth don't know those Ideas. Ask a person blind from birth as many questions as you like, but he's not going to suddenly remember how the color navy blue looks. So, Plato's theory must be false. We need another solution to the puzzle. We can find it in the works of Aristotle.

Strategy Two: Potential and Actual Knowledge: Aristotle's way of rejecting premise (2) is much more reasonable than Plato's. Aristotle distinguishes between knowing something potentially and knowing something actually. The distinction between potentiality and actuality is fairly common. A child is potentially an adult but not actually one. An unused pan is potentially hot but does not become actually hot until it is put on a stove's hot burner. I am, right now, potentially drunk but not actually drunk. I will become actually drunk if I chug a bottle of vodka. At that point I will also be potentially sober. Similarly, I can potentially know something but not actually know it.

Here's an example. I *actually* know that:

(5) Elephants are larger than cats.

And that:

(6) Cats are larger than grains of sand.

These two items of knowledge are actively before my mind. However, because I know these two things actively, I also *potentially* know that:

(7) Elephants are larger than grains of sand.

That's because (7) logically follows from (5) and (6). Now granting that I *had never before* thought about (7) but *have* thought about (5) and (6), I have just learned something new. I moved from *potentially* knowing that elephants are larger than grains of sand to *actually* knowing that elephants are larger than grains of sand.

In a similar manner, if you have taken a geometry course, you potentially know lots and lots of facts about the triangles you see around you. However, you do not yet actually know those facts just because you have not yet done the relevant geometric proofs. If you were to do those proofs, then you would move from potentially knowing those facts about the triangles around you to actually knowing those facts. In so doing you would have learned something.

Here's another example. Many people believe that, numerically speaking, a whole is always greater than its part. For example, seven and eight added together make a whole of fifteen. But the part *seven*, a part of the whole *fifteen*, is not greater than fifteen itself. Neither is the other part, eight.

Right now, however, you actually have all the relevant knowledge to learn that the previous claim is false: a whole is *not* always greater than its part. You've likely never thought of it before, but you potentially know it. Right here, right now, we will make that knowledge actual.

Let's begin with the following three things you actually know. First, you actually know that positive integers go on to infinity. Let's call this Part One:

Part One: 1, 2, 3, 4, 5, 6, . . . , ∞

Second, you also actually know that the negative integers go on to infinity. Let's call that Part Two:

Part Two: -1, -2, -3, -4, -5, -6, . . . , −∞

Third, you also actually know what it means to be equal in membership. If we were to line two sets of integers up and if for each member of the first set there is a corresponding integer for the second and vice versa, then those two sets are equal in membership. For example, the set of integers {4, 5, 6} is equal in membership to the set of integers {4, 6, 8}. Each set contains just three members. We can check it by lining those integers up:

Set {4, 5, 6}: 4, 5, 6

Set {4, 6, 8}: 4, 6, 8

Both sets have just three integers corresponding to each other (4 to 4; 5 to 6; 6 to 8). So, they are equinumerous in their membership. They each have three members.

Now that we have those three items of knowledge explicitly before us we can learn that a whole is not always greater than a part of it. Let our Whole be the set of the members of Part One and Part Two, noted above.

Now let's line up the members of Part One against the Whole as follows:

Part One: 1, 2, 3, 4, 5, 6, . . . , ∞

Whole: 1, -1, 2, -2, 3, -3, . . . , ∞

It should be clear that these integers are always going to line up to infinity. The 1 of Part One lines up with the 1 of the Whole. The 2 of Part One lines up with the -1 of the Whole. The 3 of Part One lines up with the 2 of the Whole. *And so on to infinity and beyond!* So, Part One is equal in membership to a whole of which it is a part. The Whole is not *greater* than its Part One; it is *equal* to its part! Mind-boggling, I know. But more importantly, you just moved from potentially knowing that it's false that the whole is always greater than its part to actually knowing it. Well done!

Hence, we can know something (potentially) and yet learn it. So, premise (2) is false. The antecedent can be true (we can know something potentially) while the consequent is false (we can still learn it by making our knowledge actual).

In point of fact, Aristotle's distinction between potential knowledge and actual knowledge means that we need to distinguish between two versions of the Learner's Paradox, one based on actual knowledge and one based on potential knowledge. The first statement of the paradox, the statement based on potentially knowing, runs as follows:

Let K = Anything that might possibly be known.

(1a) Either I potentially know K or I don't.

(2a) If I potentially know K, then I cannot learn it.

(3a) If I don't potentially know K, then I cannot learn it.

(4a) So, I cannot learn K.

As we have seen, premise (2a) is false. I can potentially know something and yet learn it on the basis of other information I have. The other statement of the paradox is based on actually knowing:

Let K = Anything that might possibly be known.

(1b) Either I actually know K or I don't.

(2b) If I actually know K, then I cannot learn it.

(3b) If I don't actually know K, then I cannot learn it.

(4b) So, I cannot learn K.

In this version of the argument premise (3b) is false, however. I can fail to actually know something and yet learn it *on the basis of other actual knowledge I have.* Yet, since this section is on rejecting premise (2), let's put this insight aside. We'll return to it below.

For now, let me note that this line of response isn't entirely satisfactory. Specifically, how did we get those first items of knowledge, the ones from which we are gaining new items of information? Babies, for example, are really stupid. They don't have any other background information on which to learn new things. They don't have any actual knowledge. Whenever I ask them questions, I just get blank stares. How, then, do they learn anything at all?

Strategy Three: Innate Ideas: I just noted that one problem with Aristotle's response to the Learner's Paradox is that he needs to explain where we get our first bits of information from, where we get our first items of knowledge. Another theory, proposed by René Descartes, addresses this question. He states that we have certain items of innate knowledge. On Descartes' view these are items of knowledge imprinted on our souls by God. In fact, Descartes thinks of his own position as a refinement of Plato's, claiming that even when we learn geometry it is as though we are recollecting information already possessed.

Moreover, Descartes thinks that all of our knowledge is ultimately based on our innate ideas. Everything we know about mathematics, physics, and ethics can be deduced from them. As a consequence, we already actually know some things and potentially know lots and lots of things, maybe even everything. All we have to do is get back to our innate ideas and trace out what follows from them. Descartes sets about this task in his *Meditations on First Philosophy,* which we'll discuss in Puzzle Seven.

The questions that arise, of course, are whether we really have innate ideas and, if so, what those innate ideas are. The British philosopher John Locke (1632–1704 CE) vigorously attacked the theory of innate ideas in his *An Essay Concerning Human Understanding.* Key to Locke's argument is that we do not need to appeal to a theory of innate ideas in order to give an account of knowledge. Rather, all of our knowledge can be explained through the exercise of our other mental powers (for example, perception, imagination, reasoning, etc.). As a result, innate ideas are an unnecessary hypothesis. Moreover, since Locke thinks none of the arguments in support of innate ideas are good, we ought to abandon the theory. Yet how can all of our knowledge be explained without an appeal to innate ideas? We'll take that issue up below.

Reject Premise (3)

Strategy One: Actual and Potential Knowledge, Reprise: Previously, we discussed Aristotle's distinction between actual and potential knowledge. There I noted that Aristotle can also be viewed as rejecting premise (3), or more specifically (3b), that if we do not actually know something then we cannot learn it.

Earlier I gave two examples in support of premise (3). The first example was looking for the fifth planet in the night sky. The second example was looking for a lost dog. If we keep in mind that Aristotle thinks we can gain new actual knowledge (we can learn) from other items of actual knowledge, it becomes evident why those examples fail.

First, suppose that I do not actually know where in the night sky the fifth planet from the sun is. I may still know what to look for. Namely, I'll be looking for a bright light that does not twinkle or twinkles very little compared to the other lights (planets do not twinkle as stars do) and that moves in a particular way over successive nights compared to the other lights in the sky. When I identify that light, I will have identified Jupiter. Thus, from my other actual knowledge about the difference of appearance between planets and stars and the orbit of Jupiter, I will be able to gain new actual knowledge, to learn.

Now consider the second example. All the man has to do is ask his wife what the dog looks like, what its name is, the treats it likes, and where it might have gone. Then, after finding a dog that fits the description, he can ask his wife if it is, in fact, their dog. If it is, he has now learned which dog is his even though, earlier, he did not actually know it.

Strategy Two: Abstraction: Nevertheless, I also noted that Aristotle owes us an account of how we get our first items of knowledge. To understand his account, we first need to get a handle on Aristotle's theory of nature.

Whereas Plato believes in the theory of Ideas (see Puzzle One for a discussion), Aristotle endorses *hylomorphism*. That's a fancy name for a fairly straightforward theory. The first part, *hylo-*, is from the Greek *hyle* (pronounced *whoo-lay*), which is just matter. The second part, *-morph*, should be familiar. It means *to take shape* or *to form*. So, hylomorphism is the view that matter takes shape or is formed. What forms or shapes the matter? For Aristotle, they are forms. Aristotelian forms are a lot like Plato's Ideas. They are immaterial and unchanging objects of knowledge that are of the nature of definitions. However, Aristotle did not think forms exist in another realm, as Plato thought of Ideas. Rather, Aristotle believed that forms are the intelligible parts of, or aspects of, material objects. When I see a red, round ball, that ball has the forms of redness and roundness. My knowing that the ball is red and round is possible because the ball has some intelligible parts, namely its redness and roundness.

Again, whereas Plato thinks that Ideas exist in another realm separate from material objects, Aristotle believes forms are intelligible parts of material objects. As a consequence of his view, Plato has to claim that when I see a red, round ball I am merely reminded of or *recollect* the Ideas of Redness and Roundness that I acquired before I was born, when I was hanging out with the Ideas, drinking beer and shooting the breeze. In contrast, Aristotle can claim that I have the ability to *abstract* the form, to separate the material part of the red, round ball from its intelligible, formal parts, redness and roundness.

Abstraction sounds fancy but the basic idea is simple. Look at a chalkboard. Look at a cinderblock. Look at a window. Look at a door. When you see those four things, you've received sense images or sense impressions. This is the way the world is presented to you.

Now that you have those four images in mind, figure out what is common to those four things. They're not the same color. They're not the same weight. They're not all in the exact same location. What is common to them all is that they are rectangular in some respect. In identifying them all as rectangular, you've performed an act of abstraction. In this case, you've abstracted the very same form of rectangularity from each of your sense impressions of the chalkboard, cinderblock, window, and door. In point of fact, you've performed *four* acts of abstraction, abstracting the very same form—rectangularity—from each of your sense impressions. Voila! And that is, basically, all abstraction amounts to.

Here's another example. First, look at the night sky. Now look at the pupil of your eye (you'll need a mirror for that). Now look at the letters in this book. What do they all have in common? Blackness. That's the power of abstraction at work once again. One more example: What is common to your teeth, fine china, chalk, and cirrus clouds? Whiteness.

Now to the next step: by abstracting the forms of objects we are able to make judgments about them. For example: The chalkboard is rectangular. The window is rectangular. The night sky is black. The letters in this book are black. Fine china is white. Cirrus clouds are white. And so on.

Moreover, on the basis of those judgments, we're able to make arguments like this one:

(8)　The letters in this book are entirely black.

(9)　Cirrus clouds are white.

(10)　If something is entirely black, then it is not white.

(11)　Therefore, the letters in this book are not cirrus clouds.

By making such arguments on the basis of our judgments we are able to gain more and more knowledge.

Furthermore, Aristotle thinks that the mind is a blank slate. We don't have knowledge of forms prior to our birth. However, by using our power of abstraction, we are able to abstract the forms from the objects that we see. Through this process of abstraction we are able to gain knowledge of forms like whiteness, blackness, roundness, rectangularity, gravity, levity, etc. We are then able to "write" those forms on the blank slate of our minds.

In sum, the power of abstraction enables us to separate the intelligible forms from our sense perceptions of material objects. Knowledge of forms enables us to make judgments about objects. From our judgments about objects we are able to infer new items of knowledge. And, on Aristotle's view, that is how all of science and inquiry gets off the ground. There are no innate ideas. We do not recollect knowledge we had prior to birth. Rather, we abstract the intelligible parts of objects, the forms, and reason about them.

Thus, if the theory of abstraction is true, then premise (3) is false. Although it's true that we don't now have knowledge, we can still learn. We learn by abstracting forms, making judgments, and reasoning.

But is Aristotle's theory correct? One major sticking point is his theory of hylomorphism. In particular, it is not clear what a form is supposed to *be*. *How* are intelligible forms supposed to be *intelligible parts* of material objects? Aristotle seems to think that forms are real things independent of our minds. But how is that even possible? After all, nowadays we know that objects are simply agglomerations of atoms and molecules. What aspect of that agglomeration is the *form*?

A second problem is that Aristotle thinks forms have explanatory power. They're the answer to the question: *What about it makes it as it is?* For example, suppose we ask, "What makes cinderblocks rectangular?" Aristotle would say they are rectangular because they possess the form of rectangularity.

Note that this question is different from the question of how a cinderblock *became* rectangular. Aristotle would say that it *became* rectangular because a cinderblock-maker made it that way. How did the cinderblock-maker make it that way? He imparted the form of rectangularity to it. It is the form of rectangularity *that* makes it so. By way of the cinderblock-maker imparting the form is *how* it was so made.

In fact, Aristotle distinguishes among four different explanatory principles, or causes, of substances (that is, hylomorphic composites of form and matter, such as you, me, cats, statues, cinderblocks, etc.). The explanatory principles, or causes, are answers to questions about substances. About any substance, we can ask four questions:

What about it makes it as it is? Here we are asking about the formal cause. This is the *–morph* part of "hylomorphism."

What is it made of? Here we are asking about the material cause. This is the *hylo-* part of "hylomorphism."

How did it come to be? Here we are asking about the efficient cause.

What is its purpose? Here we are asking about the final cause.

To use the example of a red ball again, we can ask the following questions:

> *What is it that makes it as it is, viz. red (formal cause)?* Redness.
>
> *What is it made of (material cause)?* Rubber, for example.
>
> *How did it come to be (efficient cause)?* A person in a factory made it.
>
> *What is its purpose (final cause)?* To play games.

We can also ask the same questions about you:

> *What is it that makes you as you are, viz. a living thing (formal cause)?* On Aristotle's view, it's your soul.
>
> *What are you made of (material cause)?* Muscle, bone, sinew, etc.
>
> *How did you come to be (efficient cause)?* Your parents made sweet, sweet love and a sperm fertilized an ovum that developed into you.
>
> *What is your purpose (final cause)?* According to Aristotle, it is to live a flourishing life.

Now back to the second problem with Aristotle's theory. On Aristotle's view, the formal cause is supposed to be an *explanatory principle.* The problem is that it doesn't really explain anything. In fact, there is an old and hilarious joke to this point. A professor and his student are studying opium. The student asks the professor, "What is it about opium that makes people sleepy?" The professor responds, "It possesses the form sleepiness!"

Get it? The professor hasn't really explained anything. He's just taken the adjective—"sleepy"—and turned it into a noun—"sleepiness"—and passed it off as an explanation. In like manner, to answer the question "What makes this red thing red?" with "Redness!" does not explain anything. Aristotelian forms don't really explain much of anything. They just restate what we already know about objects in a slightly different way. In that case, our theory of nature might be better off if we deny that material objects have intelligible parts, or forms. Forms don't contribute anything to our understanding of substances.

Descartes makes precisely this point. He notes that when we approach a fire we might *feel hot* and *feel pain*. On Aristotle's theory, we would say that the fire is hot because it possesses heatness. However, no one in their right mind would say that we feel pain because the fire possesses painness. Rather, there is something about the fire that causes a feeling of pain in us.

On Descartes' view, we should give the feeling of heat the exact same treatment that we do the feeling of pain. We should *not* claim that the fire is hot *because it possesses heatness*. Rather, we should claim that there is something in the fire *we know not what* that causes the feeling of heat in us. What's more, over 300 years after Descartes' death we now know what it is that causes the feeling of heat. It is the *high mean kinetic molecular energy* of the fire.

This consideration applies to the other examples above. We should not claim that there is the form of sleepiness in the opium. Rather, something in the opium—the chemical structure of the opium that binds with receptors in our brains—produces the sensation of sleepiness in us. Also, we should not claim that there is redness in the ball. Rather, there is something in the ball—its surface property that reflects red wavelengths of light—that produces the sensation of redness in us.

Strategy Three: The Empiricist Theory of Ideas: Empiricists—philosophers like John Locke—follow Aristotle in rejecting a theory of innate ideas. They maintain that all of our knowledge is based on our experiences. However, instead of believing that we abstract intelligible forms from objects, Locke claims that our general ideas are built *by us* out of simple ideas.

We first need to talk about simple ideas. Suppose I am walking down my street. I see one tree. I see the next one. I see the third tree, the fourth tree, the fifth tree, etc. In seeing each of those trees, I am receiving a simple idea, a perception.

Imagine, however, that I now start to reflect on each of my simple ideas. I will realize that there is a similarity among all of the trees that line my street even though they are *all different trees* and *different kinds of trees*. Even though they have differently shaped leaves, even though they're different sizes, even though they have differently textured bark, they are all tall, brown, and have leaves and branches. Moreover, they look different from everything else I see around me. They're different from houses, dogs, people, the street itself, etc.

Because of the similarities among the trees in my simple ideas and because of their differences from everything else, I can group them under one general idea, the idea *tree*. Importantly, on Locke's view I am *not* abstracting the form of treeness from the trees themselves. Rather, I am simply grouping them all under the same general idea *tree*. I see the trees. I have simple ideas of the individual trees themselves. I recognize that all of the trees I see are similar to each other and different from everything else. So I group them under one general idea, the general idea of *being a tree*. But that general idea is not abstracted from the trees. Rather, the general idea is of my own invention.

Importantly, although the general idea *tree* is my own invention, it is not arbitrary. It is based on the similarities and differences among the things I see. There is no form of treeness that is an intelligible part of the trees. But it does not follow that there is nothing in common among the trees *at all*. In fact there is something common to them. What is in common to them is the way they look.

Thus, a central point of difference between Locke and Aristotle is that Locke denies that there are forms, or intelligible parts of objects, as Aristotle conceives of them. Moreover, Locke's theory of ideas is different from Plato's theory of Ideas (note the capitalization). Whereas Plato thinks Ideas are real things existing in a separate realm and that material objects are just copies of them, Locke thinks general ideas are of our own invention and, in a way, they are just copies of what is common to our simple ideas, our perceptions of material objects. In a sense, Locke turns Plato on his head.

Just as we have invented the general idea *tree*, we have also invented the general ideas *rectangular*, *black*, and *white*. Once again, just because we have invented these ideas it does not follow that they fail to correspond to features of objects themselves. Consider again the chalkboard, cinderblock, window, and door. I recognize a similarity among all of those things, but I am not abstracting the form of rectangularity from them. Rather, I am grouping what I recognize to be similar in all of my simple ideas or impressions under one more general idea, the idea of *being rectangular*.

Finally, once we grant Locke's theory of ideas, we are in a position to adopt the rest of Aristotle's theory *without any appeal to forms as intelligible parts of objects*. We can now make judgments about the things we see by subsuming them under our general ideas. For example, now that we have invented the general idea of *tree*, we can begin applying that term to all of the trees we see from here on out. Now that we have invented the general idea of *being rectangular*, we can start applying that idea to books, computer screens, and window air conditioners. Now that we have invented the general idea of *being black*, we can apply it to car tires, dress shoes, and ants. Now that we have invented the general idea of *being white*, we can apply it to bathroom tiles, socks, and chicken feathers.

Moreover, we can start using those judgments to make arguments: this book is rectangular; rectangles are shapes; therefore, this book is shaped. My socks are entirely white. Ants are not white. So, my socks aren't ants. In this way, even though I did not previously actually know that my socks aren't ants, I have just learned it. And so premise (3) of the Learner's Paradox is false. It can be true that I do not know something and yet false that I cannot learn it. I learn it by grouping my simple ideas under more general ideas, making judgments on the basis of my simple ideas, and then making arguments based on my judgments.

Bonus Puzzle

Our focus here has been on the Learner's Paradox, but there's a riff on the argument that is equally puzzling. It comes from Aristotle's *Nicomachean Ethics*. Aristotle's puzzle isn't about learning items of knowledge but about becoming virtuous. It goes as follows:

(12) Either I'm virtuous or I'm not.

(13) If I'm virtuous, then I cannot become virtuous.

(14) If I'm not virtuous, then I cannot become virtuous.

(15) So, I cannot become virtuous.

You'll notice that this argument has the same structure as our puzzle. So, it is a valid argument. Also, the conclusion is puzzling. If I cannot become virtuous, why even try? No matter how much effort I put into it, I will fail to become any more virtuous than I am now. That can't possibly be true. In fact, I'm quite confident that I am a much more virtuous person now than I was ten years ago.

What, then, is wrong with this argument? It can't be premise (12) for the same reason we cannot reject premise (1) of the Learner's Paradox. Premise (13) is pretty obviously true. So, the only option is to reject (14). However, there's a good argument for premise (14). It's this:

(16) If I am not virtuous, then I do not do virtuous actions.

(17) If I do not do virtuous actions, then I cannot become virtuous.

(18) So, if I am not virtuous, then I cannot become virtuous.

But what is wrong with *this* argument? It can't be premise (16). It's natural to think that a person who is not virtuous is bad. Yet bad people do not do virtuous actions. They do bad ones.

It can't be premise (17) either. If I don't do virtuous acts, then I cannot become virtuous. Suppose I go around murdering, cheating, lying, drinking until I pass out, spitting in the eyes of strangers on the subway, selling meth to children in schoolyards, seducing old ladies and swindling them out of their fortunes, etc. How could I ever become virtuous if I'm performing such horrible actions? It would clearly be impossible.

Now *something* in those last two paragraphs has got to be wrong. But what? I'll leave you to puzzle through it.

References

Aristotle. *Metaphysics*. In *The Complete Works of Aristotle*. Vol. 2. Trans. W. D. Ross. Ed. Jonathan Barnes. Princeton: Princeton UP, 1984.

Aristotle. *Nicomachean Ethics*. In *The Complete Works of Aristotle*. Vol. 2. Trans. W. D. Ross. Ed. Jonathan Barnes. Princeton: Princeton UP, 1984.

Aristotle. *On the Soul*. In *The Complete Works of Aristotle*. Vol. 1. Trans. J. A. Smith. Ed. Jonathan Barnes. Princeton: Princeton UP, 1984.

Aristotle. *Physics*. In *The Complete Works of Aristotle*. Vol. 1. Trans. R. P. Hardie and R. K. Gaye. Ed. Jonathan Barnes. Princeton: Princeton UP, 1984.

Aristotle. *Posterior Analytics*. In *The Complete Works of Aristotle*. Vol. 1. Trans. Jonathan Barnes. Ed. Jonathan Barnes. Princeton: Princeton UP, 1984.

Descartes, René. *Meditations on First Philosophy*. In *The Philosophical Writings of Decartes*. Vol. 2. Trans. John Cottingham, Robert Stoothoff, and Dugald Murdoch. Cambridge: Cambridge UP, 1984.

Locke, John. *An Essay Concerning Human Understanding*. Ed. Peter H. Nidditch. Oxford: Oxford UP, 1975.

Plato. *Meno*. In *Complete Works*. Trans. G. M. A. Grube. Eds. John M. Cooper and D. S. Hutchinson. Indianapolis: Hackett, 1997.

Plato. *Phaedo*. In *Complete Works*. Trans. G. M. A. Grube. Eds. John M. Cooper and D. S. Hutchinson. Indianapolis: Hackett, 1997.

Thomas Aquinas. *Summa Theologiae*. Vol. 12. Trans. Paul T. Durbin. London: Eyre and Spottiswoode Limited, 1968.

PUZZLE THREE

The Liar Paradox

Every Cretan is a liar.
— *Epimenides of Knossos, Crete (c. sixth century BCE)*

The statement I am now making is a lie.
— *Eubulides of Miletus (c. fourth century BCE)*

One of themselves, a prophet of their own, said, "Cretans are always liars, evil beasts, lazy gluttons."
— *Paul (c. 5–67 CE), Letter to Titus 1:12*

The Philosophers

Epimenides

We know very little about the first two people who offer up our third puzzle. What we know about Epimenides is that he was an ancient prophet. According to legend, he fell asleep for 57 years in a cave in Crete. The cave was sacred to Zeus. When Epimenides awoke, he found he had gained the power of prophecy. With his powers he helped Solon reform Athens, and for his help he asked only for an alliance between Athens and Knossos.

Why does Epimenides say that every Cretan is a liar? He says it because he thinks Zeus is immortal but the Cretans claim that Zeus is mortal. However, Epimenides likely did not realize that his statement is (nearly) paradoxical. If every Cretan is a liar, and he is a Cretan, is he lying about the fact that every Cretan is a liar? We might say that every Cretan lies, just not all the time, and at this particular time Epimenides is not lying. So, this statement is only paradoxical if every Cretan *always* lies, a qualification that is added in the quotation from Paul.

Eubulides

Eubulides is most famous for originating several paradoxes and recognizing them as paradoxical. One of the paradoxes is the Liar Paradox, our current puzzle. Another paradox is the Sorites Paradox (*sorites* is Greek for *heap*), which is explained below. Eubulides despised his contemporary Aristotle (384–322 BCE), who became one of the most influential philosophers in history.

Paul

Paul is one of the founders of Christianity. He is the author of many of the books in the New Testament.

Paul was originally named Saul. A Jewish Rabbi, he hated the burgeoning sect of Christians. He persecuted them and stood by while a young Christian named Stephen was stoned to death.

When he was traveling to the city of Damascus in Syria, however, a bright light from the heavens shone into Saul's face. From the light, he heard a voice purporting to be Jesus and that asked why Saul persecuted the Christians.

The event blinded Saul, causing scales to form on his eyes. At this same time, a disciple of Jesus' named Ananias reported that he had a religious experience in which he was told that Saul was to help establish the Christian church. Ananias went to Saul. When he touched Saul's eyes, the scales fell from them and Saul's sight was restored. As a result, Saul changed his name to Paul and worked tirelessly to establish Christianity throughout the eastern Mediterranean, including in Syria, Crete, Turkey, Greece, and Macedonia.

Paul wrote "Letter to Titus" to a man named (predictably) Titus who was establishing a church on the island of Crete. Paul is encouraging Titus, who had reported that several people were trying to undermine his efforts and teaching false views about Christianity. In response, Paul notes that one of Crete's own—Epimenides, presumably—said that Cretans are always liars.

What's interesting to note, though, is that it is not paradoxical for Paul—a Jewish man and Roman citizen—to say that all Cretans are always liars. It is only paradoxical if a Cretan says it. Then again, Paul does go on to claim that the statement is true, and if we accept the claim that the Bible is inerrant, then we seem to be stuck in a paradox once again. We'll take up the issue of scriptural inerrancy in Puzzle Six.

The Puzzle and Its Premises

One of the oldest and most difficult paradoxes of all time is known as the Liar Paradox. Even today there is no clear solution to it. The paradox remains widely discussed and just as puzzling as ever. For our current puzzle we'll consider the argument and the premises together. That's because the paradox really arises from a group of logical commitments, all of which are highly plausible and all of which are still taught in any basic logic, discrete mathematics, or computer programming course. It's those commitments that allow us to move from one premise to the next in the paradox. The commitments are the real problem. If we accept all of them, we confront a paradox that violates one of them. Hence, it would seem one of those logical commitments must be false.

Warning: What I have to say in the following is dense reading. This puzzle and Curry's Paradox, our final puzzle, are the most challenging ones in the book. You will do well to read the next two sections slowly and several times.

The Premises (Our Logical Commitments)

The Liar Paradox arises from six commitments: Modus Ponens, The Principle of Contravalence, The Principle of Bivalence, Negation, the T-Scheme, and Substitution.

Modus Ponens: We were introduced to modus ponens (MP) in our first puzzle. Where S and S′ are sentences, MP is the valid inference form:

> If S, then S′.
>
> S.
>
> Therefore, S′.

Whenever we have two sentences like: "If (S) Richard is sitting, then (S′) he is not standing" and: "(S) Richard is sitting," we can infer: "Therefore, (S′) he is not standing."

The Principle of Contravalence: Our second commitment is to the Principle of Contravalence (PC).

Principle of Contravalence (PC): No sentence is both true and false at the same time and in the same respect.

In other words, the truth values (*-valence*) true and false are opposed to each other (*contra-*) in such a way that no sentence can be both true and false at the same time and in the same respect.

Consider the sentence "Richard is sitting." PC says that the sentence cannot be both true and false right now (at the time I'm writing, it's true). The same goes for sentences like "Richard is sober," "Richard is smart," "The South Rose Window is red," and "My dog is lost."

Note that it can be true that I am sober at one time and yet false that I am sober at another time. That does not violate the Principle of Contravalence because it is not at the same time. Also, it can be true that I am both smart when it comes to philosophy and not smart when it comes to advanced quantum physics. That does not violate the Principle of Contravalence because it is not in the same respect. Similar considerations follow for the South Rose Window (it can be red with respect to some part and not red with respect to some other part) and for my dog (it can be lost at one time and not at another).

From here on out, we'll drop the clause "at the same time and in the respect" for simplicity's sake.

The Principle of Bivalence: Our third commitment is to the Principle of Bivalence (PB).

Principle of Bivalence (PB): Every sentence is either true or false.

In other words, the truth values (*-valence*) only number two (*bi-*), and those two truth values are true and false. To use the previous examples, it's either true that Richard is sitting or it's false that Richard is sitting. Either it's true that the South Rose Window is red or it's false. Either it's true my dog is lost or it's false.

Taken together, PB and PC say that for any sentence S, either S is true or S is false, but S cannot be both true and false. Either it's true that I am sitting or it is false that I am sitting, but it is not both true and false that I am sitting.

Negation: Our fourth commitment is to Negation (NEG). Simple sentences have subjects and predicates. Predicates tell us something about the subject. For example, in the sentence "I am drunk," "I" is the subject and "am drunk" is the predicate.

Negation says that denying the whole simple sentence is the same as negating the predicate. For example, "I am not drunk" and "Not: I am drunk" are equivalent. We can express Negation in this way:

> *Negation (NEG):* For any sentence S of the form X is P.
> Not: S is equivalent to X is not P.

T-Scheme: Our fifth commitment is to the T-Scheme (TS). Where S is a sentence, the T-Scheme is:

> *T-Scheme (TS):* "S" is true if and only if S.

TS is called a biconditional. It is really two (*bi-*) *if . . . then . . .* (*-conditional*) claims put together. Those two claims are: if S, then "S" is true *and* if "S" is true, then S.

TS allows us to make the following sorts of arguments using modus ponens (MP). Let S = I am sitting, and suppose:

> (1) I am sitting.

TS tells us:

> (2) If I am sitting, then "I am sitting" is true.

Using MP on (1) and (2), we can conclude:

> (3) "I am sitting" is true.

When it comes down to it, TS in combination with PC and PB is really a commitment to the following *four* claims:

> *TS(a):* If S, then "S" is true.

> *TS(b):* If "S" is true, then S.

TS(c): If "S" is not true (that is, false), then not: S.

TS(d): If not: S, then "S" is not true (that is, false).

It's worth noting that, logically speaking, TS(a) and TS(c) are equivalent and so are TS(b) and TS(d). In what follows, we will be making use of TS(b) and TS(c).

Substitution: We need one more commitment, our sixth. This is a commitment to Substitution (SUB).

> *Substitution (SUB):* Whenever we have a sentence the subject of which refers to itself we can substitute the entire original sentence *in quotation marks* for the subject of the sentence.

Thus, from: "This sentence is in English" we can substitute the whole sentence for "This sentence" to get: "'This sentence is in English' is in English."

The Puzzle

That's enough logic. Let's move on to our puzzle, the Liar Paradox. The Liar Paradox begins with the *liar sentence*: "This sentence is false." The liar sentence is properly understood as: "This *very* sentence is false." It is called the liar sentence because it is like the sentence from Eubulides: "The statement I am *now* making is a lie."

The Liar Paradox arises when we ask: Is "This sentence is false" true or false? It must be one or the other, since we accept PB. It can't be both, since we accept PC. So, which is it? Let's consider each option, first that it is true and second that it is false.

We begin by supposing that:

(4) "This sentence is false" is true.

Then, by TS(b) and MP, it follows:

(5) This sentence is false.

But recall that by SUB, we can get:

(6) "This sentence is false" is false.

Clearly, then, if we suppose that: *"This sentence is false" is true*, then we are also committed to: *"This sentence is false" is false*. Yet, by PC, no sentence is both true and false. Nevertheless, by PB, it has to be one or the other.

Perhaps, then, our original supposition (4) was mistaken. So, let's begin with the other option, that the liar sentence is false:

(7) "This sentence is false" is false.

Our first step is to use SUB on the sentence inside the quotation marks:

(8) "'This sentence is false' is false" is false.

Next, by TS(c) and MP, we can infer:

(9) Not: "This sentence is false" is false.

By NEG, that is the same as saying:

(10) "This sentence is false" is not false.

If "This sentence is false" is not false, but it must be either true or false (by PB), it follows:

(11) "This sentence is false" is true.

Unfortunately, that result is inconsistent with our supposition (7). So, our original supposition (7) must be mistaken.

To conclude, we have seen that if we suppose that: *"This sentence is false" is true*, then we are committed to the claim that: *"This sentence is false" is false*. Moreover, if we suppose that: *"This sentence is false" is false*, then we are committed to the claim that: *"This sentence is false" is true*. Therefore, either: *"This sentence is false" is both true and false,* or: *"This sentences is false" is neither true nor false*. But, by PC and PB, it has to be one or the other and it can't be both. And that is the paradox.

The paradox results in something like an infinite loop in a computer program. If we begin with one supposition (that the liar sentence is true), we must reject it on pain of contradiction. That's what (4)–(6) show. But if we reject it, we must opt for the denial of that supposition (that the liar sentence is false). However, as (7)–(11) show, that supposition also requires us to reject it on pain of contradiction and opt for the negation of its supposition (again, that the liar sentence is true). We're now back at (4)–(6), which will lead us again to (7)–(11), which will take us back to (4)–(6), *ad infinitum*.

Possible Responses

The line of reasoning in (4)–(11) shows that one of our logical commitments must be false or else there is something wrong with the liar sentence itself. As we have seen, all of MP, PC, PB, NEG, TS, and SUB are used to generate the paradox. But which one should we reject? Or is there a problem with the liar sentence itself? Perhaps we should simply reject it.

There is no consensus on the issue of what to do, though there is some consensus about which options are dead ends. To begin, practically every sane person agrees that we should not reject MP, so I won't consider that option here. Instead, here are the other possibilities.

Reject the Liar Sentence Itself

There are two strategies for rejecting the liar sentence itself. The first is to claim that the liar sentence is nonsense and so neither true nor false. The second is to claim that the liar sentence is simply false.

Strategy One: The Nonsense Strategy: The first option is to reject the liar sentence itself as nonsense. On this strategy, we don't need to reject any of the logical rules. That's because the liar sentence is not a sentence at all. It is meaningless. As such, it is neither true nor false. Indeed, it is not even the sort of thing that can be true or false. In like manner, "horse apple" is neither true nor false. It's not even a sentence. Also, "Shut the t-shirt!" is neither true nor false.

There are two problems with this option. First, it's extremely hard to say why the liar sentence is nonsense. How is it different from saying, for example, "This sentence is in English" or "This sentence has five words"? It certainly does not look any different from your ordinary, run-of-the-mill sentences. As such, claiming that the liar sentence is nonsense comes off as *ad hoc*, a claim made to solve a problem but not otherwise supported.

The second and more important problem is that the paradox can be reinstated. This is known as The Strengthened Liar. It must be admitted that nonsense strings of words are not true. Thus, all we have to ask is whether:

(12) This sentence is not true.

is true or not. If it is nonsense, it is, of course, not true.

Now, suppose we rephrase PB as the Law of the Excluded Middle (LEM):

LEM: Every string of words is either true or not true.

And PC as the Law of Non-Contradiction (LNC):

LNC: No string of words is both true and not true.

When we do so and make some suitable alterations to our logical commitments above, we can generate the Liar Paradox in basically the same way that we did before. I will, however, leave that chore to you.

Strategy Two: The Truth-Implication Strategy: The second strategy is to claim that all propositions implicitly assert their own truth. Thus, "This sentence is false" also claims that it is true. However, that is obviously contradictory. Since self-contradictory sentences are false—for example, "This sentence is in English and not in English" is self-contradictory and false—the liar sentence is simply false.

This solution is usually attributed to Jean Buridan (c. 1300–c. 1358 CE) and was defended by Charles Sanders Peirce (1839–1914 CE). However, Peirce would later come to reject it. He rejected it because sentences do not assert their own truth. Much to the contrary, it is *we* who assert sentences. Assertion is something we do to sentences, not something sentences do to themselves.

Reject Substitution

Maybe we should reject SUB. After all, that one seems to be the least costly to reject in terms of logic. Once again, this solution runs the risk of being *ad hoc*. More importantly, however, yet another version of the Liar Paradox—The Postcard—can be generated without SUB. To see how, imagine that the following two sentences are written on opposite faces of a postcard:

> *Face A:* The sentence written on Face B of this postcard is false.
>
> *Face B:* The sentence written on Face A of this postcard is true.

Is the sentence on Face A true or false? Suppose it is true. If so, then it is also false. For the sentence on Face A says that the sentence on Face B is false. But the sentence on Face B says the sentence on Face A is true. If that's false, then the sentence of Face A must be false. But we just supposed it was true!

Let's consider the other possibility, that the sentence on Face A is false. If so, then the sentence on Face B is true. Now, what the sentence on Face B states is that the sentence on Face A is true. But we just supposed it was false!

In this case, we have the same result: either the sentence on Face A is both true and false or neither true nor false, in violation of PC or PB. And that occurs without an appeal to SUB. So, rejecting SUB will not help resolve the Liar Paradox.

Reject Negation

Yet another option is to reject NEG. This solution seems to run afoul of how we ordinarily use "not." Moreover, as we shall see with our last puzzle, Curry's Paradox, a paradox similar to the Liar Paradox, can be generated without using NEG. We'll save that for later.

Reject the Principle of Bivalence or the Principle of Contravalence

Our next option is to reject either PB or PC. Although a detailed account of these options cannot be given here, a brief review of them will be useful.

If we reject PB, then we can affirm that the Liar Paradox is neither true nor false (without claiming it is nonsense). Rather, there are three truth values: true, false, and neither true nor false. In that case, there is a truth value gap, the neither-true-nor-false option.

If we reject PC, then we can affirm that the Liar Paradox is both true and false. Here again there are three truth values: true, false, and both true and false. In that case, there is a truth value glut. It's interesting to note that Heraclitus (c. 535–475 BCE), the author of our first puzzle, might have endorsed such a view, since he claims that we both can and cannot step into the same river twice, in which case (by TS and NEG) it is both true and false that we can step into the same river twice. More recently, this position has been defended by Graham Priest (b. 1948 CE).

Some philosophers think that these options amount to the same thing. Whether we opt for truth value gaps or truth value gluts, we have to acknowledge that there is a third truth value option. We'll see more clearly why these are thought to be the same at the end of this section.

Yet another option is to accept four truth values: true, false, both true and false, and neither true nor false.

But we ought to ask: Why opt for a third (or fourth) truth value at all? There are at least three reasons.

First, vague sentences seem to be both true and false or neither true nor false. For example, we can all agree that one grain of sand does not make for a heap of sand. We can say the same for two, three, four, etc. grains of sand. But when, exactly, do we get a heap of sand? With 500 grains of sand? 1,000? 10,000? There seems to be no definite cut-off point between *a heap of grains of sand* and *not a heap of grains of sand*. Therefore, the sentences that occupy the middle ground—"500 grains of sand is a heap of sand," "1,000 grains of sand is a heap of sand," etc.—are both true and false or neither true nor false. This is called the Sorites Paradox. As noted above, like the Liar Paradox, it was first described and recognized as paradoxical by Eubulides.

A similar consideration applies to me being drunk and not drunk. At what line, exactly, do I transition from being not drunk to being drunk? Experience tells me that, if there is a line, it's a very thin line indeed!

Second, failed presupposition seems to require a third (or fourth) truth value. Suppose I ask you, "Have you stopped eating steel?" On the one hand, if you say *yes*, it presupposes there was a time in the past that you ate steel. Yet there was no such time. So, you shouldn't say, "I have stopped eating steel," for you never started. On the other hand, if you say *no*, it presupposes that you are still eating steel. So, you shouldn't say, "I have not stopped eating steel." Neither answer is satisfactory. Thus, we might take the view that the sentence "I have stopped eating steel" is *either* neither true nor false *or* both true and false.

Failed presupposition is especially troublesome in courts of law. Suppose someone is on the stand and a lawyer asks, "Have you stopped beating your father?" Either answer involves a worrisome presupposition. If the defendant says, "Yes, I have stopped beating my father," it presupposes he previously beat his father. If the defendant says, "No, I have not stopped beating my father," it presupposes that he continues to beat his father. What's the defendant to do?

A third reason for introducing a third (or fourth) truth value concerns sentences about the future. This is a problem first described in Aristotle's (384–322 BCE) *De Interpretatione*. He uses an example about whether a sea battle will occur tomorrow. Instead of a sea battle, let's consider the sentence, "I will eat a bagel for breakfast on May 10, 2054." If we accept PB, then it is either true or false right now that I will eat a bagel for breakfast on that day. Moreover, by PC, it is not both true and false that I will eat a bagel that day.

Granted all of that, it seems fated that I will (or won't) eat a bagel for breakfast on May 10, 2054. On the one hand, if it's *true right now* that I will eat a bagel for breakfast on May 10, 2054, then I'm going to eat a bagel for breakfast that day *no matter what*. On the other hand, if it's *false right now* that I will eat a bagel for breakfast on May 10, 2054, then it follows that I won't eat a bagel for breakfast on that day *no matter what*. Either way, it's fated *now* whether I will eat a bagel for breakfast on May 10, 2054. Sure, we may have to wait a long time to figure out whether the sentence is true or not, but that does not change the fact that it is either true or false right now. It only means we cannot yet *know* whether it is true or false. In short, in order to avoid this sort of fatalism, we might instead claim that it is neither true nor false (or both true and false) now that I will eat a bagel for breakfast on May 10, 2054.

I have just given three reasons for rejecting either PB or PC (or both). However, there is a problem with this solution. It is that rejecting either one of them commits us to a contradiction.

To begin, suppose we reject PC and claim that some sentences are both true and false. Let "S" be one of those sentences that is both true and false (a truth value glut). In that case, we would affirm:

(13) "S" is true *and* "S" is false.

But it is natural to identify the falsity of a sentence with the truth of its negation. In other words, it is natural to think of (13) as being the same as:

(14) "S" is true *and* "Not: S" is true.

That is clearly a contradiction.

Moreover, the same problem arises if we deny PB and claim that some sentences are neither true nor false (a truth value gap). We would then affirm:

(15) "S" is not true *and* "S" is not false.

If we continue to identify the falsity of a sentence with the truth of its negation, then (15) is the same as:

(16) "S" is not true *and* "Not: S" is not true.

Once again, we have a clear contradiction.

Moreover, using TS, (14)—which followed from the truth value glut option—commits us to claiming:

(17) S *and* Not: S.

Whereas (16)—which followed from the truth value gap option—commits us to claiming:

(18) Not: S *and* Not: Not: S.

But Not: Not: S seems like the same as S. In other words, (18) seems to be equivalent to:

(19) Not: S *and* S.

This is just the same as (17). Here we can finally see why some philosophers think that allowing for truth value gaps (rejecting PB) or truth value gluts (rejecting PC) amounts to the same thing. Permitting truth value gluts leads us to (17). Permitting truth value gaps leads us to (19). But (17) and (19) are the same claim.

Reject the T-Scheme

Our final option is to reject—or, what is really the case, modify—TS. Alfred Tarski (1901–1983 CE) provides us with a strategy for doing so. In order to understand how to do it, we first have to get a handle on the distinction between an object language and a metalanguage. To keep it simple, an object language is a language we use to talk directly about the way things are. For example, if I say, "The chair is red," I am using an object language (English) to talk directly about a red chair. In contrast, a metalanguage is a language we use to talk about an object language. For example, if I say, "'La silla es roja' is in Spanish," the object language is Spanish and the metalanguage is English. Also, if I say, "'The chair is red' is in English," both the object language and the metalanguage are English. Here, we might find it helpful to designate the object language English-L_0 and the metalanguage English-L_1.

Now here is the twist: on Tarski's view, the most basic object language does not have a truth predicate at all (or a falsity predicate, for that matter). Rather, whenever we assert that a sentence is true, we are making an assertion in a metalanguage. For example, in the object language I may say:

(20) The chair is red.

But if I want to say that (20) is true, then I have to say it in a meta-language L_1:

(21) "The chair is red" is true-in-L_0.

where L_0 is the object language but the assertion (21) is made in metalanguage L_1. What if I want to say that (21) is true? Then I need to make a claim in a meta-metalanguage, so to speak. In that case, I will say:

(22) "'The chair is red' is true-in-L_0" is true-in-L_1.

And what if I want to say (22) is true? Then, I need to say it in a meta-meta-metalanguage:

(23) "'"The chair is red" is true-in-L_0' is true-in-L_1" is true-in-L_2.

This could, obviously, go on forever.

What does this have to do with the T-Scheme and the Liar Paradox? First, the T-Scheme should not be expressed as:

"S" is true if and only if S.

Rather, we need a Revised T-Scheme. Where S is an assertion in language L_n, our Revised TS is:

"S" is true-in-L_n if and only if S.

S, or what is stated on the right side of the "if and only if" is an assertion in an *object language or a metalanguage one step lower than the language on the left*. This is the first-tier of expression. What is stated on the left side of the "if and only if" is an assertion made in a different language, a *metalanguage one step higher than the language on the right side*. This is a second-tier of expression.

Now, suppose we follow through with the first part—steps (4)–(6)—of the Liar Paradox above. If we do so, when we ascribe truth to the liar sentence in (4), we are doing so in a metalanguage and not in an object language. Thus, keeping in mind that the object language has no truth (or falsity) predicate, (4) should be stated as:

(4a) "This sentence is false-in-L_0" is true-in-L_1.

What follows by our Revised TS and MP is:

(5a) This sentence is false-in-L_0.

Now, suppose that we use SUB. If we do, we end up with:

(6a) "This sentence is false-in-L_0" is false-in-L_0.

But now there is no contradiction at all between (4a) and (6a) as there was between (4) and (6). Premise (4a) is a claim about truth-in-L_1, whereas (6a) is a claim about falsity-in-L_0. The paradox is stopped.

For as influential as Tarski's solution has been, it is not without its problems. First, it requires us to admit that the way we ordinarily use the word "truth" is a mistake. Tarski's *true-in-L* does not obviously correspond to our concept of truth. Indeed, on Tarski's view, our ordinary, commonsense notion of truth is paradoxical, just as the Liar Paradox shows. That's why we need to get rid of it and replace it with his conception.

The second problem, due to Saul Kripke (b. 1940 CE), is that it is not clear how Tarski's conception of truth is supposed to deal with Postcard-like cases. Suppose, for example, that two witnesses take the stand. Witness A says:

Most of what Witness B says about this case is false.

Whereas Witness B says:

Most of what Witness A says about this case is true.

How do the object languages and metalanguages fall out here? The metalanguage at which Witness A speaks would have to be higher than any of the metalanguages at which Witness B speaks and vice versa. But that is impossible. At any rate, when we make claims about the truth of the assertions of others, we don't state in advance the level—whether it is true-in-L_1 or true-in-L_2, etc.—at which we are making our claims. Complicating matters, it is not unreasonable to suppose that both Witness A and Witness B make these claims and that they are both true. They might both be true if most of what Witness A says simply states the facts of the case whereas most of what Witness B says are false accusations against Witness A.

References

Aristotle. *De Interpretatione*. In *The Complete Works of Aristotle.* Vol. 1. Trans. J. L. Ackrill. Ed. Jonathan Barnes. Princeton: Princeton UP, 1984.

Kripke, Saul. "Outline of a Theory of Truth." *Journal of Philosophy*. 72: 690–716, 1975.

The New Oxford Annotated Bible. Ed. Herbert May and Bruce Metzger. New York: Oxford UP, 1973.

Peirce, Charles. "Grounds of the Validity of the Laws of Logic: Further Consequences of Four Incapacities." In *The Essential Peirce*. Vol. 1. Ed. Nathan Houser and Christian Kloesel. Bloomington: Indiana UP, 1992.

Peirce, Charles. "The Categories Defended." In *The Essential Peirce.* Vol. 2. Ed. The Peirce Edition Project. Bloomington: Indiana UP, 1998.

Priest, Graham. "The Logic of Paradox." *Journal of Philosophical Logic*. 8(1): 219–41, 1979.

Tarski, Alfred. "The Concept of Truth in Formalized Languages." In *Logic, Semantics, Metamathematics*. 2nd ed. Trans. J. H. Woodger. Ed. J. Corocoran. Indianapolis: Hackett, 1983.

Medieval Philosophy

The Problem of Evil

The Ontological Argument

Science and Religion

PUZZLE FOUR

The Problem of Evil

We believe that everything that exists comes from the one God, and yet we believe that God is not the cause of sins. What is troubling is that if you admit that sins come from the souls that God created, and those souls come from God, pretty soon you'll be tracing those sins back to God.

—Augustine (354–430 CE), On Free
Choice of the Will, *Book One*

The Philosopher

Augustine is one of the most important figures in Christian philosophy and theology. We know a lot about his life because he wrote an autobiographical book titled *Confessions*. It's also his most famous work.

Augustine was born in the city Thagaste in modern-day Algeria. His mother was a Christian. His father was not. When he was a child, Augustine once scaled a stone wall. He stole some of his neighbor's pears and felt bad about it for the rest of his life. Augustine had a heightened sense of his own moral shortcomings.

As he matured, a patron sent Augustine to school in Carthage in modern-day Tunisia. He excelled academically. During this time, he is said to have prayed, "Grant me chastity and continence, just not yet." Chastity is sexual purity and continence is self-control, or the will to do what one thinks is right. Apparently, God complied. Augustine is known to have had several lovers.

Also during this time Augustine fell in with a group of religious people called Manichees. The Manichees practiced a religion called Manichaeism, founded by a man named Mani. Nowadays, the religion has no known practitioners.

Eventually, Augustine became disenchanted with Manichaeism. His objections to the religion were many, but two are particularly noteworthy. First, he objected to their conception of God. The Manichees thought of God as a spiritual being that pervades the entire universe. They thought God is eternal, but not all-powerful. God has a counterpart, an evil substance, which is a material being and of equal power to God. These two powers of good and evil, the Manichees believed, are at odds. In contrast, Augustine would come to believe that we ought to think of God as highly as possible. That means we should think of God as perfect, wholly good, omnipotent (all-powerful), omniscient (all-knowing), and immaterial. To do otherwise, he thought, was impious.

Second, Augustine objected to their soteriology, or theory of salvation. The Manichees believed that in order to be saved a religious devotee had to believe certain astronomical claims. However, advancements in astronomy had proven those astronomical claims to be false. Augustine thought it was bizarre that a religion required false beliefs in order to be saved. Although he realized that some of the claims recorded in the Bible were not literally true (such as that the world was created in six days—Augustine thought the creation story in the Bible was an allegory), he stressed that Christianity does not make one's salvation dependent on believing those claims. We'll discuss the relationship between science and religion more in Puzzle Six.

Augustine's disenchantment with Manichaeism might also be explained by his move to Italy. He had moved to Rome to open his own school and to teach rhetoric. Come the end of classes, Augustine's students fled without paying. As a result, he decided to leave Rome for Milan, where he gained a prominent teaching position.

While in Milan, Augustine heard a famous Manichee, Faustus, speak. Augustine had hoped he would learn the answers to many of his questions regarding their theology. In the end, though, he was thoroughly disappointed. Faustus was a bumbling speaker. In contrast, Augustine found Ambrose, a prominent Christian theologian, to be eloquent and intelligent. Unlike Faustus, Ambrose had reasonable answers to Augustine's questions.

Then one day Augustine sat in a garden. He heard children chanting, "Take up and read." He was moved to read the Bible. He picked it up and read Romans 13:13–14, written by Paul (c. 5–67 CE), mentioned in our third puzzle. It reads: "Let us conduct ourselves becomingly as in the day, not in reveling and drunkenness, not in debauchery and licentiousness, not in quarrelling and in jealousy. But put ye on the Lord Jesus Christ, and make no provision for the flesh, to gratify its desires." Finally, God did grant Augustine chastity and continence. He underwent a rapid religious conversion and devoted the rest of his life to Christianity. His mother was elated. By that time, his father was dead.

Augustine was eventually appointed bishop of the church in Hippo, Algeria, where he spent the rest of his life explaining and defending Christianity.

The Puzzle

Our fourth puzzle is the problem of evil. Like the Liar Paradox, the problem of evil is a puzzle that continues to generate considerable controversy even today.

The problem of evil is an objection not only to Christianity but to Judaism and to Islam as well. Really, it's an objection that confronts anyone who believes that God is wholly perfect and blameless, admits that God is concerned with human affairs, and yet affirms that suffering or evil exists.

The problem, in its most basic form, is this: If God is so perfect, so good, powerful, intelligent, loving, etc., then why does God allow suffering and evil to exist? Since God allows them to exist, God must be blameworthy for it. After all, they occur under God's watch. They occur with God's permission. They occur because God created—or at least manages—a world where suffering and evil *can* occur. Doesn't that make God responsible for them, at least in part?

There is no standard way to present the problem of evil. However, philosophers are in the habit of distinguishing between two different versions of the problem. The first version is usually called the logical problem of evil. This version of the problem was given its most famous statement by J. L. Mackie (1917–1981 CE). According to the logical problem of evil, believing that God is wholly good and that God is all-powerful and yet that evil exists is analogous to believing that squares have four sides, circles have no sides, and yet squares are circles. As a matter of logic, not all of those claims can go together. Obviously, we should deny squares are circles. In like manner, religious people have to either deny that God is wholly good, or deny that God is all-powerful, or deny that evil exists.

The second version of the problem of evil is called the inductive problem of evil. It was given its most famous statement by William Rowe (b. 1931 CE). According to this version of the problem, the fact that there are instances of suffering that are gratuitous—that have no purpose, that bring about no greater good and prevent no greater evil—supports the claim that there is no all-powerful, wholly good God, since any being with those attributes would prevent such suffering.

My preference is to present the problem of evil as a problem about whether God is blameworthy. This way of presenting the problem is suggested by the quotation from Augustine above. Although this way of presenting the problem has more affinities to the inductive problem of evil, it also enables us to incorporate features of the logical problem of evil. Cutting to the chase, here is the argument:

(1) Either there is gratuitous suffering or humans cause evil.

(2) If there is gratuitous suffering and God exists, then God is blameworthy for not diminishing it.

(3) If humans cause evil and God exists, then God is blameworthy for permitting it.

(4) God could not possibly be blameworthy.

(5) Therefore, God does not exist.

Obviously, some people are not religious. They don't believe in God. God, they think, is a figment of our imaginations, an illusion, a confusion, a fantastical delusion. Such people will not find this puzzle especially perplexing at all. They will simply accept the conclusion.

As for me, I am not certain whether God exists. What I do know is that very many people do believe in God. I also know that not a few extremely intelligent people—people more intelligent than I am and people who have thought much longer and more deeply about God than I have—believe in God's existence. I also know that there is an argument *for* God's existence, an argument that is just as puzzling as this argument *against* God's existence. (That will be our next, our fifth, puzzle.) So, I'm confident that it's at least plausible God exists. And if it's plausible, then it won't be a waste of time to puzzle through our current argument.

Moreover and more importantly, just because you agree with the conclusion of an argument, it does not follow that it is a sound argument. Consider, for example, this argument:

(6) If one plus one equals two, then God does not exist.

(7) One plus one equals two.

(8) Therefore, God does not exist.

If you don't believe God exists, then you concur with the conclusion of this argument. However, you'll also immediately recognize that this argument is horrible! Even though it is valid—that is, even though the conclusion follows from the premises—there is no good reason to think (6) is true. Obviously, one plus one can equal two *and* God can exist.

The question at hand for us is not whether *(5) is true* but whether *(1)–(5) is a sound argument*. It's entirely possible that (5) is true even though the argument for it in (1)–(4) is horrible. In other words, what we need to do here is set aside our personal commitments regarding God's existence. Instead of focusing on whether God exists, we need to focus on whether (1)–(5) is a good argument against God's existence. Maybe it is. Maybe it's not. That's what we need to figure out here.

One last comment: I mentioned above that there are different ways to present the problem of evil. Augustine gives us one, and Mackie and Rowe give us others. But Augustine is not the first philosopher to think of the problem of evil. That honor goes to the ancient Greek philosopher Epicurus (341–270 BCE). He argued that either (i) God can and wants to eliminate evil, (ii) God can but does not want to eliminate evil, (iii) God cannot but wants to eliminate evil, or (iv) God neither can nor wants to eliminate evil. Neither (iii) nor (iv) is befitting a God, since God is supposed to be powerful. Moreover, accepting (ii) or (iv) means God is spiteful. But God cannot be spiteful. So, the only option is (i). But then we have to wonder why there *is* evil. Epicurus concludes that God just doesn't care. Even though God wants to eliminate evil and can, he doesn't care enough to do anything about. It's akin to my desire to bench press 250 pounds. I want to do it. With training, I could do it. I just don't care enough to put in the effort.

The Premises

Each of premises (1)–(4) is plausible, even if you're a religious person. In order to see why, let's consider each in turn.

Premise (1)

I don't think anyone in this world will deny that there are evil humans and evil actions. Adolf Hitler, Joseph Stalin, Jeffrey Dahmer, and John Wayne Gacy, Jr. are examples of evil humans. Murder, rape, purposefully maiming a stranger, torturing babies, and plucking out the eyes of a dog and making the very same dog eat them are examples of evil actions. Evil humans do evil actions, even if not all of their actions are evil.

That said, not all evil actions are done by evil humans. Augustine stole pears from his neighbor. Martin Luther King, Jr. is alleged to have cheated on his wife. Theft and adultery are evil actions. Yet both Augustine and Martin Luther King, Jr. were very good people.

Granted that there are evil humans who do evil actions and good humans who do evil actions, it's not crazy to claim that humans cause evil. In fact, it's pretty clear that every human causes some evil. Augustine committed theft. Martin Luther King, Jr. allegedly committed adultery. Hitler (among many others) caused the Holocaust. Jeffery Dahmer committed rape and murder. These are all cases in which a person causes evil. Hence, humans cause evil.

You might wonder: Who decides what is moral or immoral, what is good or evil?

The answer is: I don't know. Maybe (in fact, probably) no one decides. Likely, some actions are moral or immoral quite independently of anyone's decisions or desires. In that case, morality may be an objective feature of the universe or of our very nature as humans. However, the important point here is not what *makes* an action good or evil. For theories about that, you'll have to read a book on ethics. Rather, the important point here is simply that people sometimes cause evil. Regardless of what *makes* actions evil, it's hard to deny that sometimes people do evil actions. Nonetheless, someone might press these issues: Isn't it possible that no actions are evil? And isn't morality just subjective anyway? First, if you deny that some actions are evil, then you have to admit that there is nothing evil about me locking you in my basement, chopping off your arm, applying a tourniquet, and then beating you senseless with your own severed arm every single day over the course of twenty years. And that seems like a really weird thing to say. You also have to admit that it wasn't evil for the guards of concentration camps to gas millions of people during the Holocaust. You have to admit that the genocide in Rwanda involved no evil actions. And you have to admit that if your own loved ones were raped, murdered, tortured, etc., then nothing evil has happened. Not only does saying those things sound weird, it sounds blameworthy too. Making such claims fails to recognize the harm people have endured and the injustices that demand reparation. People sometimes act evilly. When they do so, it's natural to affirm that they are the cause of evil. And to deny that people sometimes act evilly may very well be evil too.

Second, if you claim that some actions are moral or immoral but morality is really just subjective, you're probably wrong. To figure out why, however, you'll have to read a book on ethics. Nonetheless and more importantly here, even if morality is merely subjective, we sometimes act in a way contrary to what we think is good. Consider, for example, all of the times you have done things that you knew you shouldn't have done. Like the time you cheated on your girlfriend. Or the time you stole beer from the corner store. Or the time you beat up your little brother. Or the time you spread malicious lies about a romantic rival. You did those things knowing full well that you shouldn't. And so even if morality is subjective, you've still acted evilly. You have acted in a manner contrary to your own subjective views about what is good and evil.

Granted all of this, premise (1) is true. That's because all it takes to prove an *either . . . or . . .* statement true is to show that one of the disjuncts (the first disjunct is what comes after the "either"; the second disjunct is what comes after the "or") is true. For example, if you want to prove that: *Either Richard is tall or Richard is hungry,* all you have to do is prove that one of those is true. (As I'm writing this, both of them are.) Now, we've just shown that what comes after the "or" in (1) is true: humans cause evil. So, premise (1) is true. Furthermore, even the first disjunct—that there is gratuitous suffering—is plausible. To begin, we should note that not all suffering is gratuitous. Suppose I accidentally touch a hot burner on my stove and quickly move my hand. I suffer a little pain. But that pain is not gratuitous. In fact, it's a good thing I felt pain. The pain caused me to move my hand away from the burner. As a result, I avoided even greater pain, even greater harm to my person. To be sure, the suffering is undesirable. It is certainly unfortunate. But such suffering is not gratuitous. Some suffering is good.

Moreover, some suffering allows for even higher-order goods to exist. If we think of a world in which there is no pain, no suffering, it is hard to imagine how anyone could ever be compassionate, generous, or courageous. Go ahead and try to imagine such a world. You couldn't ease the suffering of others, because no one would be in pain. You couldn't give to charities, because no one would need them. You couldn't courageously run into burning buildings, because no one would be in danger anyway. A world without pain is a world devoid of higher-order goods like compassion, generosity, and courage. So, not all suffering is gratuitous. Some of it allows for greater kinds of goods.

Nonetheless, some suffering is gratuitous. Imagine a forest full of cute little animals. White-haired bunnies with floppy ears and bushy tails hop through the woods. Doe-eyed does drink from cool streams of spring water. Squirrels gracefully leap from tree branch to tree branch, gathering nuts for the winter. It's the most beautiful, lovely, and serene scene imaginable.

Now imagine a bolt of lightning strikes a dry heap of leaves and twigs. A fire consumes the forest. The bunnies, does, and squirrels start to choke on the smoke. They wheeze and cough. They run. But the ash-laden air makes breathing difficult. They can't escape the swiftly moving blaze. A ring of fire surrounds them. An impotent panic sets in. Smoldering ashes blow onto their fur. The smoke stings their watering eyes. They feel the fire licking their tails, hooves, and paws. But there's nothing they can do. Soon their fur is ablaze. They howl in pain. Only the fire's intensity matches the intensity of their guttural cries. They run to and fro, causing the fire to burn hotter and faster. The pain is unbearable, excruciating. Their only release is death, sweet and merciful death.

But for what end is their suffering? None. Does it bring about a greater good? No. (It's true that forest fires do have some good consequences, but one could have a forest fire without the suffering of animals.) Does it prevent a greater evil? No. Their suffering is gratuitous.

I have just painted the scene above as involving animals. But it can and has involved humans too. Imagine the molten lava of Vesuvius oozing over the bodies of Pompeii's citizens. Imagine the citizens of Sodom and Gomorrah—think especially of the innocent toddlers, babies, and animals, who surely did not *deserve* to suffer—consumed by fire (an act of God, according to the Bible). And we needn't think only of fires. Floods, hurricanes, tornadoes, typhoons, and earthquakes all bring with them instances of gratuitous suffering.

Moreover, even the acts of humans can result in gratuitous suffering. The suffering of the Holocaust was surely gratuitous. The suffering of justice's defenders under brutal regimes is sometimes gratuitous. The suffering of innocent children, caught in the midst of warfare or of famine, is gratuitous too. Can we really doubt that there are instances—indeed, many instances—of gratuitous suffering? It's hard to, and that is why premise (1) is so very plausible: either there is gratuitous suffering or humans cause evil. In all likelihood, both are true.

Premise (2)

The scenes I just described are terrifying and awful. If any of us were to witness them, we would try to help. In fact, even in the case of forest fires, we do try to help. We have helicopters, firefighters, and volunteers to stop or to manage such fires. If we can't save the animals, we at least try to end their suffering.

But where in all of this is God? What is that guy doing? If God exists, it seems downright cruel of him not to stop and help those floppy-eared bunnies, doe-eyed does, and industrious squirrels, not to mention all of us humans. God is all-powerful and all-loving. He can surely end their suffering. Since he doesn't but can, isn't he blameworthy for some of the suffering in this world? After all, if we could do something about it but didn't, we would be blameworthy.

And that's why premise (2) is true. If there is gratuitous suffering and God exists, then God is blameworthy for not diminishing it.

Premise (3)

Many religious people believe that everything that happens happens with God's permission. God is on the watch. God is always on the watch. And so anything that happens happens under his watch.

If that's true, then when a human does something evil, he does it with God's permission. And if God is permitting evil, isn't God partly to blame for those evils? God, after all, is all-powerful and all-knowing. God could have intervened. God could have stopped that bullet from piercing another man's heart. God could have forewarned that woman that a rapist lurked in her house. God could have stopped that torturer from pulling out his victim's fingernails. So, isn't God, in some sense, responsible for the evil that has occurred?

Compare this with us. If we could stop a murder, a rape, or torture, I hope that we would do so. If it were in my power to prevent a man's murder, or a woman's rape, or a torturer's torturing, I'd do it. But if I knew it was going to happen and if I could have stopped it but decided to sit idly by, aren't I, in some sense, responsible for what has happened? True, I didn't do the evil action myself. But I could have stopped it and I didn't. In that case, I bear some responsibility for the evil that occurred. I am, in some way, blameworthy.

Moreover, since I would be blameworthy, God is blameworthy too. God always knows when evil actions are going to happen. God always has the power to stop such evil actions. Yet God rarely, if ever, does so.

Not everyone will find this line of thought convincing. Some people think that we incur no blame even if we allow something evil to happen. In reply, our legal system disagrees, but no matter. Consider this: Suppose I can invent a gun with a really cool safety mechanism. This safety mechanism makes it such that my gun never fires when I plan to use the gun unjustly. In that case, I can't use the gun to commit murder. I can't use it to commit robbery. I can't use it for torture. And so on. But I can use the gun to prevent a murder. I can use it to fight on the just side of a just war. I can use it to defend myself. And so on.

If every gun could be made this way, it seems pretty clear that it should be. We should require every gun maker to install this safety mechanism on every gun. Also, we should blame gun makers who fail to install this really cool safety mechanism. Now consider the case of God. Suppose that God could invent us with a really cool safety mechanism. This safety mechanism makes it such that we can never act unjustly. In that case, we can't commit murder. We can't commit robbery. We can't torture. But we can still do all of the compassionate, generous, and courageous actions we've always done. Since God is all-powerful and all-knowing, God could have installed this safety mechanism on us. But God didn't. So, God is blameworthy just as a gun maker who fails to install the safety mechanism is blameworthy. Hence, if we do evil, we're responsible for it, but so is God for failing to install our safety mechanism.

One immediate objection to this will be that it means we have no free will. Free will seems to require the ability to do otherwise, to do a good rather than an evil action.

That last part, however, isn't true. I'm not sure what it means to have a free will (see Puzzle Nine). However, it's implausible to suppose that an action is free only if we can choose between a good and an evil option. Suppose a man has given me one hundred dollars. He informs me that, legally, I have to donate it either to UNICEF or to the Red Cross. In that case, there is no evil option I have. Nonetheless, I still freely choose whether to donate it to UNICEF or to the Red Cross. So why couldn't the same be true of us? God gives us a free will. We can choose to save the whales, volunteer at an adult literacy program, or plant a garden. We can't choose to maim innocent strangers or torture babies. We still have a free will precisely because we can decide to do one of the good actions. In order to have a free will, we don't have to be able to do evil actions as well.

Granted all of this, it follows that if we cause evil and God exists, then God is blameworthy for permitting it. And that is what premise (3) says.

Premise (4)

Our final premise is that God could not possibly be blameworthy. One reason to think (4) is true is because of what Augustine has said. We should think of God as highly as possible. As such, we should think that God cannot be blameworthy.

Furthermore, according to the traditions of the major mono-theistic religions, God is wholly good. If a being is wholly good, it never does anything wrong. But one is blameworthy only if one does something wrong. So, God could not possibly be blameworthy.

Possible Responses

Before considering which premises we might reject, we should note some features of this argument insofar as it is a dilemma. After that we'll look at our options for responding to the puzzle.

Responding to a Dilemma

The argument above—our statement of the problem of evil—is an example of a dilemma. Two options are presented: either there is gratuitous suffering or humans cause evil. Both options entail that God is blameworthy, if God exists.

An interesting feature of this kind of argument is that even if we deny premise (3), for example, we haven't entirely solved the puzzle. That's because there may very well be gratuitous suffering. And so premise (2) and the truth of the first disjunct of prem-ise (1)—that there is gratuitous suffering—still entails that God is blameworthy.

In a way, then, the puzzle above is really two arguments. The first argument, based on gratuitous suffering, is:

(1a) There is gratuitous suffering.

(2) If there is gratuitous suffering and God exists, then God is blameworthy for not diminishing it.

(4) God could not possibly be blameworthy.

(5) Therefore, God does not exist.

The second argument, based on humans causing evil, is:

(1b) Humans cause evil.

(3) If humans cause evil and God exists, then God is blameworthy for permitting it.

(4) God could not possibly be blameworthy.

(5) Therefore, God does not exist.

If we deny premise (3), we've responded to the second argument, the one based on humans causing evil. However, we still have to face the first argument, the one based on gratuitous suffering. The upshot of this is that there are five adequate responses to our puzzle aside from accepting the conclusion. They are:

> Reject (1a) and (1b)
>
> Reject (1b) and (2)
>
> Reject (1a) and (3)
>
> Reject (2) and (3)
>
> Reject (4)

Reject Premise (1b)

Our first step towards a solution might be to reject (1b), that humans cause evil. The problem is that rejecting (1b), as the first two options listed above do, borders on the insane. If you deny that humans cause evil, you must live a blessed and ignorant life. For every time I watch the news, I see humans causing evil. History is, by and large, the story of humans causing evil. And I myself have caused evil. I've stolen books (pathetic, I know). I've unnecessarily hurt other people. I've lied. I've cheated and I've helped other people cheat. I'm not perfect. And if you say that you are, you're either a liar or woefully unreflective.

I should note that some people have claimed evil does not exist. They say that evil is just a privation, or lack, of good. In the case of human actions, they claim that evil is really just a result of humans opting for lesser goods over their proper, higher good. Thomas Aquinas (1225–1274 CE), mentioned in our first puzzle, defends such a view. The catch, though, is this: If evil does not exist, if it is but a privation of a good, how can humans *cause* it? How can we cause evil when evil is not any *thing* at all?

Unfortunately, this response doesn't work well. It doesn't work for two reasons. First, we *can* cause privations. For example, when I dig a whole, there's a sense in which I cause a privation of dirt in a specific place (namely, where the hole is). When the fabric on the heel of my sock wears thin, there's a sense in which my walking has caused a privation of fabric on the heel of my sock. So, it's not all that strange to talk about causing privations.

Second, premises (1b) and (3) can easily be restated to accommodate such a view. All we have to do is rephrase (1b) and (3) as follows:

(1c) Humans sometimes opt for lower goods over their proper goods.

(3a) If humans sometimes opt for lower goods over their proper goods and God exists, then God is blameworthy for permitting it to happen.

(4) God could not possibly be blameworthy.

(5) Therefore, God does not exist.

Here, there is no claim that humans cause a privation. Rather, it is the very claim that those who deny evil exists endorse: humans sometimes opt for lower goods over their proper goods. With that revision, the argument still works. So, neither of the first two options—reject (1a) and (1b) *or* reject (1b) and (2)—works well.

Reject Premise (4)

The problem of evil, as noted above, is a problem for anyone who believes that God exists and is perfect. That is, it is a problem for anyone who thinks that God is wholly good, all-powerful, all-knowing, and so on. Thus, it is mainly a problem for anyone who adheres to one of the three major monotheistic religions: Judaism, Christianity, and Islam.

Yet someone might be willing to claim that God is not wholly good. In that case, we are in a position to deny (4). God may very well be blameworthy. It may turn out that God is just a big, bad guy in the sky. This, however, raises a question: Why should we worship God? Why is such a God worthy of our devotion?

One answer might be that we should worship God simply out of fear. After all, if God is not wholly good but is all-powerful, we certainly do not want to be on his bad side.

Another answer might be that we owe God our love and devotion. After all, God created us. God sustains us. And so, even though God is not wholly good, we should still worship God.

Aside from the fact that neither of those answers sounds very satisfying (who wants to worship someone out of fear?), characterizing God as not wholly good (and so blameworthy) runs contrary to all three of the major monotheistic religions. In point of fact, the God of the Bible is characterized the same way from the beginning to the end: as abounding in steadfast love and faithfulness. Thus, Genesis 24:27 reads, "Blessed be the Lord, the God of my master Abraham, who has not forsaken his steadfast love and his faithfulness towards my master," and 1 John 4:8, 10 reads, "God is love. . . . In this is love, not that we loved God but that he loved us."

In sum, even though we might reject (4), doing so is sharply contrary to all three major monotheistic religions and it raises the question of why we should care about God at all.

Thus far we have seen that neither rejecting premise (1b) nor rejecting premise (4) is a promising option. That means we *have to* reject premise (3) if we are to have an adequate response to the problem of evil. It also means that we will have to reject one of (2) or (1a). Let's now examine how that might be done.

Reject Premise (2)

Perhaps our first positive step toward a solution should be to reject premise (2). We should admit that even though there is gratuitous suffering and even though God exists, God is not blameworthy for failing to diminish it. But why might God not be blameworthy? Let's consider four different strategies.

Strategy One: Deny That God Is All-Powerful or Deny That God Is All-Knowing: Our first strategy is to claim that God is not blameworthy for failing to diminish suffering just because God is not *able* to diminish suffering. We cannot be blamed for failing to do what we are unable to do. For example, I cannot be blamed for failing to give 1,000,000 dollars to charity. Why? Because I don't, in fact, have 1,000,000 dollars to give. I cannot be blamed for failing to save the lives of people in a burning building in China. Why not? Because I'm in the United States and so I am unable to save them. In like manner, God might not be able to diminish suffering either because God is not powerful enough to (in other words, God is not all-powerful) or God is simply unaware of it (in other words, God is not all-knowing).

Whereas either of these strategies would solve the problem, they are also sharply contrary to the traditions of the major monotheistic religions. Moreover, we might wonder why such a weak and ignorant being is worthy of our devotion. Consequently, we face the same problems we faced in rejecting (4).

Strategy Two: God's Comparative Greatness: One of the most well-known stories in the Bible is that of Job (pronounced so that it rhymes with "robe" rather than "rob"). Job was an upright man. He had lots of land and cattle, a large family, a lovely wife, great friends, and his health. He loved and worshiped God.

One day, however, The Accuser (commonly understood to be Satan or the Devil) met up with God. The Accuser said that Job only loved God because God had made him prosper. He urged God to allow him to afflict Job. The Accuser believed that Job would curse God as soon as things started going badly. God disagreed. So, God allowed him to make poor Job suffer.

The Accuser began by destroying Job's cattle and crops. But Job didn't curse God. Next, The Accuser killed all of Job's children. Still, Job didn't turn his back on God. But The Accuser persevered. He caused painful sores and boils to fester on Job's skin. Job sat and scraped the sores off with broken pieces of pottery. His wife told him to curse God and die. Job's friends gathered around him and blamed Job for his suffering. But Job remained faithful to God.

Yet why did God allow Job to suffer like this? Surely it wasn't so he could win an argument with The Accuser. After all, if God is all-knowing, God knew he would win. So, is God blameworthy for Job's gratuitous suffering, assuming Job's suffering was gratuitous?

In the end, the book of Job exculpates God of Job's suffering. God doesn't offer us a reason for it. Instead, God claims that he can't be blamed for Job's suffering, saying, "Shall a faultfinder contend with the Almighty? He who argues with God, let him answer it. . . . Will you even put me in the wrong? Will you condemn me that you may be justified?" (Job 40:2, 8).

In short, God is saying: stuff it. Neither Job nor any of his friends are in a place to blame the Almighty. They may think that Job's suffering was gratuitous. They may think God is blameworthy. But, when it comes right down to it, they're in no position to say so. After all, they're mere mortals. They didn't lay the foundations of the earth. They didn't make the beasts of the fields. They didn't make the giants of the sea. They're not all-powerful. They're not wholly good. They're not all-knowing. So, they should zip it.

It's important to stress that the claim being made is *not* that God had a perfectly good reason for allowing Job's suffering. Rather, the claim being made here is that God is so great we are simply not in a position to blame God. Even if there is gratuitous suffering, God is outside of our jurisdiction, so to speak. We have no legal standing to blame God. After all, we're mere mortals. God is divine.

Strategy Three: This Is the Best of All Possible Worlds: Our third and fourth strategies are based on the same general notion: the best of all possible worlds. The third strategy uses the claim that this *is* the best of all possible worlds, and so God is not to be blamed for any of the suffering. Even though it's gratuitous, God couldn't make a world with any less. The fourth strategy uses the claim that this *may be* the best of all possible worlds, and so we're not in a position to blame God for any suffering. Both positions are to be attributed to Gottfried Leibniz (1646–1716 CE).

To begin, we might claim that this really is the best possible world. After all, if God were perfect, then God would make the best possible world. God is perfect. And so this must be the best of all possible worlds.

One problem with this argument is that it begs the question. To beg the question is to assume in one's argument what one needs to prove. In the present context, the very issue at stake is whether God exists and, if he does, whether he is perfect. So, to reply to the problem of evil by claiming that God is perfect is to assume what is at issue. That is begging the question.

A second problem with this strategy is that it is pretty obvious this is not the best possible world. All you have to do is look around. If just one instance of suffering were eliminated, and at least one of them clearly could be, the world would be better. Thus did Voltaire (1694–1778 CE) lampoon the claim that this is the best of all possible worlds in his novel *Candide*. Poor Candide, under the tutelage of Dr. Pangloss, had come to believe that this is the best of all possible worlds. In the course of the novel, he struggles mightily to maintain that belief in the face of life's hardships.

Yet a third problem with this solution is that it is tantamount to denying that there is gratuitous suffering at all, premise (1a). That is because God has made the world as best as he could. He could not make it such that there is less suffering. None of it is excessive. None of it is gratuitous.

Strategy Four: This May Be the Best of All Possible Worlds: For our fourth strategy, we might claim that God is not blameworthy because we are simply not in a position to claim that this is *not* the best possible world. We're just not in a position to say that this world is worse than some (or any) other possible world. We don't have the relevant information. We don't have enough information about how much suffering there is in this world. We have even less information about how much suffering there would be in any other possible world. Hence, while there is gratuitous suffering, we cannot blame God. We don't have enough evidence to blame, or convict, God for failing to make a better world.

One problem with this solution is that it does not seem very hard to conceive of worlds that are better than this one. As a consequence, it is strange to claim we do not know that this is not the best possible world. If we can conceive of a better world than this one, surely we do know that there is a better possible world. It's the very world we are conceiving of!

Reject Premise (1a)

As noted above, claiming that this is the best of all possible worlds may be tantamount to denying that there is gratuitous suffering. But there are other strategies for denying that there is gratuitous suffering. When we reject (1a) we are claiming that there is no gratuitous suffering. All of the suffering we see around us may *appear* to be gratuitous, but it is not *really* gratuitous.

Note that this line of response is different from rejecting (2). When we reject (2), we admit that there really is gratuitous suffering. What we deny is that just because there is gratuitous suffering God is blameworthy. Here, unlike with rejecting (2), we are not admitting that there is gratuitous suffering.

Strategy One: Suffering Has a Purpose: Above I discussed the story of Job. Another way to understand the story is that it explains why Job's suffering is not really gratuitous. On this view, God did have a good reason for allowing Job's suffering. But what could that reason be?

Some people have claimed that God allowed it as a test for Job. Others have claimed that God allowed it as an opportunity for Job to improve his own soul. Job's friends thought that his suffering was a just punishment for his wrongdoing. In these cases, we end up saying that Job's suffering was not gratuitous just because God had a good reason for allowing it.

Unfortunately, this strategy doesn't work very well, at least in the case of Job. First, why did God need to test Job? If God is all-knowing, he already knew whether Job would pass the test or not. So, why make Job take it?

Second, why was making Job suffer so much the only way to improve Job's soul? Couldn't God have done it another way? In fact, why did Job's soul need to be improved in the first place? According to the Bible, he was already a righteous man who had done no wrong. What was wrong with his soul such that it needed to be improved?

Third, according to the Bible, Job had done nothing wrong, so his suffering wasn't a punishment for wrongdoing.

A fourth problem is this: How could these claims possibly excuse the suffering of our fluffy-tailed bunnies and doe-eyed does burning in a forest fire? Sure, these claims about tests and improving Job's soul might excuse some suffering, but they don't excuse all suffering.

Strategy Two: Our Inability to Know Final Causes: Our first stab at denying gratuitous suffering wasn't very successful. Our second and third strategies require two different claims. The first claim is that we're not in a position to assert that there really is gratuitous suffering. The second claim is to argue that because we're not in a position to assert that there really is gratuitous suffering, we are at liberty to deny that there is gratuitous suffering.

One attempt at this strategy is found in René Descartes' (1596–1650 CE) famous book *Meditations on First Philosophy*. Descartes claims that he has found the study of final causes to be useless in the study of nature. The study of final causes is the study of the purposes or proper functions of things in the natural world. We all know that some things in the world have specific purposes or functions. The purpose of a heart is to pump blood. The purpose of eyes is to see. The purpose of baskets is to hold or to carry things. These are examples where the final cause of something is clear.

But what is the purpose of the universe itself? What is the purpose of the myriad stars in the sky? What is the purpose of other planets orbiting different suns? What is the purpose of a particular wave lashing the shore, of a particular grain of sand, or of a particular flea? In these examples, the answer isn't forthcoming. It's really hard to say what their purposes are.

That said, neither are we in a position to claim that such things have no purposes at all. Maybe they do, we're just not in a position to know what it is. For example, for a long time people thought that the appendix served no purpose. They claimed it was a vestigial organ, an evolutionary remnant. However, studies have recently shown that the appendix does have a purpose. It holds important intestinal bacteria so that the bacteria can be repopulated in case of illness. Perhaps the same is true of the universe itself, of the myriad stars, and of the other planets orbiting different suns. We don't know their purposes now, and maybe we never will, but they do have a purpose.

The very same considerations can be applied to suffering. In some cases the purpose of suffering is fairly obvious. When I put my hand on a stove's hot burner and feel pain, the purpose is clearly to get me to move my hand. In other cases, the purpose of suffering is less clear. Such may be true of Job's suffering. But just because we can't tell what the purpose of such suffering is, it doesn't follow that it has no purpose. The appearance of gratuitous suffering may be just that, an appearance. And that's the import of Descartes' point: if the study of final causes is useless in the study of nature, we can't show that apparently gratuitous suffering really *does* have a purpose.

Yet that's a double-edged sword. Why? It's a double-edged sword because neither can a proponent of the problem of evil show that such suffering *does not* have a purpose.

That is the first claim we needed to make to get this strategy to succeed: we're not in a position to say that there really is gratuitous suffering. The second claim we need to make is that the first claim puts us at liberty to reject (1a). But why should that be so? Some people claim that if we're not in a position to pass judgment, then we should suspend our belief. They will say that we're not at liberty to deny that cases of apparently gratuitous suffering are really gratuitous. Rather, our only option is to say that we just don't know. We should be agnostic about the issue and, consequently, agnostic about God's existence.

This claim, however, is mistaken. To see why, suppose that your best friend Steve has been brought up on charges of grand larceny. There is not enough evidence to convict him, but neither is there evidence showing he is innocent. Should you now be agnostic about whether Steve is guilty? Considering that Steve is your good friend, what you should do is give him the benefit of the doubt. You should deny that he is guilty of the crime.

The same consideration applies to God and gratuitous suffering. We're not in a position to conclude that there is (or is not) gratuitous suffering. Now the religious believer thinks of God as a good friend. So, a religious believer should give God the benefit of the doubt. The religious believer should deny that there is gratuitous suffering, just as you should deny that Steve is guilty of grand larceny.

Strategy Three: Our Cognitive Condition: William Alston (1921–2009 CE) develops a second way of showing that we're not in a position to claim instances of suffering really are gratuitous. Alston doesn't deny that there may be instances of gratuitous suffering; he just claims that we are not in a rational position to say that there are. The question of whether there is gratuitous suffering is simply too complex and we lack sufficient data.

To give a taste of how complex these issues are, Alston points to a variety of claims that might be made with respect to supposedly gratuitous suffering. It's important to note that he is not affirming these claims really do show that there is no gratuitous suffering, as our first strategy in this section does. Rather, he is affirming that because the issue is so complex, we're not yet in a position to claim that purported instances of gratuitous suffering really are gratuitous. Perhaps, after all, a person's suffering is proportioned to his sinfulness. Perhaps the suffering is for the purpose of improving someone's soul. Perhaps some suffering contributes to the improvement of others, as (for example) the suffering of martyrs has led other people to turn to God. Perhaps suffering brings about greater goods. Perhaps some suffering is necessary for a good, a good like having a free will. Perhaps suffering is necessary to retain the lawful ordering of the universe. All of these possible explanations—and more besides—must be taken into account if we are to conclude that there are in fact instances of gratuitous suffering.

Now here is the kicker: the complexity of the issue and our current cognitive condition entail that we are incapable right now of making a determination as to whether any suffering really is gratuitous. It may be. It may not be. What we need is more evidence. On Alston's view, it's not that we are literally incapable of figuring out whether instances of suffering are gratuitous. We are capable of figuring it out. The problem is simply that we lack all of the information we need to make a determination at this time.

At this stage we need to make recourse to the second claim made in the previous section. If Alston is correct, then we cannot conclude that some instance of *supposedly* gratuitous suffering is *in fact* gratuitous suffering. Granted that that is so, a religious believer does not need to be agnostic about God's existence. Rather, once again, because God is the religious person's good friend, God should be given the benefit of the doubt. The religious believer is at liberty to reject (1a) since there is no conclusive evidence for it.

Strategy Four: The Nature of Bodies: Lastly, let's consider another way to claim that there really is no gratuitous suffering. This strategy is to deny that suffering can rightly be described as gratuitous in the first place. To be sure, suffering is undesirable. No one wants to suffer. Certainly, suffering is unfortunate. But suffering itself is never gratuitous. It is simply a consequence of the way natural beings like humans, bunnies, and does are made or "designed."

An example will be helpful. Imagine a sheep. He is grazing in the field, enjoying the tender shoots of spring grasses. The sun warms his thick, soft fleece. Cool water babbles in a nearby brook. Then, suddenly, a lioness lunges. She grabs the sheep with her razorlike claws. She sinks her sharp teeth into the sheep's hind. The sheep bleats, writhes, and dies.

Clearly, the sheep suffered. But that suffering wasn't gratuitous. The sheep's body reacts and behaves as sheep bodies do and should. Sheep bodies have nerves. Those nerves are necessary to interact with the world. They are necessary to avoid harm. They are necessary to enjoy pleasures. Unfortunately for the sheep, though, those very same nerves can also cause great pain when a lioness grabs him with her claws and sinks her teeth into his hind. That's unfortunate, but it's not gratuitous. It's just the way that nerves and bodies like those of a sheep work.

Consider another example. Imagine a person grabs my hand and holds it to a stove's hot burner. I am going to suffer. The pain will be incredibly intense. But is there something wrong with my suffering *itself*? Is it gratuitous? Unquestionably, there is something deeply wrong with a person holding my hand against a burner. No one would deny that. Yet the question here is whether there is something wrong with my suffering, with the very pain I feel, such that we should call my suffering gratuitous.

In this case, it's not clear that there is. My hand has nerves. Those nerves cause me to feel pain. As we know from cases where I accidentally put my hand on a burner, feeling that pain is a good thing. It enables me to avoid a greater harm. Unfortunately, those same nerves can also cause great pain when my hand is held to a burner. It's unfortunate. It's undesirable. But it's not gratuitous. That's just the way bodies like mine work. I'd rather be able to feel the pain than risk severe burns every time I accidentally touch something hot.

As these examples show, it is important to distinguish an animal's suffering from the cause of its suffering. The sheep suffers. Yet his body has done nothing wrong. A lioness has caused that suffering. Yet the lioness hasn't even done something wrong. Lionesses aren't morally blameworthy for their actions. They have to hunt prey to survive.

Again, when a person holds my hand to a hot burner, I suffer. But my body has done nothing wrong. It's functioned as it's supposed to function. It's functioned as a body like mine functions. My suffering isn't gratuitous, just undesirable and unfortunate. Of course, the person who holds my hand to the burner has done something wrong. But that is a separate issue, one to be taken up in the next section.

What about bodies that do not function properly? What about bodies where the nerves don't behave as they ought? What about instances when a person feels pain not because some other agent like a lioness or a human causes it but because the body itself causes it?

In response to these questions, we must point out that bodies are corruptible. They fail. They get out of whack. A slipped disc in one's back will cause excruciating pain. Genetic anomalies can cause severe suffering. Yet again, it's possible to respond that even in these cases the nerves and genes are merely functioning as nerves and genes do. Pinched nerves cause pain. That's just what nerves do. Similarly, genes mutate. That's their nature. Do these things cause suffering? Yes. Is it undesirable and unfortunate? Yes. Is it gratuitous? No. It's just the way the world works.

Reject Premise (3)

As noted above, an adequate response to the problem of evil will require denying (3). What we must do is show that it can be true that humans cause evil and God exists *and yet* false that God is blameworthy.

Strategy One: God's Comparative Greatness: First, we can deny God is blameworthy for permitting evil just as the story of Job denies God is blameworthy for gratuitous suffering. God is out of our jurisdiction. We're mere mortals. Who are we to say that God is blameworthy for permitting humans to cause evil? That's like drawing a picture, the very picture as you want it to be, and then the picture complaining you didn't do a better job of drawing it. Who's the drawing to complain? After all, it wouldn't even exist if you hadn't drawn it.

The problem here is that we're the ones to complain precisely because we're the ones suffering from the evil God permits. We're the ones who have to deal with the consequences, not God. Though it's possible our suffering itself isn't gratuitous, it doesn't follow that God should permit the evil that causes our suffering. And when God does so, we are surely within our rights to complain.

Strategy Two: Descartes or Alston, Reprise: Alternatively, we might respond in the way that Descartes or Alston does. We can admit that humans cause evil. However, we're not in a position to claim that God is blameworthy for permitting it to happen. Perhaps there is a good reason that God permits humans to cause evil, even though we're not in a position to know what the reason is. Perhaps we're not in that position because the study of final causes is, as Descartes claims, useless. Perhaps we're not in that position because the questions are so complex. In either case, if God is our good friend, we're at liberty to deny (3).

Strategy Three: The Free Will Defense: One of the most common strategies for explaining why God is not blameworthy for our evil actions is that we have free will. God cannot be held responsible for our free actions. So, God is not blameworthy.

An analogy is helpful. You're someone's child, though you're now an adult. Moreover, you have a free will. Also, you've done things that are wrong. Maybe you stole something. Maybe you unnecessarily harmed another person. Maybe you've driven drunk. Whatever evil action you've done, you did it freely. But suppose you had been caught (maybe you were!). Would your parents have been arrested? Would they have been held responsible for your crimes? The answer is no. You alone are blameworthy for your actions.

The same may be true of God with respect to us. Just because we do something wrong, it doesn't follow that God is responsible for our actions. We're the one's who are blameworthy, not God. We did the action of our own free will.

Does this strategy work? We have already seen two reasons for thinking it does not. First, why didn't God install a "safety mechanism" on us such that we can do no wrong? Second, why doesn't God intervene when we're about to act evilly? After all, our parents (hopefully!) would if they could.

Defenders of the free will strategy have replies to these two objections. To the first, they may reply that a free will is such that it can have no safety mechanism. Descartes takes this view. He claims that our will does nothing but pass judgment on, or make decisions about, objects of appetite or aversion. It either says yes or no, it seeks out or avoids. Moreover, Descartes thinks it is essential to the very nature of a will to be unlimited. If God were to limit our wills such that they can only say "yes" or only say "no" on certain occasions, we would no longer be talking about a will. So, God cannot put a "safety mechanism" on our wills.

It's important to note that this sort of reply does not threaten God's omnipotence. God, many philosophers assume, cannot do what is logically impossible. God cannot make squares with only three sides. God cannot make married bachelors. God cannot make red things that aren't colored. God cannot make bodies that occupy no space. And, Descartes would say, God cannot make wills with "safety mechanisms."

In response to this, other people have claimed that while God may not be able to restrict our wills, God could have given us dispositions that strongly incline us to always choose good actions over evil actions. For example, I am strongly disinclined to physically harm other people or animals. I have never even punched another person (except my older brother, but he deserved it). Nevertheless, when I refrain from punching my very loud, very annoying downstairs neighbor and kicking his yappy dog, I still do it freely. If that's true, why didn't God give us dispositions that strongly incline us to always choose the good option over the evil one?

Here again defenders of the free will strategy have a response. They can claim that moral dispositions are by their very nature things that have to be cultivated. If we were born strongly and naturally disposed to be compassionate, generous, and courageous, then we would not have moral dispositions at all. These would be natural dispositions, not dispositions deserving of praise or blame. To compare, our bones are naturally disposed to break when they are hit with a baseball bat. But that's not a moral disposition. It's just the way things are. It's a natural disposition. Such a natural disposition deserves neither praise nor blame. In contrast, moral dispositions, the things that incline us to do good or evil actions, have to be developed. They cannot be inborn, for then they would not be *moral* dispositions at all.

This brings us to the second objection: Why doesn't God intervene when we're about to do evil actions? This is a very difficult question. One possible answer is that if God intervened whenever we were about to do evil actions then it would rob us of praise whenever we did good actions. Suppose that a father stopped his child every time she were about to do something blameworthy.

Instead, he only allowed her to proceed when she were about to do something praiseworthy or blameless. In that case, praise just doesn't seem right. His child did the only action she could have done. Similarly, we wouldn't deserve praise if God stopped us every time we were about to do something blameworthy. The praiseworthy action is the only action we could have done. For that reason, to preserve praiseworthiness, God does not intervene. Unfortunately, this line of response doesn't work well. Some actions are so very evil that it is better the action be stopped than that we deserve praise. Did the Holocaust really have to happen so that we could preserve praiseworthiness? It would be much better that we not be deserving of praise, at least in that time period, and for the Holocaust to have never happened.

Another way to respond to this question—Why doesn't God intervene?—is to appeal to the strategy of Job, of Descartes, or of Alston. Once again, we're simply not in a position to blame God for not intervening. Perhaps that is because God is so great. Perhaps it is because we don't have enough information. Whatever the case, if God is our good friend, we're at liberty to deny that God is blameworthy for failing to intervene.

Accept the Conclusion

Perhaps you find none of these attempts to reject the premises plausible. Perhaps you do not think of God as your good friend. Perhaps you think it is obvious that this is not the best of all possible worlds. If so, you might accept the conclusion of the argument: God does not exist. Reaching that conclusion may be troubling or liberating. It may depress you; it may delight you. Whatever the case may be, we should accord our beliefs to the best evidence. And, whether it makes you happy or sad, the best evidence may very well weigh against God's existence.

References

Alston, William. "The Inductive Problem of Evil and the Human Cognitive Condition." In *Philosophical Perspectives*. Vol. 5. Atascadero: Ridgeview Publishing, 1991.

Augustine. *Confessions*. 2nd ed. Trans. F. J. Sheed. Ed. Michael P. Foley. Indianapolis: Hackett, 2007.

Augustine. *On Free Choice of the Will*. Trans. Thomas Williams. Indianapolis: Hackett, 1993.

Descartes, René. *Meditations on First Philosophy*. In *The Philosophical Writings of Descartes*. Vol. 2. Trans. John Cottingham, Robert Stoothoff, and Dugald Murdoch. Cambridge: Cambridge UP, 1984.

Leibniz, Gottfried. *Theodicy*. Trans. E. M. Huggard. Ed. Austin Farrer. New Haven: Yale UP, 1952.

Mackie, J. L. "Evil and Omnipotence." *Mind*. 64(254): 200–12, 1955.

The New Oxford Annotated Bible. Ed. Herbert May and Bruce Metzger. New York: Oxford UP, 1973.

Rowe, William. "The Problem of Evil and Some Varieties of Atheism." *American Philosophical Quarterly*. 16(4): 335–41, 1979.

Thomas Aquinas. *Summa Contra Gentiles: Book Three, Part One: Providence*. Trans. Vernon J. Bourke. Notre Dame: University of Notre Dame Press, 1991.

Voltaire. *Candide*. Trans. and Ed. Robert M. Adams. New York: W. W. Norton, 1991.

PUZZLE FIVE

The Ontological Argument

And surely that than which a greater cannot be thought cannot exist only in the understanding. For if it exists only in the understanding, it can be thought to exist in reality as well, which is greater. So if that than which a greater cannot be thought exists only in the understanding, then that than which a greater cannot be thought is that than which a greater can be thought. But that is clearly impossible. Therefore, there is no doubt that something than which a greater cannot be thought exists both in the understanding and in reality.

—Anselm (1033–1109 CE), Proslogion, 2

The Philosopher

Anselm's was a life of controversy. In his adult life, that controversy mainly stemmed from his position within the Catholic Church. He was the Archbishop of Canterbury in England centuries before the Church of England split from the Roman Catholic Church in 1538. Nonetheless, even in the eleventh century, the relationship between the king of England and the Catholic Church was highly contentious. In fact, it resulted in Anselm being exiled from England twice.

Yet even in youth, Anselm's life was one of controversy. Born into nobility in northern Italy, at the tender age of fifteen Anselm wanted to join a monastery. However, his father refused to grant him permission to do so. Anselm was heartbroken, crestfallen.

After getting over his heartbreak, Anselm became a free spirit. At that time it was common for young men seeking wisdom to wander about Europe in search of teachers. So when his mother died and his father became a royal pain in the neck, Anselm decided to strike off on his own. He was twenty-three.

Anselm eventually wandered all the way across France. In 1060, he ended up in Normandy. The reputation of a great scholar, Lanfranc, had drawn Anselm to the monastery of Bec. Anselm quickly gained a reputation as a bright student. One year later he became a monk at Bec. Two years after that Lanfranc left Bec for another monastery. As a result of Lanfranc's departure, Anselm became the primary teacher at Bec.

Anselm's students encouraged him to write his teachings down. He did so, first in a book titled *Monologion* (written c. 1075 CE) and then in a work titled *Proslogion* (written c. 1077 CE). By 1085, Anselm's works were widely read throughout Western Europe. His reputation grew. In 1093 Anselm was asked to succeed his former teacher Lanfranc as Archbishop of Canterbury. He reluctantly accepted the post, which he held—controversy and all—until his death in 1109.

The Puzzle

Anselm's argument for the existence of God may be one of the very coolest arguments ever made. It's a fascinating and puzzling argument, an argument that continues to receive attention even today.

To begin, suppose you are thinking of X. If you can think of something greater than X, then X is not that-than-which-nothing-greater-can-be-thought. On the other hand, if you're thinking of X and it is impossible to think of anything greater (not impossible because of your lack of imagination but because there really is nothing greater), then you're thinking about that-than-which-nothing-greater-can-be-thought.

Take yourself, for instance. You probably think you're pretty great. For the sake of argument, I'll admit that you are. But are you that-than-which-nothing-greater-can-be-thought? I suspect not. After all, you'd be greater if you were just a bit stronger. You'd be greater if you were just a bit smarter. You'd be greater if you never did an evil action. And you'd be greater still if I were to put you in a giant blender, turn it on, and it didn't harm you in the least. In short, we can think of something greater than you. So, you're not that-than-which-nothing-greater-can-be-thought. You might be close, but you're not it.

What makes Anselm's argument awesome is that from the very idea of that-than-which-nothing-greater-can-be-thought we can prove that that-than-which-nothing-greater-can-be-thought really exists. That-than-which-nothing-greater-can-be-thought isn't just a creation of your mind. It isn't just a figment of your imagination. To the contrary, that-than-which-nothing-greater-can-be-thought really exists. And we can know it exists just from the fact that we can think of that-than-which-nothing-greater-can-be-thought! If Anselm's argument is sound, that's pretty awesome.

We can express Anselm's argument in this way:

Let TTWNGCBT = That-Than-Which-Nothing-Greater-Can-Be-Thought.

(1) If TTWNGCBT exists in thought and not in reality, then we can think of something greater than TTWNGCBT, namely TTWNGCBT existing *both* in our thought and in reality.

(2) We cannot think of something greater than TTWNGCBT.

(3) TTWNGCBT does exist in thought.

(4) Therefore, TTWNGCBT exists in reality.

It may not be obvious, but this is a valid argument. If you accept premises (1)–(3), then you *have* to accept the conclusion. But can you really argue from the mere fact that you have the *thought* of TTWNGCBT to its *actual existence*? After all, we can think of lots and lots of things that don't really exist. For example, we have thoughts of unicorns, Sherlock Holmes, Pegasus, gold mountains, and socially adept philosophers. All of those things are figments of our imaginations. We don't conclude from the mere thought of them that they exist. But it seems to be otherwise with TTWNGCBT. We can conclude from the mere thought of it that it exists. And that's a very strange—and surprising—conclusion indeed!

The Premises

What can be said in defense of the premises in Anselm's argument? Let's consider each in turn.

Premise (1)

Existence in thought and in reality is greater than existence in thought alone. I remind myself of this every time I check my bank account. Thinking I have 1,000 dollars in my bank account *and really having it* is far better than thinking I have 1,000 dollars in my bank account and *not really having it*. After all, I can do something with 1,000 dollars I really have. I can't do anything with a merely imagined 1,000 dollars. Trust me, I've tried.

In like manner, TTWNGCBT existing in thought and in reality is greater than TTWNGCBT existing in thought alone. Wouldn't it be nice if TTWNGCBT really existed? Then it could actually do things. It might answer my prayers for 1,000 more dollars in my bank account, for example. So, existing in thought and in reality is greater than existing in thought alone. And that is why premise (1) is true.

It might be objected that existence in reality is not always greater than existence in thought alone. Evil existing in reality and thought does not seem to be better than evil existing in thought alone. Assuming evil exists at all (see Puzzle Four) this is a good point. But Anselm's argument does not actually depend on the general claim that existence in reality and in thought is always greater than existence in thought alone. Rather, it only depends on the claim that TTWNGCBT existing in reality and thought is greater than TTWNGCBT existing in thought alone. And that, at least, is quite plausible.

Nonetheless, if you're skeptical of that line of thought, another reason to think that (1) is true is that if something exists in thought and not in reality, it follows that the thing is *contingent*. It does *not have to exist*. For example, I am a contingent being. If you put me in a giant blender and turn it on, I'll die. I'll get pureed into delicious bits and pieces. I'll cease to exist. So, I'm contingent.

But some beings might be *necessary*. Necessary beings are the sorts of things that *cannot* die. If you put a necessary being in a blender and turn it on, the necessary being will still exist. It's *incapable of inexistence*.

Being a necessary being would be pretty great. It would be greater than just being a contingent being. Contingent beings fall apart. They die. They break. Their bits and pieces scatter to the ends of the earth. In a word, they're physically corruptible. Necessary beings aren't like that. They don't fall apart. They don't die. They

don't break. They're incorruptible. Being a necessary being, therefore, must be a whole lot greater than being a contingent being.

In sum, if TTWNGCBT exists in thought and not in reality,
then TTWNGCBT must be contingent. But if TTWNGCBT
is contingent, then we can think of something that is greater than TTWNGCBT. Specifically, we can think of a being like
TTWNGCBT but that is necessary rather than contingent, which
is incapable of inexistence. So, if TTWNGCBT exists in thought
and not in reality, then we can think of something greater than
TTWNGCBT.

Premise (2)

The second premise of Anselm's argument is obviously true. If you
can think of something greater than *what you think is TTWNGCBT*,
then *what you think is TTWNGCBT* is not in fact TTWNGCBT.
You need to rethink your grasp of TTWNGCBT.

By analogy, suppose you think the number four is the greatest
number thinkable. If you can think of a number greater than the
number four (and you can!), then the number four is not the greatest number thinkable. So, you are wrong. You need to rethink your
grasp of the greatest number thinkable. It's not in fact the number four. Similarly, if you realize that you can think of something
greater than *what you took to be TTWNGCBT* it turns out that what
you took to be TTWNGCBT wasn't TTWNGCBT after all. You
simply cannot think of something greater than TTWNGCBT.

Premise (3)

I'm pretty weak. I'm not the weakest person I know. Babies are
weaker than me. Whenever I get into fights with them I win, barely.
But every time I watch a football game, a baseball game, or a bas-
ketball game—or pretty much any sporting event—I realize that
there are people stronger than me. So, I'm not the strongest being
thinkable.

The same goes for intelligence. I'm pretty smart. I know quite
a few things. But there are people who know way more than me.
Sure, there are people a lot less intelligent than me too. Nonetheless,
some people are smarter than me. So, I'm not the smartest being
thinkable.

I'm a pretty good person. I'm not a drunkard. I'm not a glutton. I don't abuse any animals or any people. I try to help others out when I'm in a position to do so. But I'm not perfect. I've stolen books, for example. I've insulted people for no good reason. I've hurt the feelings of my loved ones. I've cheated. I'm not the best person thinkable, and so I'm not TTWNGCBT.

Nevertheless, even though I'm not super strong, super smart, and super moral, I can think of a being that is. I can think of a being that can do anything (omnipotent), a being that knows everything (omniscient), and a being that is morally perfect. And so I can think of TTWNGCBT. That's why premise (3) is true. TTWNGCBT exists in my mind, in my thoughts.

Possible Responses

What are we to make of Anselm's argument? Let's begin by considering ways to reject one of the premises and then move to the option of accepting the conclusion.

Which premise might we reject? First off, it should be pretty clear that we cannot reject premise (2). Premise (2) is true by definition. Nothing can be greater than TTWNGCBT. So, we cannot think of something greater than TTWNGCBT. Therefore, the only premises that we are able to reject in this argument are premises (1) and (3). Let's start with the latter.

Reject Premise (3)

Strategy One: The Paradox of Omnipotence: One peculiarity of Anselm's argument is that he talks about TTWNGCBT as existing in thought. What does it mean for something to exist in thought? Is it even right to say that a thing—anything—"exists" in thought?

Fortunately, Anselm's argument does not hinge on the notion of things "existing" in thought. All that really matters is the fact that we can think of TTWNGCBT.

But what does it take to think of TTWNGCBT? To be thinking of TTWNGCBT, what do we have to be doing?

To begin, we must note that just because we can articulate the words and know what each individual word means, it does not follow that we really have the thought of TTWNGCBT. By comparison, we can articulate the words "square circle" and we know what each word—square and circle—means individually. But it is impossible to really think of a square circle. That's like having the thought of a non-red red or of a married bachelor. So being able to string the words together and knowing the meaning of each word does not show that we can think of TTWNGCBT.

What *does* it take to think of TTWNGCBT? I'm not entirely sure. But the prior comments do show that we *cannot* think of anything that is self-contradictory. The very idea of a square circle is self-contradictory, for squares have sides and circles do not. The very idea of a non-red red is self-contradictory because all reds must be red. The very idea of a married bachelor is not conceivable because no bachelors are married. Hence, if TTWNGCBT involves a contradiction in the ways that "square circle," "non-red red," and "married bachelor" do, then we can deny premise (3). TTWNGCBT cannot be thought. It does not exist in thought.

Some people have claimed that the idea of TTWNGCBT is self-contradictory. To see why, suppose that TTWNGCBT is omnipotent. That is certainly plausible, for an omnipotent thing is greater than a thing that is not omnipotent. Now we can ask: Can an omnipotent TTWNGCBT make a boulder so heavy it cannot lift it? If so, then TTWNGCBT must not be omnipotent for there is something that it cannot do (namely, lift such a boulder). If not, then TTWNGCBT is not omnipotent for there is something that it cannot do (namely, make such a boulder). Either way there is something an omnipotent being cannot do. But that means it is not really omnipotent. So, the very idea of an omnipotent TTWNGCBT is self-contradictory. This is known as the paradox of omnipotence.

This line of argument, however, does not prove that TTWNGCBT is unthinkable. It only shows that TTWNGCBT is not omnipotent in the sense of "being able to do anything." So, it turns out that if our conception of TTWNGCBT is one of an omnipotent being, we've just made a mistake. It's like we've tried to think of a square circle. In the end, we haven't really thought of any*thing* at all.

Yet if we dial back the power of TTWNGCBT a little bit we can still preserve premise (3). Instead of thinking of TTWNGCBT as an omnipotent being and of omnipotence as "being able to do anything," all we have to do is think of TTWNGCBT* as omnipotent* and think of omnipotence* as being "as powerful as is thinkable." While an omnipotent being might be unthinkable, an omnipotent* being is surely thinkable. In this way, we still have to admit that *that* being—TTWNGCBT*—can be thought even granted the paradox of omnipotence.

To put the above point another way, Anselm is not staking a claim on what the properties of TTWNGCBT are other than that it is TTWNGCBT. Now if TTWNGCBT really is thinkable, it *follows* that TTWNGCBT must also be conceivable. It must not be like thinking of a square circle or of a non-red red. But Anselm is not *assuming* that TTWNGCBT is conceivable.

Strategy Two: Experience: Maybe there are yet other reasons we cannot think of TTWNGCBT. One possible line of attack—found in the work of Anselm's contemporary Gaunilo (c. 1090 CE)—is to claim that in order for TTWNGCBT to exist in thought we have to have had some *encounter* with it before or some *experience* of it. In order for me to think of a cat I have to have experienced a cat. In order for me to think of a chair I have to have experienced a chair. In order for me to think of water I have to have experienced water. In order for me to think of TTWNGCBT I have to have experienced TTWNGCBT. But I've never done that. I hang out at bars and on street corners all the time and still have yet to meet TTWNGCBT. So, I do not have the thought of TTWNGCBT.

This objection fails, however, because we can think of things without having experienced them. I have the thought of a unicorn, but I have never encountered a unicorn (except in my most wonderful dreams). I have never encountered a goat that lives on sunshine, but I have the thought of it. So, having an experience of something is not a requirement for having the thought of it.

Someone might reply to this objection in the following way: While it is true that you've never encountered a unicorn, you have encountered horses and horns. So, you can develop or construct the thought of a unicorn. Also, while it is true that you have never encountered a goat that lives on sunshine, you have encountered goats and photosynthetic plants. So, you can put these thoughts together and develop the idea of a goat that lives on sunshine. Accordingly, to think of something it is not required that you experience the thing but it is required that you experience the features of the thing that the thought is built out of. In the case of unicorns, that's horses and horns. In the case of a goat that lives on sunshine, you have to encounter goats and organisms that live on sunshine.

Those claims may very well be correct. Unfortunately, it doesn't help prove premise (3) false. That is because I *can* build up the thought of TTWNGCBT from my experiences. I have never experienced TTWNGCBT, but I have met some people who are more moral than others. I have met some people who are stronger than others. I have met some people who are smarter than others. With these experiences in mind, I can build up a thought of a being that is the *most* moral, the *most* strong, and the *most* smart. That being is TTWNGCBT. Consequently, I can think of TTWNGCBT.

Strategy Three: Complete Understanding: Maybe there is another way to reject premise (3). We can argue that in order to think of TTWNGCBT we have to understand it fully. We have to understand it in all of its aspects. Since we can never *fully* understand TTWNGCBT, we cannot think of it. After all, presumably such a being is infinite. And I, finite thing that I am, am incapable of fully thinking of infinity.

Unfortunately, this strategy won't work either. It's too strong. I assume that we can all think of the number two. But to understand the number two, do I have to know it in all of its aspects? I know that one and one are two. But three and negative one are also two. A half and one and a half are also two. Do I have to know all of the sums that equal two to think of the number two? That would mean no one can think of the number two, but that sounds crazy. So, thinking of something doesn't require understanding it in every aspect.

Another example may be helpful. If I go hiking and look out from a scenic ledge at a distant mountain, I am thinking of that mountain. But do I have to understand that mountain in every aspect in order to think of it? Do I have to be able to fully understand it? The answer is surely no. Similarly, to think of TTWNGCBT, I don't have to understand it fully. I only have to understand it in some aspects. Most important for Anselm's argument, I have to understand that it *existing in reality and thought* is greater than it *existing in thought alone.* Once I realize that, I cannot but avoid concluding that TTWNGCBT exists.

Reject Premise (1)

Another way of responding to Anselm's argument is to reject premise (1). One way of doing so is owed to Immanuel Kant (1724–1804 CE). Kant's response is really directed at another version of the ontological argument, one developed by Descartes and explained below, but we might try to adapt it as a response to Anselm's.

Kant argues that existence is not a real predicate. As a consequence, the mere fact that something *is* does not make it any greater than anything else. To see why Kant thinks existence is not a real predicate we first need to understand what a predicate is. A simple sentence, such as "The chair is red," has two parts. The first part is the subject. The subject of *the chair is red* is *the chair*. The other part is the predicate. The predicate of *the chair is red* is *is red*.

Predicates tell us something about the subject. They might tell us something that is essential to the subject itself, something we cannot separate from the idea of the subject. For example, *is four-sided* is a predicate essential to the very idea of a square. Alternatively, predicates might tell us something about the subject even though the predicate is not essential to it. For example, *is red* is a predicate of *the chair*, but we could easily reupholster the chair to be blue. We can separate redness from the idea of the chair.

The question becomes: What does the concept of "existence" add to our thought of TTWNGCBT? For starters, we should note that to say that something *exists* is nothing more than to say that it *is*. "To exist" and "to be" are synonymous. They mean the same thing.

Moreover, the verb "to be" is conjugated as follows:

I am . . .	We are . . .
You are . . .	You are . . .
He/ She/ It is . . .	They are . . .

Now granted that "to exist" and "to be" are synonymous, to affirm that:

TTWNGCBT exists.

is no more than to affirm:

TTWNGCBT is.

Yet this raises a question: *What* or *how* is it? TTWNGCBT is *what?* Here we get to the crux of the issue. Predicates are supposed to tell us something about their subjects. However, "is" all by itself doesn't tell us anything about the subject. "Is red" tells us about the color of the chair. "Is four-sided" tells us about how many sides squares have. But "is" doesn't tell us anything about TTWNGCBT. In like manner, *the chair is* doesn't tell us anything about the chair. Moreover, *the square is* doesn't tell us anything about the square. So, saying that something exists, that it is, doesn't add anything to our idea of it. It doesn't make it greater. It doesn't make it lesser. It doesn't tell us anything at all. As a consequence, it is not a real predicate. Why? Because real predicates *do* tell us something about their subjects.

In short and in sum, the thought of an existing TTWNGCBT is *equal* to the thought of a non-existing TTWNGCBT, not *greater* than it. That's because "existing" isn't a real predicate. It doesn't add anything to our thought of TTWNGCBT. So, premise (1) is false.

Kant's argument, however, seems to miss the mark here, though it may succeed as a response to Descartes' version of the argument. It misses the mark here because "is real" does add something to our thought of TTWNGCBT. For example, the predicate "is real" in "London is real" and "Sherlock Holmes is not real" does tell us something about both London and about Sherlock Holmes.

Accept the Conclusion

We turn now to two further options. The first option is to accept the conclusion straightforwardly. The second option is to accept the conclusion but with a huge caveat. Let's consider each here.

Strategy One: Accept the Conclusion Straightforwardly: Our first option is to simply accept the conclusion as it stands. TTWNGCBT exists, just like I exist, just like you exist, and just like any other object in the world exists.

Note that if we accept the conclusion we don't have to think that any particular religion is true. TTWNGCBT might be something like God. But it may not be. After all, we surely don't understand TTWNGCBT fully even if we do understand it partially.

Moreover, even if TTWNGCBT is like God there is nothing about admitting its existence that proves Judaism, Christianity, or

Islam is true. In fact, TTWNGCBT might be like Brahman, the ineffable cosmic force discussed in Hindu theology and philosophy. Nothing about the present argument can rule that out.

In short, admitting the conclusion only requires admitting that there is some great being in the universe, something greater than you, me, or any other thing. It doesn't tell us much of anything else about what that being is like.

Strategy Two: Accept the Conclusion with a Caveat: A second strategy is to accept the conclusion with a huge caveat. To see how this strategy works, it can be helpful to think about Santa Claus. Consider this argument:

> (5) Santa Claus has a white beard.
>
> (6) Anything with a white beard is bearded.
>
> (7) Therefore, Santa Claus is bearded.

Notice that I can admit the conclusion of this argument without claiming that Santa Claus *actually* exists *in fact*. I am just saying something about *the nature of the idea of Santa Claus*, not something about *a factually existent thing*.

Let's take this a step further. Suppose now that we live in a universe where there are no squares at all, a squareless universe. Even so, we would admit the following argument is a good argument:

> (8) Squares are four-sided closed polygons with equal angles and equal sides.
>
> (9) If squares are four-sided closed polygons with equal angles and equal sides, then each angle of any square equals 90 degrees.
>
> (10) Therefore, each angle of any square equals 90 degrees.

That would be a good argument *even though there are no squares in the entire universe*. It's a good argument about the *idea of squares*.

Now we can apply these ideas to Anselm's argument. Suppose that there is *in fact* no being in the entire universe that *actually* is

TTWNGCBT. If so, we might still admit that this argument, which
is akin to Anselm's, is a good argument:

(11) Being incapable of inexistence (that is, being a
necessary being) is greater than being capable of
inexistence (that is, being contingent).

(12) TTWNGCBT is the greatest being thinkable.

(13) If something is incapable of inexistence, then it
exists.

(14) Therefore, TTWNGCBT exists.

That might be a good argument even though, as stipulated
above, TTWNGCBT does *not actually exist in fact*! Why might it
be a good argument? It might be a good argument because it tells
us something about *the nature of the idea of TTWNGCBT* rather
than about what actually, in fact, exists in the universe itself. In this
way, the argument parallels the argument about squares in (8)–(10),
which tells us something about the nature of the idea of squares
even though in the universe there are in fact no squares.

In other words, we need to distinguish between two ways
of understanding what Anselm's argument concludes. One
way of understanding Anselm's argument is that it proves that
TTWNGCBT actually does, in fact, exist like you and I exist.
The other way of understanding Anselm's argument is that it
shows what belongs to the nature of the *idea* of TTWNGCBT,
namely existence. In this way, even though the argument is a
good argument, it does not prove that TTWNGCBT *actually*
does *in fact* exist. We can accept the conclusion with the major
caveat that it does not prove TTWNGCBT actually does in fact
exist.

Anselm's contemporary Gaunilo, mentioned above, takes exactly
this view regarding Anselm's argument. Speaking of a place called
the Lost Island, Gaunilo asks us to imagine that-island-than-which-
no-greater-island-can-be-thought. Parodying Anselm's argument,
it would follow that the lost island must exist:

Let TITWNGICBT = That-Island-Than-Which-No-
Greater-Island-Can-Be-Thought

(15) If TITWNGICBT exists in thought and not in reality, then we can think of an island greater than TITWNGICBT, namely, TITWNGICBT existing both in our thought and in reality.

(16) We cannot think of an island greater than TITWNGICBT.

(17) TITWNGICBT does exist in thought.

(18) Therefore, TITWNGICBT exists in reality.

But what has Gaunilo really proven? He has proven that it belongs to the idea of TITWNGICBT that it exists. He has not proven that the island *actually in fact* exists.

Thus, Gaunilo maintains that *if it were possible to prove that TTWNGCBT actually does in fact exist somewhere in the universe*, it would follow that existence belongs to its very nature. In like manner, if it were possible to prove that TITWNGICBT actually does in fact exist somewhere in the world, it would follow that existence belongs to its very nature. Moreover, to draw an analogy to the square argument above where we live in a squareless universe, if it could be shown that there actually is in fact a square somewhere in the universe, it would have to be admitted that having angles of 90 degrees really does belong to its very nature. However, the argument above doesn't prove the island actually does in fact exist. The square argument doesn't prove there actually are in fact squares. And Anselm's argument does not prove there actually exists in fact TTWNGCBT.

Still, there seems to be something strange about claiming that it belongs to the nature of TTWNGCBT that it exists in reality and yet it may not actually exist in fact. To understand why this is not so strange it is helpful to have recourse to another point that Immanuel Kant makes.

Imagine that you claim:

(19) Santa Claus is bearded.

Suppose, further, that I deny that claim and say:

(20) That's false! Santa Claus isn't bearded.

I might make that claim for one of two reasons. First, I might make it because Santa Claus doesn't even actually exist in fact. In that case, I would follow up the prior comment by saying:

> (20a) That's false! Santa Claus isn't bearded. He doesn't even actually exist in fact.

Alternatively, I might deny it because I think Santa Claus is actually clean-shaven. In that case, I would say:

> (20b) That's false! Santa Claus isn't bearded. I was looking at a depiction of him just yesterday and he was clean-shaven.

What this shows is that in "canceling" (that is, rejecting) a claim like "Santa Claus is bearded" I might either be canceling the predicate as being properly attributed to Santa Claus (20b) *or* I might be canceling the claim that there actually exists in fact a Santa Claus at all (20a).

To put it another way, claiming that *Santa Claus is bearded* might mean either:

> (21a) There actually is in fact a Santa Claus *and* that very thing, Santa Claus, is bearded.

Or it might mean:

> (21b) There is no Santa Claus *but* his depicted nature is such that he is bearded.

In (20a) I deny all of (21a). There is no Santa Claus and so there is no thing that is both Santa Claus and bearded. In contrast, in (20b) I only deny the second part of (21b), that Santa Claus' depicted nature is such that he is bearded.

Now again consider the example of squares having angles of 90 degrees. Suppose, however, that I don't know whether or not this is a squareless universe. In that case, in claiming that squares have angles of 90 degrees, my claim might be interpreted as meaning:

> (22a) There actually are in fact squares *and* those very things by their conceptual nature have angles of 90 degrees.

Or as:

> (22b) There may or may not be squares *but* by their
> conceptual nature they have angles of 90 degrees.

Furthermore, if you deny that squares have angles of 90 degrees,
you might be claiming either:

> (23a) There actually are in fact no squares at all.

Or that:

> (23b) It is not true that by their conceptual nature
> squares have angles of 90 degrees.

In (23a) you deny both conjuncts of (22a). In (23b) you only
deny the second part of (22b). But notice that you could deny both
conjuncts of (22a) *while or without* denying the second part of (22b).

In like manner, accepting the conclusion of Anselm's argument
might be understood as making one of the following two claims:

> (24a) There actually is in fact a TTWNGCBT *and* that
> very thing's conceptual nature has the property of
> existence.

Or it might mean:

> (24b) There may or may not be a TTWNGCBT *but* its
> conceptual nature has the property of existence.

Now suppose I *do* deny that God exists. Am I denying all of (24a)
as I do with respect to Santa Claus in (20a) and squares in (23a)? If
so, I would still be able to claim that by TTWNGCBT's *conceptual
nature* it has the property of existence. Analogously, in denying there
actually are in fact squares in (23a), I am still permitted to claim that
that the conceptual nature of squares is such that they have angles
of 90 degrees. And this is the position that anyone who opts for our
second strategy for accepting the conclusion of Anselm's argument
might take with respect to TTWNGCBT. Such a person might
deny TTWNGCBT actually in fact exists while simultaneously

conceding it belongs to the conceptual nature of TTWNGCBT to exist. To put it another way, all Anselm's argument is doing is unpacking the idea of TTWNGCBT, its conceptual nature. It is not proving that TTWNGCBT actually does in fact exist.

Bonus Puzzles

There is, in fact, no single version of the ontological argument. Rather, an ontological argument is any argument that tries to prove the existence of God by appealing to nothing other than the idea of God. Thus, such arguments are in contrast with arguments that try to prove God's existence based on observing the world around us.

Accordingly, a second example of an ontological argument is found in René Descartes' (1596–1650 CE) *Meditations on First Philosophy*. His version of the argument is:

(25) God is supremely perfect.

(26) A supremely perfect being possesses every perfection.

(27) Existence is a perfection.

(28) Therefore, God exists.

A third example comes from the work of Alvin Plantinga (b. 1932 CE). His argument is based on possible worlds and the idea of a maximally greatest being. It goes as follows:

(29) There is a possible world in which the maximally greatest being exists.

(30) A maximally greatest being exists in every possible world.

(31) This actual world is also a possible world.

(32) Therefore, the maximally greatest being exists in this actual world.

The question now arises: Do any of the responses above apply to these arguments too? If not, is there anything wrong with these arguments? I'll leave those questions for you to puzzle through.

References

Anselm. *Proslogion: With the Replies of Gaunilo and Anselm.* Trans. Thomas Williams. Indianapolis: Hackett, 1995.

Descartes, René. *Meditations on First Philosophy.* In *The Philosophical Writings of Descartes.* Vol. 2. Trans. John Cottingham, Robert Stoothoff, and Dugald Murdoch. Cambridge: Cambridge UP, 1984.

Gaunilo. "On Behalf of the Fool." In *Proslogion: With the Replies of Gaunilo and Anselm.* Trans. Thomas Williams. Indianapolis: Hackett, 1995.

Kant, Immanuel. *Critique of Pure Reason.* Trans. and Ed. Paul Guyer and Allen W. Wood. Cambridge: Cambridge UP, 1998.

Plantinga, Alvin. *The Nature of Necessity.* Oxford: Clarendon Press, 1974.

PUZZLE SIX

Science and Religion

The heretics in our times have heard the awe-inspiring names of people like Socrates, Hippocrates, Plato, Aristotle, etc. They have been deceived by the exaggerations made by the followers of these philosophers—exaggerations to the effect . . . that the principles they have discovered are unquestionable: . . . and that with all the subtlety of their intelligence and the originality of their accomplishments they repudiated the authority of religious laws: denied the validity of the positive contents of historical religions, and believed that all such things are only sanctimonious lies and trivialities.

. . . When I saw this vein of folly pulsating among these idiots, I decided to write this book in order to refute the ancient philosophers. It will expose the incoherence of their beliefs and the inconsistency of their metaphysical theories. It will bring to light the flimsiest and the obscurest elements of their thought, which will provide some amusement for, and serve as a warning to, the intelligent men.
—*Al-Ghazali (a.k.a. Algazel, 1058–1111 CE),*
Incoherence of the Philosophers

Now since this religion [Islam] is true and summons to the study of which leads to knowledge of the Truth, we the Muslim community know definitely that demonstrative study does not lead to conclusions conflicting with what Scripture has given us; for truth does not oppose truth but accords with it and bears witness to it.
—*Ibn Rushd (a.k.a. Averroës, 1126–1198 CE),*
Decisive Treatise

The Philosophers

Many people assume that the contemporary controversy between religious belief and scientific discovery is distinctly, well, *contemporary*. But it's not. From the moment that the major monotheistic religions (Judaism, Christianity, and Islam) began to incorporate the ideas of ancient philosophers like Socrates (469–399 BCE), Plato (429–347 BCE), and Aristotle (384–322 BCE), religion and philosophy have been at odds. What's more, philosophy *just was* science back then. In ancient and medieval times, philosophy included all of the sciences like physics, meteorology, and astronomy. So, religion and science have been at odds for well over 1,000 years. The controversy is nothing new.

Within Islam the controversy between religious belief and scientific discovery started to take shape with the writings of Ibn Sīna (a.k.a. Avicenna, c. 980–1037 CE). (Before proceeding, I should note that the "a.k.a." names here and above are the way the names of Islamic thinkers were translated into Latin. For Ibn Sīna and Ibn Rushd, it is common to use their Latin names Avicenna and Averroës but less so for al-Ghazali; I shall follow what is standard.) Avicenna was a Persian philosopher and theologian. He is reported to have known the Qur'an by heart at age ten. At the age of sixteen he began studying and practicing medicine. By the age of twenty-one he had written one of the most important texts in the history of medicine, *The Canon of Medicine*.

Avicenna had endorsed several claims that almost all Islamic scholars rejected. Most notably, he argued that (i) God created the universe out of necessity rather than freely; (ii) God created the earth through intermediaries rather than directly; and (iii) there is no resurrection of the body. With respect to (iii), he thought of the afterlife as a disembodied, immaterial existence.

It may be surprising to learn that, prior to Avicenna, Muslim scholars denied that the afterlife is a disembodied, immaterial existence. But the truth is that the view that the afterlife is immaterial and disembodied is not to be found in the primary religious texts of the major monotheistic religions, such as the Bible or Qur'an. Rather, it was a view of the afterlife developed on the basis of arguments from Plato.

Al-Ghazali, another Persian thinker, believed that Avicenna's views were fundamentally at odds with the Qur'an. Al-Ghazali wasn't as precocious as Avicenna. However, he did hold some of the most important teaching positions of the time. Perhaps because of the stress, he stopped teaching in 1095. Claiming he was heading to Mecca and after making arrangements for his family, he went into seclusion.

Al-Ghazali believed that adopting theological views on the basis of arguments from Plato and Aristotle, as Avicenna did, led scholars to deny the authority of the religious law. He worried that this could result in people turning away from Islam. Moreover, he thought that the views espoused by thinkers like Avicenna were deeply mistaken. He undertook to show that such views are incoherent, if not internally then with the Qur'an.

Averroës, a philosopher from Spain who was incredibly influential for his commentaries on Aristotle, disagreed. He believed that religion, rightly understood, and philosophy, correctly conducted, could not be at odds. Whatever the conclusions of well-conducted religious inquiry are, they cannot possibly conflict with the conclusions of philosophical inquiry. Why he thought this we shall see below.

The Puzzle

Like the problem of evil, our fourth puzzle, this puzzle is perplexing only for religious people. The present puzzle requires that the religious person believes that some religious text is the word of God. Here is the argument, where S is some sentence (such as "The universe was created in six days"):

(1) Sometimes my religious text states S, whereas our very best science concludes not: S.

(2) My religious text is never wrong.

(3) Therefore, whenever my religious text states S and our very best science concludes not: S, our very best science is wrong.

Generally speaking, however, it's a bad idea to reject our very best science. As it happens, good science is quite good at figuring out what is true. Of course, it's not infallible. But it is reliable. So, this puzzle, if sound, puts religious people in a very uncomfortable position: that of having to reject truths. And that's a surprising conclusion indeed! Before proceeding, a comment about this argument is in order. It is important to point out that there are (i) times when science concludes S but the religious text is silent about the truth of S, and (ii) times when the religious text states S but science is silent about S. As examples of (i), science tells us about the causes of eclipses and cell division, but religious texts say nothing about either. As examples of (ii), religious texts tell us that Luke (author of the books Luke and Acts of the Apostles) was a doctor and that Abraham was married to a woman named Sarah. However, science does not pronounce on the truth of either of those claims. So, to be clear, this puzzle is only a problem when the religious text and science are inconsistent, when the religious text states *S* and our very best science has concluded *not: S*. The problem does not arise otherwise; the religious text *might* be correct with regard to every other claim it makes.

If you're an atheist, if you don't believe in God, then you'll reject premise (2) of this argument. You'll probably think that religious texts are wrong about lots and lots of things, most notably that there's a God. So, instead of arguing from (1) and (2) to (3), you'll likely endorse an argument along these lines:

(1) Sometimes religious texts state S, whereas our very best science concludes not: S.

(4) Our very best science probably isn't wrong.

(5) Therefore, the religious text is probably wrong about S.

You'll put the "probably" in there because sometimes the very best science is wrong *and conflicts with what the religious text states*. For example, if we were assessing this argument in the eighteen hundreds, then some of our "very best science" took it to be established "fact" that women should not have the right to vote and that African peoples are not fit to rule themselves but should be made subject to the European races. Such claims were "supported" by appeals to smaller brain sizes and smaller cranial capacities of women and Africans, for example. (Some of these claims are detailed in the work of Stephen Jay Gould [1941–2002 CE].) To be sure, those appeals were supported by shoddy science, but it was the "best science" of the time.

Moreover, such conclusions stand in sharp contrast with claims from the Bible that we ought to "despise the gain of oppression" (Isaiah 33:15) and "to let the oppressed go free and to break every yoke" (Isaiah 58:6). So, here is an issue and a particular time when, arguably, the religious text got it right and the very best science got it wrong. That is true even in spite of the fact that our very best science *today* has disproven the claims made in the eighteen hundreds.

Yet if you're an atheist you might also wonder: Are religious people just stupid? After all, who would reject the conclusions of our very best science? As for me, I have met many religious people who are way smarter than me and, I would venture to guess, are way smarter than you. So, the answer is that religious people are not just stupid. How, then, do they respond to this puzzling argument? To answer that question, let's first examine what can be said in support of the premises.

The Premises

Premise (1)

Premise (1) states that there are times when a religious text states S but our very best science denies it. What are some examples of where religious texts state S but our very best science denies it? Here are two from the Hebrew canon, two from the New Testament, and two from the Qur'an:

(A) According to the book of Genesis (1:1–31), the universe was created in six days (the seventh day was a day of rest). However, according to our very best science, it wasn't.

(B) According to the book of Joshua (10:12–13), Joshua commanded the sun to stand still in the sky and it did. But this suggests that the sun moves around the earth, and the very best science tells us that it doesn't. The very best science also tells us that the sun won't stand still just because someone commands it to.

(C) In the book of Matthew (13:31–32), Jesus says that the smallest seed is the mustard seed. However, according to our very best science, it's not.

(D) The book of Luke (1:26–35) states that Mary was a virgin when she conceived Jesus. Our very best science says that's not possible.

(E) According to the Qur'an (18:86), the sun sets in a muddy spring. Our very best science concludes the sun does not set in a muddy spring.

(F) The Qur'an also states that procreation occurs by way of a fluid secreted from between the loins and the ribs (86:6–7). That is false. Semen is secreted from the testes and ovaries do not secrete a fluid.

It's because of examples like (A)–(F) that premise (1) is true.

Premise (2)

Premise (2) claims that the religious text is never wrong. It's inerrant; it contains no errors. Of course, which religious text you think is inerrant will depend on which religion you belong to. But whether you're Jewish, Christian, or Muslim, chances are you endorse (2).

Premise (2) is widely endorsed for two reasons. The first reason is that the authors of the religious text—whether Moses, Luke, or Muhammad—are thought to have been inspired by God. After all, the religious text is supposed to be the word of God.

Yet if the religious text errs it suggests either that God was deceiving the people who wrote the religious text or that the authors of the religious text were themselves deceivers. In the first case, God would have had to tell the authors something that wasn't true, and since God knows everything, God would have been deceiving them. In the second case, if God did tell the authors the truth, then the authors knew the truth (after all, God is a great source of knowledge!) but opted to write something else. The other possibility is that they were passing off claims as the word of God that, presumably, they knew were not in fact the word of God. If so, the authors were being deceptive.

Neither of these options, however, is acceptable. First, God is not a deceiver. What sort of God deceives his own people about the nature of reality? Also, the authors of the religious text are supposed to be revered, holy men. If they are deceivers, they do not deserve our reverence.

The second reason that denying premise (2) is unacceptable for religious people is that denying it introduces a deep suspicion of the religion itself. If the religious text is wrong about some matters, why think it is correct about others? Why think that it is a reliable guide to the eternal resting place of our souls when it is not a reliable guide to the world around us? Thus, denying premise (2) undermines one's confidence not just in the religious text but in the religion itself.

Possible Responses

What can be said in response to this argument? What can be said on behalf of the religious person? First, let's begin by considering the option of accepting the conclusion. Second, we'll consider rejecting premise (2). Third, we'll consider rejecting premise (1).

Accept the Conclusion

One option is to accept the conclusion. We can affirm that our very best science is wrong. We may distinguish among three strategies that follow on accepting the conclusion of the argument.

Strategy One: Show the Science Is Wrong: First, we might accept the conclusion but then go on to show why our very best science is wrong. This, for example, is what al-Ghazali does. He admits that Socrates, Plato, and Aristotle were great thinkers. Nonetheless, he thinks that their arguments—and the arguments endorsed by Avicenna—are fallacious. In his book *Incoherence of the Philosophers*, he proceeds to show why.

Such a strategy can also be used with respect to "hard" scientific theories like evolution. For example, I was raised in a religious, evangelical household. At my church people rejected the theory of evolution, believing instead that God created the universe in six days. One person who endorsed this view—I won't tell you his real name; let's call him Les Watson—actively argued that the very best science was wrong and tried to provide countervailing scientific evidence disproving evolution. One such argument, I recall, was that the strength of the earth's electromagnetic field declines at a constant rate. If we track that constant decline backwards 250 million years, we would find that the earth's electromagnetic field would be so strong that nothing could possibly live on earth. Yet people who believe in evolution think that there was life on earth 250 million years ago, and so they must be wrong.

Les' argument fails, of course. Even if it's true that the strength of the electromagnetic field is *now* declining at a constant rate, it doesn't follow that it has *always* declined at a constant rate.

One peculiar feature of following this strategy is that it ultimately ends up rejecting premise (1) of the argument above. That's because the people who endorse this strategy think that while the very best *scientists* believe in, say, evolution, the very best *science* shows that evolution is false. Of course, there is the implicit assumption that people like al-Ghazali and Les Watson are in tune with the very best science even if they're not the very best scientists. In other words, this strategy accepts the conclusion but only tentatively. It says that while our best scientists *now* claim not: S, in due time they will come around and realize that S—what the religious text says—is true after all.

Strategy Two: Appearance and Reality: Another way to accept the conclusion is to affirm that the science is wrong but that scientists are not blameworthy for thinking the science is right. Following this strategy, someone might affirm that the earth really was created in six days approximately 6,000 years ago. However, when God created the universe 6,000 years ago, he made the earth so that it *looks* as though the earth is billions of years old, that humans evolved from apes, that dinosaurs roamed the earth for millions of years, etc. In this sense, the science is, strictly speaking, wrong. However, the scientists can't be blamed for getting it wrong. After all, that's the way God made things appear.

By way of reply, we might wonder why God would create the universe to look much older than it is. Wouldn't that mean God is deceiving us into thinking the earth is really old when it's not? And if God does that, doesn't it follow that God is a colossal jerk? After all, many people have rejected their faith on scientific grounds. By making the world look older than it is, God is essentially encouraging their unbelief.

One response to this reply is that God made the world to look older than it is to test our faith. Will we choose to believe in science or to believe in God? Unfortunately, I don't think this response works very well. Couldn't God have tested our faith in better ways, in ways that don't involve outright deception? After all, God has given us the power of reason to figure out what is true. Why would God give us that power and yet make it such that reasoning leads us astray about one of the most important decisions we could ever make?

Another and more significant problem is that this strategy does not resolve all of the inconsistencies between religious texts and science. For example, how does this response account for the claim that humans are made from a fluid secreted between the loin and ribs? Or account for the claim that the smallest seed is the mustard seed? Is God only making it appear as though semen is secreted from the testes? Is God only making it appear as though there are seeds smaller than mustard seeds?

Strategy Three: Tenacity: A third strategy for accepting the conclusion is simple, straightforward tenacity. According to this strategy we should claim the conclusion is right, the best science is wrong, and that's that. There's nothing else to be said, nothing about how a little more inquiry will show that our very best science is wrong and nothing about how God made the world to look older than it is.

The problem with this strategy is that it's deeply unsatisfying. We can't just reject our very best science out of hand and we shouldn't. Scientific inquiry leads us to the truth. To claim otherwise is sheer lunacy. Moreover, it's unacceptably arbitrary to claim that *some* of our very best science is right *but* the very best science that contradicts a religious text is always wrong. Why should we get to claim that science gets it right almost all of the time but goes wrong when its claims are inconsistent with our most cherished beliefs?

That's like saying that justice is almost always a good thing, but it is bad when it conflicts with what I want most in the world. What warrants the exception in these specific circumstances?

Reject Premise (2)

Another strategy is to reject premise (2). We can claim that the religious text is sometimes wrong.

Above, I noted that this is an uncomfortable option for many religious people. However, we can ease the discomfort by taking note of three claims. The first claim is that we need to be sensitive to the genre in which the claims are made. There are many different literary genres. Among them are poetry, historical nonfiction, legal writing, and philosophy. When it comes to poetry, no one thinks that a poet's use of metaphor and simile should be taken literally. For example, when David writes in Psalm 139:13 that God knitted him together in the womb, no one thinks that God literally went into the womb of David's mother with knitting needles and yarn and made him. So, this is a time that the religious texts "errs" but only trivially so. It's not really an error so long as we realize that this is a simile and not a literal description of how David came into being.

The second claim is that we need to be sensitive to the cultural context in which the religious text was written. Suppose that Moses had written the first two chapters of Genesis but that it contained an exposition of the theory of evolution. Would the people who read the text have understood what Moses was saying? Not one iota. First, they didn't have the relevant concepts to understand the theory. The very idea of a gene was totally unfamiliar to people even 250 years ago. Second, they didn't even have a notion of science or of its methods to understand that evolution is a scientific theory. In short, the theory of evolution would sound even crazier to people 5,000 years ago than the creation story in Genesis sounds to us today. So, what did Moses do to explain the origins of the universe to people 5,000 years ago? He co-opted an ancient Babylonian myth and used it to explain to the ancient Israelites that God created, sustains, and cares for the universe and us.

This doesn't make Moses (or God) a liar or even a misinformer. Sometimes when we teach people we have to meet them where they are. For example, you could not walk into the midst of a never-before-contacted Amazonian tribe and immediately start teaching them the theory of gravity. They wouldn't be ready for it. However, you could (I suppose) teach them that there is a spiritual power keeping them connected to the ground rather than flying into the air like smoke. That would be false, of course, but it would go some way in teaching them about the way the universe works. In like manner, the creation story is false, but it does go some way in teaching ancient peoples about God's relationship to the world.

The third claim is that the religious text never errs with respect to its purpose: to teach us truths about God and what is proper for our lives. Consider Jesus' claim that the mustard seed is the smallest seed but grows into the greatest bush. That's false. The mustard seed isn't the smallest seed and it doesn't grow into the greatest bush. But Jesus' aim is not to teach people about botany. His aim is to teach people about faith: even a little bit of faith can have great consequences. It doesn't really matter if he's right about mustard seeds. What matters is that he's right about faith.

In sum, we might reject premise (2) while opting for a weaker claim:

(2a)   The religious text is never wrong with respect to what it states about God and what is proper for our lives.

One problem with this strategy is that it concedes too much ground. If we are willing to admit that some portions of the religious text are just ways of "reaching out" to ancient peoples, why should we not think that other claims—for example, that God made a covenant with David, that Jesus was born of a virgin and was the son of God, and that Muhammad ascended to Heaven and conversed with God—are not similarly fictitious claims? Why not think any talk of God is just a way of reaching out to ancient peoples? Perhaps when it comes down to it all these religious texts are just moral tales wrapped in ancient mythologies. But in that case we might jettison the whole of religion in favor of a good ethical theory.

A second problem with opting for (2a) is that the entire puzzle above could be reframed in this way:

(1a)   Sometimes my religious text states S about God or what is proper for our lives, whereas our very best science concludes not: S.

(2a) My religious text is never wrong with respect to what it states about God and what is proper for our lives.

(3a) Therefore, whenever my religious text teaches S about God or what is proper for our lives and our very best science concludes not: S, our very best science is wrong.

The question, then, becomes whether the religious text ever teaches things that are inconsistent with what science concludes regarding God or what is proper for our lives.

One point of inconsistency might simply be that our very best science teaches God does not exist (or, at least, probably does not exist), whereas the religious text teaches God does exist. Some scientists, such as Richard Dawkins (b. 1941 CE) and Lawrence Krauss (b. 1954 CE), have argued that science rules out the "God hypothesis." Although their general objection that science renders the hypothesis that God exists unnecessary is nothing new (for example, Thomas Aquinas [1225–1274 CE] mentions it), the details of their arguments are certainly novel insofar as they take into account advancements in evolutionary biology and quantum physics.

A second point of inconsistency might be over ethics and politics (recall that for al-Ghazali and Averroës science includes not just natural science but all of philosophy). The religious texts, for example, require various immoral actions (such as putting psychics and wizards to death, as Leviticus 20:27 requires) and forbid some actions that many people today consider morally permissible (for example, getting tattoos, which Leviticus 19:28 forbids, or men wearing women's clothes, which Deuteronomy 22:5 describes as an abomination). In these cases, it does appear as though the religious text states things that are inconsistent with our best political science or ethical philosophy.

Reject Premise (1)

Strategy One: Simple Allegorical Interpretation: Our final option is to reject premise (1). This may seem like an odd option since, as noted above, there are very many passages in the religious texts that are inconsistent with what our very best science concludes.

However, rejecting (1) becomes more palatable if we distinguish between what the religious text *states* and what it *means*. As we noted in the previous section, some passages should not be interpreted literally. For example, the claim that David was knitted together in his mother's womb should not be taken as a statement of fact.

David's claim, of course, is but a simile, a poetic device. Yet sometimes, entire stories are like similes. In such cases the stories are allegories. One good candidate for a Biblical story that is an allegory is the first two chapters of Jonah. According to the story, Jonah is called by God to go to the city of Nineveh and urge them to change their immoral ways. Jonah does not want to go. Instead, he flees on a boat, planning to cross the Mediterranean Sea. God is displeased and summons up a great storm. The ship is tossed to and fro. The sailors are terrified. The ship is at risk of sinking. To save them and the ship, Jonah tells the sailors to throw him overboard. They do so and a whale (or whalelike fish) then swallows him. He lives for three days in its belly. Finally, Jonah prays to God and the whale vomits him out on to dry land.

Now science tells us two things that are inconsistent with this story. First, you cannot live in the belly of a whale for three days. Second, there are no whales or whalelike fish in the Mediterranean Sea. So, we should interpret the story allegorically. We can do so by claiming that while the story is not literally true it illustrates the saving love of God. Even though we are pursued by powerful and terrifying forces, even though we are urged to do difficult tasks, even though we find ourselves in challenging situations, God is faithful and loves us.

Such a claim might also be made about other stories in the Bible. For example, the creation story in Genesis can be read as an allegory revealing deeper truths about God's relationship to the world. In fact, Augustine (354–430 CE; and see Puzzle Four) reads the creation story in this way.

Averroës also endorses reading the religious text allegorically whenever it conflicts with what our very best science affirms. Moreover and more importantly, he offers us an argument concluding that our knowledge based on the religious text and our knowledge based on science can never conflict. His argument is this, where S and S′ are sentences:

(6) If I know S based on my religious text, then S is true.

(7) If I know S′ based on our very best science, then S′ is true.

(8) The truth cannot conflict with itself.

(9) Therefore, S and S′ cannot conflict, if we know both of them (or, to state it slightly differently, if S′ is identical to not: S, then one of them is not known).

Premises (6) and (7) are generally conceded to be true based on contemporary theories of knowledge: you know S only if S is true. In other words, there is no such thing as false knowledge (or so many philosophers think). Premise (8) is generally accepted as a rule of logic. It is nothing other than the Principle of Contravalence, discussed in Puzzle Three.

Since Averroës believes in the truth of Islam, this argument compels him to maintain that whenever the statements of his religious text conflict with the very best science, the religious text must be interpreted allegorically. That is, whenever these inconsistencies arise, we must interpret the religious text in a manner other than what it apparently *states*. We must find in the religious text a *deeper meaning*.

You might wonder: Why can't we interpret science allegorically and the religious text literally? The answer is that science is supposed to tell us what the facts are. Its conclusions are supposed to be true, taken just as they are. Science cannot be interpreted allegorically and still be science. The theory of gravity, for example, isn't just an allegory for the love that massive bodies have for each other. It's a theory about the way massive bodies actually affect each other.

Nonetheless, this solution is not without problems. First, even if we opt for Averroës' solution, we can rephrase the entire puzzle as follows:

(1b) Sometimes my religious text *means* S, whereas our very best science concludes not: S.

(2b) My religious text is never wrong with respect to what it means.

(3b) Therefore, whenever my religious text means S
and our very best science concludes not: S, our
very best science is wrong.

The question now becomes whether the meaning of the religious text is ever inconsistent with what our very best science
concludes. Once again, an inconsistency might arise over the nature
of God. For example, what the religious text may mean is that God
loves us, whereas our very best science may conclude God does not
exist and so could not possibly love us.

There are two other more significant problems if we opt for
Averroës' solution. First, it is not clear that the religious text can be
read as an allegory in every instance where an inconsistency arises
between the religious text and science. What, for example, is the
allegory when Joshua commands the sun to stand still?

Second, it is not clear that all of the religious stories that conflict
with science can be interpreted allegorically without undermining
the religion itself. For example, we know scientifically that people
cannot be resurrected from the dead. However, it is a core belief of
the Christian faith that Jesus was resurrected from the dead. How
can that story be allegorized into something else without undermining Christianity itself?

Strategy Two: Complex Allegorical Interpretation: In cases like the story
of Joshua and the resurrection of Jesus, we may have to combine
the strategy of allegorical interpretation with an appeal to some of
the insights from the previous response, rejecting premise (2). This
is also a strategy that Averroës employs. If we adopt this strategy, we
will claim that the religious text never conflicts with our very best
science over what it *means to teach us about God and what is proper
for our lives.* Since the religious text doesn't mean to teach us about
astronomy, the example of Joshua would be ruled out. Since the
religious text does mean to teach us that Jesus has conquered death,
we can regard the story as reporting a miraculous event.

In this case, the entire puzzle would once again have to be reframed as follows:

(1c) Sometimes my religious text *means to teach me S
about God and what is proper for our lives,* whereas
our very best science concludes not: S.

(2c) The religious text is never wrong with respect to what it means to teach me about God and what is proper for our lives.

(3c) Therefore, whenever my religious text means to teach me S about God or what is proper for our lives and our very best science concludes not: S, our very best science is wrong.

One problem that remains is that it is possible science rules out God's existence. However, a second and more pressing problem that arises is how we are to figure out what the religious text *means to teach us about God and what is proper for our lives.* We need to establish rules, principles, of interpretation. First, we don't want to allow people to read whatever claims they please into the religious text. For example, we wouldn't want to permit a person who changes his name to Solomon to allegorically interpret the Biblical story that King David had a wise son named Solomon as a prophecy of *his own* birth and religious authority. Second, we need to make sure our interpretations are not undermining the religion itself. In short, interpretations need to be principled. And if they're to be principled we need to establish principles of interpretation.

In fact, there is a whole science of interpreting texts called hermeneutics. Although it can hardly be denied that Averroës was dealing with the same issues, Friedrich Schleiermacher (1768–1834 CE) is widely regarded as the modern founder of the science and, more recently, Hans-Georg Gadamer (1900–2002 CE) is regarded as a seminal figure. However, a discussion of hermeneutics is far beyond the purview of this book. I encourage you to study it on your own.

References

Al-Ghazali. *Incoherence of the Philosophers.* Trans. Sabih Ahmad Kamali. Lahore: Pakistan Philosophical Congress, 1958.

Augustine. *On Genesis.* Trans. Edmund Hill and John Rotelle. New York: New City Press, 2002.

Averroës. *Decisive Treatise, Determining the Nature of the Connection Between Religion and Philosophy.* Trans. George F. Hourani. London: Luzac and Company, 1961.

Avicenna. *The Metaphysics of the Healing*. Trans. Michael Marmura. Provo: Brigham Young UP, 2005.

Dawkins, Richard. *The God Delusion*. New York: Houghton Mifflin, 2006.

Gadamer, Hans-Georg. *Truth and Method*. Trans. J. Weinsheimer and D. G. Marshall. New York: Crossroads, 2004.

Gould, Stephen Jay. *The Mismeasure of Man*. New York: W.W. Norton, 1996.

Krauss, Lawrence. *A Universe from Nothing: Why There Is Something Rather than Nothing*. New York: Free Press, 2012.

The New Oxford Annotated Bible. Ed. Herbert May and Bruce Metzger. New York: Oxford UP, 1973.

Plato. *Phaedo*. In *Complete Works*. Trans. G. M. A. Grube. Eds. John M. Cooper and D. S. Hutchinson. Indianapolis: Hackett, 1997.

Qur'an. Trans. M. A. S. Abdel Haleem. Oxford: Oxford UP, 2005.

Schleiermacher, Friedrich. *Hermeneutics and Criticism: And Other Writings*. Trans. and Ed. Andrew Bowie. Cambridge: Cambridge, UP, 1998.

Thomas Aquinas. *Summa Theologiae*. Vol. 2. Trans. Timothy McDermott. London: Eyre and Spottiswoode Limited, 1963.

Modern Philosophy

Cartesian Doubt

Psychological Egoism

Free Will and Determinism

PUZZLE SEVEN

Cartesian Doubt

Given, then, that our efforts are directed solely to the search for truth, our initial doubts will be about the existence of the objects of sense-perception and imagination. The first reason for such doubts is that from time to time we have caught out the senses when they were in error, and it is never prudent to place too much trust in those who have deceived us even once. The second reason is that in our sleep we regularly seem to have sensory perception of, or to imagine, countless things which do not exist anywhere; and if our doubts are on the scale just outlined, there seem to be no marks by means of which we can with certainty distinguish being asleep from being awake.

Our doubt will also apply to other matters which we previously regarded as most certain—even the demonstrations of mathematics and even the principles which we hitherto considered to be self-evident. One reason for this is that . . . we have been told that there is an omniscient God who created us. Now we do not know whether he may have wished to make us beings of the sort who are always deceived even in those matters which seem to us supremely evident; for such constant deception seems no less a possibility than the occasional deception which, as we have noticed on previous occasions, does occur. We may of course suppose that our existence derives not from a supremely powerful God but either from ourselves or from some other source; but in that case, the less powerful we make the author of our coming into being, the more likely it will be that we are so imperfect as to be deceived all the time.

—René Descartes (1596–1650 CE),
Principles of Philosophy

The Philosopher

René Descartes is the bane of all high school geometry students, for the Cartesian coordinate system we all know and love is based on his work in geometry. Indeed, it was Descartes' ability to fuse geometry—conceived by the ancient Greeks—and algebra—conceived by medieval Arabians—that made him famous in the sixteen hundreds.

When Descartes was one year old, his mother died. When he was eight, his father sent him to study with the Jesuits, an order of Catholic priests. Descartes' father wanted him to become a lawyer, and he did earn a degree in law. However, he never practiced. Instead, he turned his attention to philosophy and mathematics. He eventually sold all of his possessions and invested in bonds so that he could live off of their interest for the rest of his life.

Although he was born in and studied in France, Descartes spent most of his time in the Netherlands. While there he set about his plan to write a book titled *Treatise on the World*. He intended to argue in favor of heliocentrism, the theory that the sun is at the center of our solar system. However, shortly before publication, he learned that the teachings of Galileo—an advocate of heliocentrism—had been condemned. Rather than spend his afterlife in the fiery pits of hell, Descartes decided to stop publication of his book.

Instead, his efforts then centered on publishing portions of his original book as essays. One was an essay on meteors. A second was an essay on optics. A third was an essay on geometry (on which the Cartesian coordinate system is based). Descartes' famous *Discourse on Method* served as the introduction for the third work. In that book, Descartes declares, "I think; therefore, I am."

Descartes also made advancements in anatomy. In one of my favorite—simply because it is so twisted—experiments, he confirmed that the heart is the organ that pumps blood by taking a live dog, slicing it open, clipping off the bottom of its heart, and sticking his finger inside so as to feel the contraction of the muscle around his finger.

As a result of his fame and immense intellect, Descartes' friends urged him to write a book establishing the sciences on an indubitable, unshakeable foundation. He did so, writing a book called *Meditations on First Philosophy*. The *Meditations* consists of six meditations, the first of which calls into doubt the existence of the material world and the reliability of sense perceptions and inferences (or reasoning). The quotation above is a succinct restatement of Descartes' arguments in the first meditation.

Descartes asked a friend of his, Marin Mersenne, to circulate the *Meditations* among other intellectuals for objections. Mersenne did so, and Descartes wrote a series of responses to those objections. One of those thinkers was Thomas Hobbes (1588–1679 CE), who is the author of our eighth puzzle.

Although his works were controversial, in 1647 Descartes earned a pension from the king of France. In late 1649, he went to Sweden to tutor Queen Christina. Christina wished to study early in the morning, specifically at 5:00 a.m., and Descartes had to oblige. She was, after all, the queen. Unfortunately, a few months later Descartes died of pneumonia. Supposedly he became more susceptible to the illness because he was used to reading in bed until noon. Queen Christina felt pretty bad about inadvertently killing poor Descartes. Forty years later she died of pneumonia too.

The Puzzle

What is Descartes' puzzling argument? We can state it like this:

(1) Every belief I have I formed either on the basis of sense perception or on the basis of inference.

(2) I cannot be certain that forming beliefs on the basis of sense perception generally results in true beliefs.

(3) I cannot be certain that forming beliefs on the basis of inference generally results in true beliefs.

(4) If I cannot be certain that forming beliefs by way of some method (for example, sense perception or inference) generally results in true beliefs, then I cannot be certain that any of the beliefs formed using that method is true.

(5) Therefore, I cannot be certain that any of my beliefs is true.

Once again we have a valid argument. But is the argument sound? Are its premises true? Let's consider what can be said in their defense.

The Premises

Premise (1)

When we form a belief on the basis of sense perception, we form that belief based on what we see, hear, smell, touch, or taste. For example, you believe that you have a friend with at least one eye. But why do you believe this? Because you've seen your friend and noticed that he has an eye. On the basis of seeing your friend (a sense perception), you form the belief that your friend has at least one eye.

When we form a belief on the basis of inference, we form a belief because we have some argument for it. For example, you believe that all squares have at least one side. Why? Because when you read the previous sentence, you probably had the following line of thought:

(6) All squares have four sides.

(7) If something has four sides, then it has at least one side.

(8) Therefore, all squares have at least one side.

In this case, you came to believe that all squares have at least one side on the basis of an inference.

Premise (1) is plausible just because it's hard to think of a counterexample. What belief do you have that you did not form on the basis of sense perception or on the basis of inference? You believe that you are right now reading this book. Why? You believe it because you see the book. That's sense perception. You believe in the Pythagorean theorem. Why? At first you probably believed it because your teacher told you it's true. In that case, the belief is based on sense perception, on hearing your teacher say it. Later, when you took geometry, you likely learned a proof for the Pythagorean theorem. In that case, your belief is based on an inference. Can you think of a belief you gained without it being based either on sense perception or on inference (or both)? If not, the absence of a counterexample is an argument in favor of premise (1).

Premise (2)

I cannot be certain that forming beliefs on the basis of sense perception generally results in true beliefs. Descartes himself gave two arguments for this claim. His first argument is based on the fact that we have suffered illusions. It goes like this:

> (9) I have been deceived by sense perceptions in the past, for example when I have suffered an illusion.
>
> (10) I shouldn't completely trust that which has deceived me even once.
>
> (11) Therefore, I shouldn't completely trust sense perception.

I don't think anyone would deny premise (9). Nonetheless, if you do doubt it, I invite you to look up the checkerboard shadow illusion. After that, you might look up the café tiles illusion and Müller-Lyer illusions.

Premise (10) is true so long as we interpret "completely" in a really strong way. If we've been deceived by something even once, we shouldn't trust it 100%. That said, we might still trust it 99.99999%.

For this reason, Descartes realizes the argument is not very strong. It only shows that I cannot be *absolutely* certain that forming beliefs on the basis of sense perception does not result in true beliefs. (See our first puzzle for a discussion of degrees of certainty.)

Because Descartes realizes his argument is not very strong, he offers a second argument. His second argument is based on how hard it can be to distinguish being awake and being asleep. If you're like me, you've had dreams that you thought actually happened. More than likely, later on you discovered that what happened in those dreams didn't actually happen. For example, when I was in college I once dreamt that I had a conversation with my friend about a philosophy assignment. However, the next time I saw him, I brought up what we were talking about and he said we never had the conversation in the first place. I realized I must have dreamt it.

Yet isn't it possible for you to have a dream, for you to think that the events in the dream really happened, and yet for you *never* to find out it was a dream? Furthermore, if you've ever seen the movie *Inception*, you can at least *conceive* of dreams being in dreams. So, it is *possible* that every time we think we're awake, we are in fact asleep. What we call our dreams might be but dreams within dreams.

We're now in a position to see what Descartes' second argument in favor of premise (2) is. It goes like this:

(12) There are no sure signs by which I can distinguish being awake and being asleep.

(13) If (12), then any time I think I am awake I might actually be asleep.

(14) If any time I think I am awake I might actually be asleep, then I cannot be certain that forming beliefs on the basis of sense perception generally results in true beliefs.

(15) Therefore, I cannot be certain that forming beliefs on the basis of sense perception generally results in true beliefs.

In short, the possibility that all of the beliefs we form on the basis of sense perception might actually have been formed on the basis of dreams—and the fact that what we dream about need not be true—means that we cannot be certain that forming beliefs on the basis of sense perception generally results in true beliefs.

Maybe all this dreaming stuff just isn't convincing to you. Fine. It doesn't really matter. There are lots of ways to get the same conclusion that Descartes wants. One way is to think about the movie *The Matrix*. In that movie, people think they're having all sorts of different experiences but all of their experiences are like dreams or hallucinations. That's because they are hooked up to machines that cause them to have experiences of, for example, the blue sky, cats, and brick buildings even though the sky is not blue, there are no cats, and there are no brick buildings. Granted that this is conceivable—that we are humans hooked up to machines feeding us experiences—so it follows that we cannot be certain that forming beliefs on the basis of sense perception generally results in true beliefs. Perhaps we too are in the Matrix.

Another way to generate Descartes' conclusion is to imagine the possibility that all of our experiences are self-generated. Just as your liver secretes bile (or you *think* you have a liver that secretes bile) and you have no voluntary control over whether it secretes bile, maybe your brain (or what you *think* is your brain) actually generates all of your sense perceptions and you have no voluntary control over whether and how it creates those experiences.

Another way to generate Descartes' conclusion is to imagine the possibility that we're simply virtual reality creations. All of our first-person experiences might be like the first-person experiences of our video game creations, only of much better design. In that case, we might just be the avatars of other creatures, blissfully unaware that we're but the ones and zeroes of a very complex computer program.

Alternatively, maybe we are actually rational octopuses sleeping in an octopus garden and dreaming that we're having these experiences. Or maybe we're baby kittens who just ate some hallucinogenic mushrooms and are now having experiences that make it seem as though we're humans. Or maybe we're just the dreams of demented demon spirits. It doesn't matter how you go about supporting it, for the key point is that there may be nothing in reality that corresponds to what we see, hear, feel, taste, or smell. If so, we cannot be certain that forming beliefs on the basis of sense perception generally results in true beliefs. That's why premise (2) is true.

Premise (3)

Premise (3) is supported in much the same way as premise (2). However, instead of considering the possibility that all of our experiences are dreams, Descartes considers the possibility that an evil demon is tinkering with our thoughts and deceiving us. As we perform the inference from (6)–(8)—or any of the other arguments—it is conceivable that an evil demon tinkers with our thought process. That evil demon can make it such that when we move from (6) and (7) to (8) in our process of reasoning, he makes it *seem* as though (8) follows from (6) and (7) when in fact it does not. The evil demon just tinkers with our thoughts to make it appear as though (8) follows from (6) and (7).

Maybe that sounds silly to you. Maybe you think this talk of evil demons is just silly stuff. Fine. Once again, it doesn't matter. We can generate the argument in other ways. You would surely admit it is possible that you suffer from a cognitive defect. That cognitive defect might cause you to infer (8) from (6) and (7), even though (8) does not in fact follow from (6) and (7). Granted that is true, then you can't be certain that forming beliefs on the basis of inference generally results in true beliefs. Maybe a cognitive defect causes you to infer (8) from (6) and (7) when it is simply not true that (8) does follow from (6) and (7).

Here's another example: You might admit that all of your thoughts depend on your brain. If that's true, then why is it not possible that you are right now a brain in a vat of gelatinous goo? And if that is possible, why is it not possible that an evil scientist manipulates your neurons in such a way that he gets you to conclude that (8) follows from (6) and (7) even though it does not? It is certainly possible to make fallacious arguments or to follow a fallacious line of thought and really think that the conclusion follows from the premises. If you've ever added a large column of numbers and reached the same wrong sum on several occasions, you know that that is possible. Why couldn't a mad scientist put your brain into such a state with respect to all *arguments*?

The argument, then, can be stated in this way:

(16) It is possible that I suffer from a cognitive defect that causes me to make fallacious inferences without realizing it.

(17) If (16), then it is possible that every time I make an inference that seems sound I am actually mistaken.

(18) If it is possible that every time I make an inference that seems sound I am actually mistaken, then I cannot be certain that forming beliefs on the basis of inference generally results in true beliefs.

(19) Therefore, I cannot be certain that forming beliefs on the basis of inference generally results in true beliefs.

That is why premise (3) of Descartes' argument is true.

Premise (4)

Premise (4) is extremely plausible. If I cannot be certain that a method results in true beliefs, how can I be certain that any of the beliefs resulting from the application of that method is true? Imagine, for example, that there is some formula that can tell you the exact location of the planet Jupiter if you just plug some data— say, the location of the planet earth—into it. But suppose, moreover, that you cannot be certain the formula actually generates a true statement of the location of the planet Jupiter *and that there is, in principle, no way to check that it does* (for example, you can't just look for the planet Jupiter in the sky). Can you be certain that any of its results is true? Clearly you cannot.

In like manner, suppose that there is some machine and you've been told that by dropping a box of ingredients into it, it will make a soufflé. However, suppose that there is actually no way for you to ascertain whether the machine really generates a soufflé or not and that you didn't even know what was in the box of ingredients. Could you be certain the machine has actually made a soufflé? Clearly you cannot.

Yet this is precisely the position we find ourselves in with respect to sense perception and inference. There is some method (sense perception or inference, the formula or machine in our analogy from above) that generates statements about the way the world is (the location of Jupiter or a soufflé in our analogies above). But we cannot, in principle, check that the method generates *true* statements. That's because even when we're checking we might be dreaming or we might be deceived by an evil demon. Consequently, we cannot be certain that any of our beliefs based on sense perception or on inference is true. This is what premise (4) states.

Possible Responses

What are we to make of Descartes' argument? Is there a response to be made to it? Let's begin by considering the option of accepting the conclusion. After that, we'll consider rejecting premises (2) and (3) in turn. Then we'll turn to premise (1). Lastly, we'll consider the option of rejecting premise (4).

Accept the Conclusion

Strategy One: Straightforward Acceptance: One option is to accept the conclusion. We can concede that none of our beliefs is certain. Importantly, accepting the conclusion allows that most of our beliefs may be true. It only entails that we cannot be *certain* that they are true. Our beliefs that the sky is blue, that there are kittens, and some buildings are made of brick might be true even if we cannot be certain that they are.

One problem with this solution is that an appeal to certainty has an important role to play in the way we converse with each other and conduct our lives. For example, if we protest an injustice, we want to be able to claim we are *certain* that an injustice really has been committed and that we are *certain* that the injustice needs to be redressed. Otherwise, the protest is impotent.

As another example, if we are waiting for a train and a person asks us what time it is, we should tell that person if we know the time. But if the person making the inquiry asks, "Are you certain? I really need to know because I don't want to miss my job interview," are we to respond that certainty, with respect to any of our beliefs, is impossible? Should we reply that no one can be certain what time it is because we cannot be certain that forming beliefs on the basis of sense perception (here, looking at one's watch) generally results in true beliefs? That seems absurd. Yet accepting the conclusion of our present argument entails that we must rid ourselves of certainty-talk.

Strategy Two: Degrees of Certainty: A second way to handle Descartes' argument is to distinguish between being absolutely certain and being highly certain. As discussed in Puzzle One, we can distinguish between 100% certainty and 99.999999% certainty. We might then distinguish between two versions of Descartes' argument, the first being about absolute certainty:

(1a) Every belief I have I formed either on the basis of sense perception or on the basis of inference.

(2a) I cannot be 100% certain that forming beliefs on the basis of sense perception generally results in true beliefs.

(3a) I cannot be 100% certain that forming beliefs on the basis of inference generally results in true beliefs.

(4a) If I cannot be 100% certain that forming beliefs by way of some method (for example, sense perception or inference) generally results in true beliefs, then I cannot be 100% certain that any of the beliefs formed using that method is true.

(5a) Therefore, I cannot be 100% certain that any of my beliefs is true.

And the second being about high degrees of certainty:

(1b) Every belief I have I formed either on the basis of sense perception or on the basis of inference.

(2b) I cannot be highly certain that forming beliefs on the basis of sense perception generally results in true beliefs.

(3b) I cannot be highly certain that forming beliefs on the basis of inference generally results in true beliefs.

(4b) If I cannot be highly certain that forming beliefs by way of some method (for example, sense perception or inference) generally results in true beliefs, then I cannot be highly certain that any of the beliefs formed using that method is true.

(5b) Therefore, I cannot be highly certain that any of my beliefs is true.

According to this strategy, we might accept the conclusion (5a) but reject one of the premises (1b)–(4b). Let's look at the options of rejecting (2b) and (3b) now.

Reject Premise (2)

Can we even be highly certain that forming beliefs on the basis of sense perception generally results in true beliefs? Can we reject (2b)?

The first question we should ask is what it would take to be certain that forming beliefs on the basis of sense perception generally results in true beliefs. Presumably what we would need is some sort of *argument* for the *reliability* of sense perception. We would need some way to show that sense perception does not generally lead us astray. But can we offer such an argument?

One strategy might be to argue that because sense perception is so successful, we can conclude that forming beliefs on its basis generally results in true beliefs. For example, I see a baseball heading toward me. I believe it will hit me in the head and it does. My belief, formed on seeing the baseball, was true. I believe a knife is before me. I reach for the knife and pick it up. My belief must have been correct; a knife really was before me. I see snow falling. I believe it will be cold. I touch it and it is cold.

A second strategy might be based on the theory of evolution. Organisms that perceive the world accurately and have true beliefs are more likely to survive. So, we can be sure that sense perception is reliable, and forming beliefs on the basis of sense perception generally results in true beliefs.

But can these arguments succeed? They cannot. They cannot work because, to use just one of the ways to support premise (2), all of our experiences might be self-generated. Consider the first line of argument: I not only generate the experience of the baseball flying toward my head, I also generate the experience of the ball actually hitting me in the head. I generate the experience of the knife and the experience of picking it up. I generate all of my experiences of snow and its feeling cold. In these cases I have astonishing success, but that's just because I have generated the entirety of the experiences all by myself. The experiences in fact correspond to nothing in reality and so they are not true. There is no baseball. There is no knife. There is no snow. Nonetheless, I'm successful just because my self-generated experiences are consistent with each other.

Now consider the second line of argument: any proof of the theory of evolution will depend on forming beliefs on the basis of sense perception. We must observe the fossils. We must study the earth's geological history. Yet doing so must already assume that forming beliefs on the basis of sense perception generally results in true beliefs. But that is what we need to prove. We have worked in a circle: we tried to prove sense perception is reliable by the theory of evolution but we assumed sense perception is reliable to prove the theory of evolution.

Recently, William Alston (1921–2009 CE) has persuasively argued that all of the attempts to prove that sense perception is reliable assume that sense perception is reliable. All such arguments are *epistemically circular*. That is the problem with the arguments based on success and evolution above. Claiming that forming beliefs on the basis of perception is reliable because of my success assumes that the beliefs I previously formed on the basis of sense perception were generally true. Claiming that forming beliefs on the basis of perception is reliable because the theory of evolution is true assumes that the beliefs I formed about evolution on the basis of my perceptions were true.

Reject Premise (3)

What about rejecting premise (3)? Can we offer an argument showing that inference is a reliable belief formation process, that forming beliefs on the basis of inference generally results in true beliefs? That is what it would take to be highly certain that inference is a reliable belief formation process.

We might begin by arguing that some inferences are obviously good because they are logically true. For example, we can be certain the inference form modus ponens (the mode of positing, discussed in Puzzle One) is valid because it is logically impossible for the premises to be true and for the conclusion to be false. It is on par with claiming *if squares have four sides, then squares have four sides*. Those beliefs are true quite independently of sense perception or inference. They are logically, necessarily true. (This also suggests a strategy for rejecting premise (1), to be discussed below.)

That might work for valid deductive arguments. Valid deductive arguments are arguments such that if their premises are true, then their conclusions must be true as well. However, there are two concerns. The first concern is how we get content for the premises of our deductive arguments. It is one thing to be certain that modus ponens is a valid argument form:

If S, then S'.

S.

Therefore, S'.

It is yet another thing to be certain that substitution instances of modus ponens are valid arguments:

(20) If it is raining, then the uncovered ground will be wet.

(21) It is raining.

(22) Therefore, the uncovered ground will be wet.

And it is yet a third thing to be certain that:

(22) The uncovered ground will be wet.

My certainty of (22) depends not merely on being certain modus ponens is a valid argument form and not merely on being certain that (20)–(22) are valid but also on being certain that (20) and (21) are true. However, my certainty that (20) and (21) are true depends on sense perception. Yet we have just seen that we cannot be certain that forming beliefs on the basis of sense perception is reliable. In short, even if we grant that we can be certain some argument forms are valid, it does not get us very far. It does not get us anything like certainty about what is happening in the world, certainty based on the senses, empirical knowledge.

A second problem with this strategy is that deduction is not the only kind of argument. Another kind of argument is induction. Typically, inductions are arguments that reach a general conclusion based on prior experiences. For example, from the fact that every time it has rained the uncovered ground has gotten wet, I might make the following argument:

(23) Every time it has rained in the past the uncovered ground has gotten wet.

(24) Therefore, if it rains, then the uncovered ground will be wet.

There is nothing about (23) that requires us to accept (24), as with deductions. After all, it is perfectly conceivable that it rains on some future occasion but for some bizarre reason the uncovered ground does not get wet. So, (24) does not follow from (23) as a matter of logic.

The problem now becomes whether we can be highly certain that forming beliefs on the basis of inductive inferences will generally result in true beliefs. Here again the answer is *no*. David Hume (1711–1776 CE) provides us with the key as to why. Hume argues that any attempt to prove that inductive inferences are reasonable inferences will require assuming that inductive inferences are reasonable inferences. If he is right, then any argument supporting inductive inference would be circular.

For example, suppose I believe that the next time it rains the uncovered ground will get wet. On what basis do I believe that? I believe it on the basis of the fact that every time in the past that it has rained the uncovered ground has gotten wet *and* I assume that the future will continue to resemble the past. But what is my support for the claim that the future will continue to resemble the past? It is that in the past the future has always resembled the past. But that is what I need to prove: that the future will continue to resemble the past. Once again, we have worked in a circle.

Much like the problem of circularity with respect to arguments for the reliability of sense perception, any attempt to argue that we can be highly certain that forming beliefs on the basis of inductive inferences will generally result in true beliefs will assume the very belief. Drawing on the insight of Hume, we can construct the following argument:

(25) If I am highly certain that forming beliefs on the basis of inductive inferences generally results in true beliefs, then I am certain of it on the basis of my experiences *and* the assumption that my future experiences will continue to resemble my past experiences.

(26) However, any attempt to prove that my future experiences will continue to resemble my past experiences must assume that my future experiences will continue to resemble my past experiences.

(27) We cannot be certain of beliefs based on unsupported assumptions.

(28) So, I cannot be highly certain that forming beliefs on the basis of inductive inferences generally results in true beliefs.

In sum, we have seen that our attempts to show we can be highly certain that sense perception is reliable are circular and any attempt to show that we can be highly certain that inductive inference is reliable will be circular. It follows that we cannot be highly certain of either.

Reject Premise (1)

If we cannot reject (2) and we cannot reject (3), perhaps we can instead reject (1). Descartes himself rejected premise (1). Moreover, he thinks that he can reject (2) and (3). Let's see why.

To begin, Descartes argues that there is one belief of which we can be absolutely certain. It is that "I am a thinking thing." Descartes believes that this proposition—"I am a thinking thing"—is known neither by sense perception nor by inference. Instead, it is known by intuition.

Intuition is both a mental power—as sense perception, imagination, and inference are—and a kind of belief. As a mental power, intuition is the ability to recognize the truth of a proposition immediately and directly. The truth of a proposition is recognized immediately because we need not prove it on the basis of other premises (in other words, it's not inferred). Also, the truth of a proposition is recognized directly, intellectually, and not through the senses. Descartes sometimes calls this faculty for immediately and directly recognizing the truth of propositions "the natural light of reason."

As a kind of belief, an intuition is a proposition that—as Descartes says—cannot be denied without manifest contradiction. Denying that "I am a thinking thing" involves a manifest contradiction because I must be thinking to deny "I am a thinking thing." How could I deny I'm a thinking thing unless I'm thinking of the denial?

Other intuited ideas are "squares are four-sided" and "something cannot come from nothing," or so Descartes thinks. It is built into the very definition of a square that it is four-sided. So, if we deny that squares are four-sided, then we are saying something manifestly false. The same goes for "something cannot come from nothing." How could some thing come from no thing at all? In fact, intuitions are nothing more than innate ideas, as discussed in Puzzle Two.

Descartes also thinks "God exists" is an intuited, innate idea. That's because he endorses a version of the ontological argument, as discussed in Puzzle Five. Since God is supremely perfect, and existence (or being incapable of inexistence) is a perfection, it follows that God must exist. Once we realize that, we realize that "God exists" is necessarily true, just like "squares are four-sided" is true. Moreover, Descartes thinks all deception depends on some imperfection. Consequently, he believes that a supremely perfect God cannot be a deceiver. That also leads Descartes to conclude that God would have given him the ability to root out any errors with respect to sense perception and with respect to inference. As a result, Descartes cannot be systematically deceived. We can be certain that forming beliefs on the basis of sense perception and that forming beliefs on the basis of inference are methods that generally result in true beliefs just because God would not endow us with faculties—mental powers like imagination, perception, and reason—that lead us astray and make it such that those errors cannot, in principle, be corrected.

In a nutshell, Descartes' attempt to resolve the problem follows this line of thought:

(A) I am a thinking thing.

(B) I am certain, by way of intuition, that I am a thinking thing.

(C) Because of (B), I must know what is required to be certain. Specifically, whatever sentence, when denied, involves a manifest contradiction must be certain.

(D) "God exists" cannot be denied without manifest contradiction.

(E) So, God exists.

(F) "God is not a deceiver" cannot be denied without manifest contradiction.

(G) So, God is not a deceiver.

(H) If God is not a deceiver, God would not design me in such a way that I am systematically and irredeemably misled by my sense perceptions and inferences.

(I) So, I can be highly certain that forming beliefs on the basis of sense perception and inference generally results in true beliefs.

Descartes' attempt to respond to our present puzzle is brilliant and beautiful. However, most philosophers think it fails miserably. This is for at least two reasons. First, it depends on Descartes' proofs of God's existence. However, as discussed in Puzzle Five, many philosophers believe the ontological argument does not prove that God in fact exists. Descartes has other arguments for God's existence, but the general consensus is that they don't fare any better. So, Descartes' line of thinking falters at step (D).

Second, many philosophers doubt that we have a power of intuition, or that, even if we do, we cannot be certain as to what is known by intuition and what is not. This line of objection is first found in the work of Charles Sanders Peirce (1839–1914 CE) and pursued further by Willard Van Orman Quine (1908–2000 CE). To begin, some philosophers doubt that we ever know anything immediately and directly. They doubt it because language is acquired and based on conventions. We must first gain knowledge of how to use the term 'square' and its significance to know that the term picks out four-sided figures. In that case, we don't know that "squares are four-sided" immediately and directly. Rather, we only know it through a process of language acquisition and convention. The claim that "squares are four-sided," for example, is known on the basis of a convention about the term 'square' and the roles that convention plays in our body of mathematical knowledge.

Moreover, even if Descartes is right that we have a power of intuition, how can he be certain that "I am a thinking thing" is known by intuition? After all, philosophers have been mistaken many, many times about what is known by intuition. One example of this error was discussed in our second puzzle. Many philosophers thought it was self-evident—or known by intuition— that a whole is always greater than its part. However, we have seen that this supposed intuition is false. Since intuitions are, by definition, true, it follows that it wasn't an intuition after all. Maybe the same is true of "God is not a deceiver," "I am a thinking thing," and "something cannot come from nothing." In fact, many physicists deny that last claim. Moreover, those who deny that there is a self must deny that we are thinking things (see Puzzle Eleven). Thus, Descartes' project may well fail at step (B) or even (A).

Reject Premise (4)

Premise (4) states that we can be certain of the truth of our beliefs only if we can be certain that the method by which we came to our beliefs generally results in true beliefs. In other words, I can be certain of my beliefs only if I can be certain sense perception and inference are reliable. But is that correct?

One point we should make off the bat is that it *is* correct so long as we mean by *certainty*, with respect to our individual beliefs, *absolute* certainty. We cannot be absolutely certain that any of our beliefs is true if we can always hold it out as a possibility that the method by which we came to our beliefs may be fundamentally flawed. In short, we should accept (4a).

Nonetheless, can't we have a *degree* of certainty regarding the truth of our beliefs, even if we cannot be absolutely certain that the methods whereby we came to our beliefs are reliable? Can't we reject (4b)?

Many philosophers have argued that even though it is true that we cannot be highly certain that sense perception and inference are *reliable belief formation processes*, we can still be certain of our *individual beliefs* formed by way of sense perception and inference. Let's examine two strategies for doing so. The first strategy belongs to the Scottish philosopher Thomas Reid (1710–1796 CE) and the second belongs to Crispin Wright (b. 1942 CE).

Strategy One: Thomas Reid's Commonsensism: I am, right now, looking at my computer as I type this. I believe I am looking at a computer. I am certain right now that I am looking at a computer. No matter how many clever arguments Descartes produces, I am thoroughly convinced I am right now looking at my computer.

Thomas Reid maintains that it is part of my nature, of my very constitution, to believe such claims about the external world simply on the basis of my sense perceptions. My very nature demands that I accept my experiences. It demands that I accept my beliefs formed on the basis of sense perception.

Reid readily admits that he has no proof for the conclusion that sense perception is a *reliable belief formation process*. Nonetheless, it is commonsense to admit that the *individual beliefs* I have formed on the basis of sense perception are, generally, true. That is the nature of my constitution, after all. I cannot but admit I am looking at my computer even if I acknowledge it is possible my experience is self-generated.

In this sense, I can be certain of my individual beliefs formed on the basis of sense perception. I can be certain of them just because my nature requires me to accept them. I am constituted in such a way that I cannot help but admit their truth.

Of course, I may come to doubt my sense perceptions. I may, for example, come to realize that I suffered an illusion or was dreaming. Reid does not question that. But these are, by far, exceptions to the rule. By and large, for the most part, I simply concede the truth of my perception-based beliefs. I cannot but do otherwise.

Thus, I cannot be certain that sense perception is a reliable belief formation process. However, my nature, my very constitution, is such that I cannot help but accept my beliefs about the world as formed on the basis of my sense perceptions. As a consequence, I can be certain of my individual beliefs formed on the basis of sense perception. My certainty is based, not on some argument for the reliability of sense perception, but on my very nature. It is because my constitution demands that I accept my perception-based beliefs that I can be highly certain of them.

Strategy Two: Entitlement: Crispin Wright agrees that we cannot be certain that sense perception and inductive inference are reliable belief formation processes. We cannot offer any arguments to support such claims.

Nevertheless, he does think that we are *entitled* to accept the claims that sense perception and inference are reliable belief formation processes. Because we are *entitled* to accept them, we can be certain of our *individual beliefs* that are formed on the basis of sense perception or of inference.

Being entitled to a belief—in this case, our belief in the reliability of sense perception and inference as *belief formation processes*—is not the same as knowing it. When you know something, you have some justification for it. You have good epistemic grounds for believing it, like an argument. (For more on justification, see Puzzle Ten.) However, as we have already seen in our attempts at rejecting premises (2) and (3), we cannot offer an argument for rejecting (2) or for rejecting (3).

But it does not follow from the fact that we cannot justify a belief that we have no grounds for accepting the belief at all. On

Wright's view, the facts that (i) sense perception and inference are vitally important for our all of our cognitive projects; (ii) we have no reason to think sense perception and inference are not reliable belief formation processes; and (iii) any attempt to justify either would involve using claims no more certain than the belief in their reliability (as was shown in our attempts to reject (2) and (3) above) *entitles* (but does not justify) us to claim that forming beliefs on the basis of sense perception or of inference generally results in true beliefs. We are permitted to *take it to be true* that sense perception and inference are reliable belief formation processes even though we cannot *prove it to be true*.

Since we can take it to be true that forming beliefs on the basis of sense perception or inference is reliable, we can still be highly certain of our *individual beliefs* formed using them. Our uncertainty about the reliability of sense perception and inference does not harm our certainty about the individual beliefs we form using sense perception or inference. Rather, our entitlement serves as a foundation on which we build our individual beliefs. The certainty of our individual beliefs is based on our entitled beliefs in the reliability of sense perception and inference. Thus, although it is true we cannot be certain that forming beliefs on the basis of sense perception or of inference generally results in true beliefs, it is false that we cannot be certain of our beliefs formed using sense perception and inference. We can be certain of them because they have our entitled beliefs as their foundation.

Bonus Puzzle

I have been presenting Descartes' puzzling argument as being concerned with certainty. However, a variation on Descartes' argument can also be presented. In the variation, the puzzle is not about certainty but about knowledge. Descartes' argument, then, runs as follows:

(1) Every belief I have I formed either on the basis of sense perception or on the basis of inference.

(2) I cannot know that forming beliefs on the basis of sense perception generally results in true beliefs.

(3) I cannot know that forming beliefs on the basis of inference generally results in true beliefs.

(4) If I cannot know that forming beliefs by way of some method (for example, sense perception or inference) generally results in true beliefs, then I cannot know that any of the beliefs formed using that method is true.

(5) Therefore, I cannot know that any of my beliefs is true.

Premise (1) is plausible for the same reasons as mentioned above. Premise (2) is plausible because it is possible there is no external world. It is possible, for example, that all of my experiences are self-generated. Premise (3) is plausible because I could suffer from a cognitive defect. And (4) is plausible for the same reasons provided above.

Now we can ask: Do the same considerations as discussed in the "Possible Responses" section apply to this argument about knowledge as well? If so, how do the arguments against rejecting (2) and (3) need to be modified? If they do not, then why not?

References

Alston, William. *The Reliability of Sense Perception*. Ithaca: Cornell UP, 1996.

Descartes, René. *Meditations on First Philosophy*. In *The Philosophical Writings of Decartes*. Vol. 2. Trans. John Cottingham, Robert Stoothoff, and Dugald Murdoch. Cambridge: Cambridge UP, 1984.

Descartes, René. *Principles of Philosophy*. In *The Philosophical Writings of Decartes*. Vol. 1. Trans. John Cottingham, Robert Stoothoff, and Dugald Murdoch. Cambridge: Cambridge UP, 1984.

Hume, David. *An Enquiry Concerning Human Understanding*. 2nd ed. Ed. Eric Steinberg. Indianapolis: Hackett, 1993.

Peirce, Charles Sanders. "Questions Concerning Certain Faculties Claimed for Man." *The Essential Peirce*. Vol. 1. Ed. Nathan Houser and Christian Kloesel. Bloomington: Indiana UP, 1992.

Quine, Williard Van Orman. "Two Dogmas of Empiricism." *Philosophical Review.* 60: 20–43, 1951.

Reid, Thomas. *An Inquiry into the Human Mind on the Principles of Common Sense.* Ed. Derek R. Brookes. University Park: Pennsylvania State UP, 1997.

Wright, Crispin. "Warrant for Nothing (and Foundations for Free?)." *Proceedings of the Aristotelian Society Supplement.* 78: 167–212, 2004.

PUZZLE EIGHT

Psychological Egoism

Endeavor, when it is toward something which causes it, is called appetite, or desire. . . . And when the endeavor is from ward something, it is generally called aversion. . . . But whatsoever is the object of any man's appetite or desire, that is it which he for his part calleth good; and the object of his hate and aversion, evil. . . .
. . . [O]f the voluntary acts of every man the object is some good to himself.
—Thomas Hobbes (1588–1679 CE), Leviathan

The Philosopher

Thomas Hobbes was the son of Thomas Hobbes. The former was a famous philosopher. The latter was an infamous clergyman.

Thomas Hobbes the elder was an infamous clergyman for two reasons. First, one Saturday night he stayed up into the wee hours of the morning playing cards. He was so tired the next morning that he fell asleep during the church service. He is reported to have shouted out, "Clubs is trump!" while dreaming. Second, when a young clergyman joined the church, Thomas Hobbes the elder had a heated argument with him. In the midst of the argument he struck the younger clergyman. Hobbes the elder had to flee.

By the time his father was off beating other clergyman, Thomas Hobbes the younger was off studying at school. Hobbes must have distinguished himself as a student, for he was recommended to tutor the son of William Cavendish, who was also named William Cavendish. (Apparently the English weren't very creative with names.) William Cavendish the elder was the First Earl of Devonshire (he died of the plague) and William Cavendish the younger was the Second Earl of Devonshire (he died of overindulgence). They both served in the House of Lords.

Hobbes strongly supported English royalty. After all, they wrote his paychecks. This became a problem for him just prior to the beginning of the English Civil War. Hobbes' defense of the royals made him a target of contempt by the Parliamentarians who sought to depose the royal family. Hobbes had to flee. He made his way to Paris. Hobbes had been there previously, making acquaintances with the French thinker Marin Mersenne (1588–1648 CE). Mersenne was also good friends with René Descartes (1596–1650 CE), the author of our seventh puzzle. Descartes had recently completed his masterpiece, *Meditations on First Philosophy*. Mersenne asked Hobbes to write a set of objections to Descartes' *Meditations* so that Descartes could respond to them and dispel misunderstandings concerning his work.

Hobbes gladly undertook the project. He and Descartes were at odds both philosophically and personally. Whereas they respected each other outwardly, Hobbes thought that Descartes should have stuck to geometry and not bothered his pretty little head about philosophical issues. For his part, Descartes worried that Hobbes was trying to make a reputation for himself by riding his coattails.

Fortunately for Hobbes, he didn't need to ride Descartes' coattails. As the English Civil War raged, many supporters of royalty made their way to Paris and into Hobbes' company. There's nothing like keeping company with royalty and their friends to make you famous, and so Hobbes' philosophical renown spread rapidly.

Hobbes had fled from England in 1640 and would not return until 1651. He had to return. In 1651 he published his most famous book, *Leviathan*. Although it argued for a strong, absolute sovereign, the book angered the Royalists. That's because Hobbes' book did not obviously support the Church of England, let alone Catholicism. Hobbes was a materialist. He did not believe that we have immaterial souls that go to heaven. He did not believe we have any higher good than the perpetual satisfaction of our own desires. And he did not believe that the source of political power comes from God. Rather, he thought that it derived from the need for people to enforce their contracts with each other. This angered the king's exiled supporters in Paris, and so Hobbes had to return to England.

Hobbes was permitted to return and eventually settled into a quiet life. However, his writings were reviled. The Royalists hated them for the reasons just mentioned. The Parliamentarians hated them because Hobbes argued for an absolute sovereign. Poor Hobbes had no allies. In fact, his writings were so detested that the Royalists and Parliamentarians worked together to pass a law forbidding him to publish books in England. At least they could see eye-to-eye on that.

Hobbes died of a bladder infection at the ripe old age of ninety-one.

The Puzzle

Thomas Hobbes' argument purports to show that, at root, all of our actions are ultimately motivated by self-interest. When we act, we are always ultimately motivated by the promise of promoting our own interests. This theory is called *psychological egoism*.

Five preliminary points are in order. First, psychological egoism is to be distinguished from another theory called *ethical egoism*. Ethical egoism is a theory about what we *ought* to do. The theory of ethical egoism is that we ought to always promote our own interests exclusively and over the long run. In contrast, psychological egoism is a theory about the way we *in fact* are. When we act we are in fact ultimately motivated by self-interest. Whether we *ought* to act so is a different question.

Second, when psychological egoists affirm that all of our actions are ultimately motivated by self-interest, they mean to exclude involuntary behaviors and forced actions. Sneezing, for example, is excluded because it is an involuntary behavior. Also, if someone should grab my hand and force me to punch myself in my own face, it is a forced action and so excluded from the theory.

Third, psychological egoists do not deny that we may fail to promote our interests. Youthful smokers, for example, fail to promote their own interests because smoking puts them at greater risk for future diseases. What psychological egoism states is that we are ultimately *motivated* by self-interest. Whether we have any clue as to what *really is* in our own interest is a separate question.

If we are mistaken about what is in our interest, we will fail to promote our own interests (unless we do so by luck). Nevertheless, the psychological egoist will say that we are still *motivated* by self-interest. An analogy is helpful here. A competitive archer who believes that striking the outer ring of an archery target will get him the most points is still motivated to win the contest even though he is mistaken about how to win it. In like manner, a young person who believes that smoking will best promote his interests is still motivated to promote his interests. He is just mistaken about how to do it.

Fourth, endorsing psychological egoism does not require claiming that everyone else's interests are *totally* irrelevant. It does not require claiming that the only person who matters is the agent. Rather, there are both *extreme* and *moderate* versions of psychological egoism, as Elliot Sober (b. 1948 CE) has pointed out.

To illustrate the difference, suppose that you and a psychological egoist are going to the movies. However, you have to come to an agreement about which movie to see. One of two things might happen:

Possibility One: You both want to see the same movie.

Possibility Two: You want to see different movies.

Obviously, if you both want to see the same movie (Possibility One) you will go see that movie. Call this *Outcome One.* But suppose you do not want to see the same movie, Possibility Two. In that case, you will do one of the following:

Outcome Two: Go to the movie the psychological egoist wants to see.

Outcome Three: Go to the movie you want to see.

Outcome Four: Go to a movie neither of you wants to see.

The difference between extreme and moderate psychological egoism lies in how those outcomes are rated.

For starters, both extreme and moderate psychological egoists will rate Outcome One as the best and Outcome Four as the worst.

The difference between extreme and moderate psychological egoists lies in how they rate Outcome Two and Outcome Three. The extreme psychological egoist thinks that Outcome Two is *just as good as* Outcome One. Also, he thinks Outcome Three is *just as bad as* Outcome Four. That's because the extreme psychological egoist thinks that your desires, your wants, are totally irrelevant. All that matters to him are his own desires, his own wants.

In contrast, the moderate psychological egoist will rank Outcome Two as worse than Outcome One but better than Outcome Three. Also, he will rate Outcome Three as better than Outcome Four. In other words, the best is Outcome One. Outcome Two is good. Outcome Three is fair. Outcome Four is bad. That's because the moderate psychological egoist thinks your desires and wants matter. They just don't matter as much as his.

Our fifth point is that some people might think that psychological egoism is clearly false. After all, if everyone ran around pursuing his or her own interests the world would be chaotic. Our lives would be nasty, miserable, brutish, and short.

This objection to psychological egoism, however, is simply mistaken. It turns out that even among egoists cooperation can emerge. This has been amply shown in game theoretic modeling of egoistic behavior by Robert Axelrod (b. 1943 CE) and by Brian Skyrms (b. 1938 CE). Even egoists can work together to promote their own interests. In fact, a society of psychological egoists might look very much like our own.

Now that we have made these clarifications, just what is Thomas Hobbes' argument for psychological egoism? His argument may be expressed as follows:

(1) If you act, then you expect to accrue some benefit to yourself or to avoid some harm to yourself when you act.

(2) If you expect to accrue some benefit to yourself or to avoid some harm to yourself when you act, then you are ultimately motivated by self-interest.

(3) Therefore, if you act, then you are ultimately motivated by self-interest.

The conclusion (3) is, of course, the theory of psychological egoism. If we accept (1) and (2), then we are committed to (3). There are no two ways about it. The argument is logically valid.

Before we turn to a consideration of what can be said in defense of these premises, I want to point out why so many philosophers have found the argument in (1)–(3) troubling. Many philosophers believe that we cannot be morally required to do what is beyond our powers or abilities. For example, I am not right now morally required to run into a burning building in China and save the people inside. That is because I am now in the United States and cannot possibly get to China in time to save those people. In like manner, I am not morally required to donate 1,000,000 dollars to charity. Why? Just because I do not have 1,000,000 dollars to donate. More generally, many philosophers endorse this claim:

> (4) We are not morally required to do what we cannot do.

The conclusion (3) above, however, states that we cannot ultimately be motivated to help others for their sake alone. Rather, whenever we help others, we always ultimately do it for ourselves. Consequently, (3) and (4) together prove that:

> (5) Therefore, we are not morally required to do an action if in doing it we are not ultimately motivated by self-interest.

Yet (5) is a very disturbing conclusion. Imagine that there is some man whose conscience will not pang him in the least if he lets a child drown. Moreover, assume that everyone already reviles this man and that they will never praise or honor him. In that case, such a man is not morally required to save a drowning baby. He will gain nothing from it. He will avoid no harms by failing to do it. And so we cannot hold him morally responsible. He was not morally required to help the baby because he could not possibly be motivated by self-interest.

Similarly, suppose an extremely wealthy man will gain nothing from being charitable. Suppose he is already praised and honored by his countrymen. Suppose he derives no pleasure from charity. If the above argument is correct such a man is not morally required to be charitable. However, he surely *is* required to be charitable.

And what of us normal folk? Suppose that humiliating a co-worker will bring me great pleasure and a pay raise but absolutely no harm. Am I morally required to refrain from humiliating my co-worker? If the above argument is correct, then I am not. For I cannot be morally required to do an action if I am not, ultimately, motivated by self-interest.

Thus, the present puzzle is puzzling on two counts. First, it denies that we ever act in a manner that is not ultimately motivated by self-interest. That's quite surprising, for it means that whenever I help my child or a stranger I'm ultimately in it for myself, not them. Second, it means that much of what we think about morality might be mistaken. For traditional moral demands must be mistaken insofar as they require us to set aside our own interests for the sake of others.

In what follows, I will take premise (4) for granted (though it is doubtful). My focus shall be on premises (1) and (2).

The Premises

Premise (1)

Why is premise (1) true? It's hard to imagine why a person would do any action if that person did not expect some benefit or to avoid some harm when doing it. What other motivation could possibly explain a person's action?

You might reply: oh, there is a very simple reason you might act. You might act to help another person. That has nothing to do with benefitting yourself. For example, if you bring soup to a sick friend you aim to help your friend, not yourself.

Very well. I admit that *appears* to be true. However, if we desire to help another person, we also desire the satisfaction of that desire. If I want to volunteer for a charity, then I also desire that my want be satisfied. I not only want to volunteer, I desire that my want to volunteer be satisfied *by volunteering*. Yet that means that whenever I act to benefit another I also expect to benefit myself. Namely, I expect the benefit of the satisfaction of my desire to help that other person. Similarly, if I bring soup to my sick friend I do so because I want to. Yet I also desire the satisfaction of my want. I want to help my friend and I want to satisfy my desire to help my friend. That is the benefit I expect to accrue by virtue of my action.

We can approach the same point from another angle. Suppose that I have two equally strong desires, one to volunteer at a charity and one to care for a sick friend. These are my first-order desires.

I prefer doing one of the actions to doing neither. However, since my first-order desires are equally strong, I cannot decide between them. Since I have a second-order desire to do one of the actions rather than nothing, I have a second-order desire that at least one of my first-order desires—to volunteer or to care for my friend— be satisfied *by acting*. Hence, when I act (either volunteer or care for my friend) I at the very least expect to satisfy my second-order desire to satisfy a first-order desire. Granted that this is the right account whenever I have competing desires, and we can generalize and claim that it is the right account whenever I act at all: I only act on a (first-order) desire when I (second-order) desire to satisfy that (first-order) desire. Acting, then, will always at least bring the benefit of satisfying one of my desires, namely, my second-order desire to satisfy my first-order desire.

In sum, we act only if we want something (whether something for ourselves or for another person). However, if we want something when we act, then we also desire the satisfaction of our wants by virtue of the action. Yet if we desire the satisfaction of our wants by virtue of the action, then we are expecting a benefit. We expect the benefit of satisfying our wants. Hence, if we act, then we expect some benefit. And that is why premise (1) is true.

Premise (2)

Based on what we said with respect to premise (1) we can also see why premise (2) is true. Premise (2) is true because the expected *satisfaction* of our wants explains why we *act* on our wants in the first place. So, if we are to expect some personal benefit or to avoid some personal harm by virtue of our actions, then we are ultimately motivated by self-interest. The expected satisfaction of our wants ultimately explains why we acted at all.

Possible Responses

Reject Premise (1)

Maybe we can reject premise (1). In order to do so we need to find some occasion when a person acts but that person does not expect to accrue some personal benefit or to avoid some personal harm by virtue of her action. We needn't look far for such examples. Any time a person performs a heroic action—for example, rushing into a burning building to save a family or throwing oneself on a grenade to save the lives of one's fellow soldiers—is just such an example. To take the second case, what possible benefit could accrue to a dead person? What harm does a dead person avoid? To the argument for premise (1) presented above, how does throwing herself on a grenade satisfy her want to save her fellow soldiers? After all, dead people no longer have wants and so such a want cannot be satisfied.

Moreover, we needn't look only to heroic actions. Consider again the example of going to see a movie. We've all been in that situation, a situation where we disagree about what movie to see. Moreover, many of us have sacrificed our own interests and gone to see the movie that the other person wanted to see. In that case, we have acted in a manner contrary to moderate psychological egoism. We have sacrificed our own interests to the interests of our friends.

A psychological egoist, however, can respond to these cases by attributing a self-interested motivation to such persons. For example, the person who rushes into a burning building might expect to be honored or to make the family indebted to her. The soldier who throws herself on the grenade might avoid the pangs of conscience that she would have suffered had she not done so. Or she might expect to accrue the benefits of going to heaven. Moreover, perhaps her want is satisfied at just the moment the grenade explodes, as she momentarily considers the good she has done. As for the movie example, the psychological egoist may claim that you gave into your friend because you wanted to avoid the pain of further argument or to ensure that the next time you go to the movies you get to see the movie you want.

Moreover, let's suppose that the psychological egoist grants the example of heroism. Let's suppose that the psychological egoist grants that sometimes people perform actions for which they neither expect a benefit nor the avoidance of harm. Does this pose a significant problem for the underlying puzzle of psychological egoism?

The answer is *no*. Even granting heroic actions, it may still very well be true that in the vast majority of cases—99.999999% of cases—people expect a personal benefit or to avoid a personal harm. After all, how often does a person do something truly heroic? This means that a psychological egoist can trade in her theory for a slightly weaker theory called *predominant egoism*. Predominant egoism is the theory that *nearly all* human actions are ultimately motivated by self-interest. It makes exceptions for truly heroic actions. But since hardly anyone is a true hero, pretty much everyone's actions are ultimately motivated by self-interest. In that case, a predominant egoist can present a slightly weaker argument to support her claim and get around examples of heroism. She can argue as follows:

(1a) For nearly every action you will ever do (indeed, probably for every action *you* will ever do) you expect to accrue some benefit to yourself or to avoid some harm to yourself when you act.

(2a) If you expect to accrue some benefit to yourself or to avoid some harm to yourself when you act, then you are ultimately motivated by self-interest.

(3a) Therefore, for nearly every action you will ever do (indeed, probably for every action you will ever do), you are ultimately motivated by self-interest.

This argument is every bit as puzzling as the first one.

What about the example of going to the movies, of deferring to your friend in seeing the movie he wants? Such cases are fairly common, and so even a predominant egoist will need to deal with them. However, here the predominant egoist can explain away your deference in the same way the psychological egoist does: you want to avoid further argument or you want to ensure you get to see the movie you want next time. That is a fairly plausible reply here.

Reject Premise (2)

In order to reject premise (2) we need to show that while it is true that we expect some benefit or to avoid some harm from our actions, it is false that we are ultimately motivated to promote our self-interest. Is it possible to show this?

Strategy One: Sometimes We Expect Benefits But Anticipate Even Greater Misery: One way to reject premise (2) is to point out that sometimes people do actions when they expect some benefit but anticipate even greater misery. Hence, their ultimate motivation must not be to promote their own interests.

An example of this is a corporate whistleblower. Corporate whistleblowers are employees of a company who report unethical actions by their employers. Such a corporate whistleblower expects a benefit—the cessation of her pangs of conscience for working with an unethical company—but she also expects significant harm. If she is not fired she will at least be ostracized within the company. If she is fired, it will be virtually impossible for her to find another job in her sector. In such cases a person expects a benefit. However, she can be assured of much greater misery. Hence, it is very peculiar to claim such a person is ultimately motivated to promote her own interests.

Unfortunately, a psychological egoist can resist this point. A psychological egoist might insist that, to the whistleblower, cessation of the pangs of conscience really does outweigh the foreseen harms of whistleblowing. In other words, whereas it seems to us that such whistleblowers are better off keeping their secrets to themselves, the whistleblower herself does not feel that way and that is why she blows her whistle.

Strategy Two: Butler's Stone: I'm not sure that whistleblowers really do expect the cessation of conscience's pangs to outweigh the foreseen harms of whistleblowing, but let's grant the point. Is there another way to reject premise (2)? Joseph Butler (1692–1752 CE) provides us with a way of doing so. Butler notes that we need to distinguish between the satisfaction of our desires and our desires themselves. Whereas the former—the satisfaction of our desires—may well be a benefit to us, Butler points out that what our desires themselves are *for* is something external to us, not their own satisfaction.

For example, I desire to eat something. As such, eating something will satisfy my desire. But what is my ultimate motivation in eating? My motivation is not merely the pleasure of satisfying a desire to eat something. For suppose I have before me an apple and a stone. Obviously, I am going to eat the apple, not the stone. But what does this show? It shows that my ultimate motivation in eating is not simply to satisfy my desire to eat something. Rather, my ultimate motivation in eating is *the apple*. If I were ultimately just aiming to satisfy my desire to eat something, a stone would be just as satisfactory as an apple. In both cases I would have eaten something. And here is Butler's point: It is true that I expect some satisfaction from eating the apple. I expect to satisfy my desire to eat something. However, it is false that satisfying my desire to eat something is my ultimate motivation in acting. If it were my ultimate motivation I may as well have eaten the stone.

A similar consideration applies to other examples. For instance, suppose you bring soup to your sick friend. We might now ask: Why did you bring soup to your sick friend? The psychological egoist will claim that you expected the benefit of satisfying your desire to help your friend. But that is wrong. It is true you expect that benefit. However, your ultimate motivation is *to help your friend by bringing her soup*. If that were not your ultimate motivation, you may as well have just transferred the five dollars that the soup costs you to her bank account. After all, if you had done that you would have still satisfied your desire to help your friend.

Strategy Three: Multiple Motivations without Ultimacy: Can we say anything else to reject premise (2)? We can. To understand the response, we need to point out that the very same action can have two motivations, neither of which is ultimate. That is, we can have two motivations in acting such that either alone is sufficient to lead us to do the action, even though one of the motivations is not self-interested.

Let's begin with a simple scenario. I might go jogging because I am both motivated by the promise of good health and by the hope of winning a marathon. But which is my ultimate motivation? Plausibly, neither is the ultimate motivation because I would still jog for either aim individually. Even if I were not motivated to improve my health, I would jog. Also, even if I were not motivated to win a marathon, I would jog. Of course, a psychological egoist has no problem handling this case, for both aims are in my own interest. But this example helps us get a handle on understanding how an action can have two motivations without either one being ultimate.

To continue, consider again the example of going to a movie with a psychological egoist. Suppose that you both want to see different movies, but you give into the psychological egoist and go see the movie he wants to see. Nonetheless, the psychologist egoist wants to make it clear that you really did it to promote your own interests. That is, he wants to make sure that you realize psychological egoism is true even though you *appear* to be putting his interests before your own. In that case, you might have the following conversation:

Conversation One:

PE: Why did you agree to go see the movie I wanted to see?

You: Because I wanted to make you happy.

PE: Okay, but really you did it not because you want to make me happy but because it makes you happy to make me happy, right?

You: Well, it does please me to see that you're happy.

PE: So, you ultimately did it to make yourself happy.

You: Yes.

But now imagine a slightly different conversation, one where you are unwilling to admit the truth of psychological egoism. In that case, the conversation might go as follows:

Conversation Two:

PE: Why did you agree to go see the movie I wanted to see?

You: Because I wanted to make you happy.

PE: Okay, but really you did it not because you want to make me happy but because it makes you happy to make me happy, right?

You: No, I did it because I genuinely wanted to make you happy.

PE: I know you like to attribute finer motives to yourself than you in fact have, but let's face it: you really did it to make yourself happy, because it pleases you. That's why you really did it.

You: No, that's not right. I did it to make you happy *and*
because it pleases me. But I would have done it just
to make you happy. And I would have done it just
because it pleases me.

In your last comment you are giving expression to the strategy being pursued here. Sometimes we can do an action with two
different motivations. However, neither one is the singular, ultimate motivation for the action. Either alone would be sufficient to
explain why the action is done.

To further this line of thought, both Charles Sanders Peirce
(1839–1914 CE) and Elliot Sober ask us to imagine a scenario
where you will undergo a surgery that will make it such that you
will no longer feel pleasure when you do an action that benefits
another person. Consider again the movie example where both
you want to make the other person happy and you want to make
yourself happy by making the other person happy. Imagine that
you have decided in advance that you will give into the psychological egoist and go see whatever movie he wishes. You now
have two motivations in acting: to make him happy and to make
yourself happy. But suppose just beforehand you knowingly underwent a surgery that made it such that you will feel no pleasure
at all in giving into the psychological egoist, in going to see the
movie he wants to see. Keeping in mind that you had decided
in advance to give into the psychological egoist, would you still
do it even though you will no longer derive any pleasure from
doing so?

If you answer the previous question in the affirmative (and it is
quite plausible to do so), then psychological egoism is false. Your
ultimate motivation wasn't your own pleasure. After all, you will
feel no pleasure (because of the surgery) and you know so. Peirce's
point is that because you decided in advance to give into the psychological egoist, because you have *resolved* to do so and are *determined* to do so, you will go through with the action. You will
go through with it even though you will receive no benefit from
doing so.

Similar considerations apply to actions we do not want to do.
Suppose, for example, that you have made plans with a friend to
hang out. You're really looking forward to it, and you're sure you're

going to have a great time. However, a few hours before you're to get together your friend calls and tells you that Steve—a guy you really can't stand to be around, a guy whose very existence repulses you, a guy who makes you throw up a little in your mouth every time his name is even mentioned—is going to come over too. You now realize that you're going to have a horrible, miserable time. However, you already made plans. You were already intending to go. So, you go anyway. Even though you will get no pleasure from it, you go just because you had already resolved to and were determined to do so.

To return to the example of going to the movie the psychological egoist wants to see, it is obvious that you have not and will not undergo surgery to cut your pleasure nerves. Consequently, you will still take pleasure in making the psychological egoist happy. Nonetheless, the fact that you *would* have undertaken the action had you undergone surgery shows that your pleasure is not your ultimate motivation when you act. You're motivated to make him happy. You're motivated to make yourself happy. However, neither motivation is ultimate. Either alone suffices to explain your action. So, even if for every action we expect a benefit or to avoid some harm when we act, it does not follow that our *ultimate* motivation is self-interest. It only follows that self-interest is one motivation among many.

Accept the Conclusion

Finally, we can accept the conclusion. We can maintain that, whenever we act, our ultimate motivation is self-interest. That conclusion may have important implications for morality. However, as noted above, it does not mean we will fail to help each other out. It does not mean society will dissolve into a chaotic mess of self-seeking, self-interested people. It may, however, be disheartening and disillusioning to admit that every nice thing anyone has ever done for you was just an instance of self-interested pursuit. Every time your father pushed you on a swing, every time a friend consoled you when you were sad, every time you relied on the kindness of strangers, the person was always ultimately in it for himself or herself. And, of course, if you ever do anything nice for another person, you're really just in it for yourself too.

References

Axelrod, Robert. *The Evolution of Cooperation*. Rev. ed. Cambridge: Basic Books, 2006.

Butler, Joseph. "Upon the Love of Our Neighbor." In *Five Sermons*. Ed. Stephen L. Darwall. Indianapolis: Hackett, 1983.

Hobbes, Thomas. *Leviathan*. Ed. Edwin Curley. Indianapolis: Hackett, 1994.

Peirce, Charles S. "What Makes a Reasoning Sound?" In *The Essential Peirce*. Vol. 2. Ed. The Peirce Edition Project. Bloomington: Indiana UP, 1998.

Skyrms, Brian. *The Stag Hunt and the Evolution of Social Structure*. Cambridge: Cambridge UP, 2003.

Sober, Elliot. "What Is Psychological Egoism?" *Behaviorism*. 17(2): 89–102, 1989.

PUZZLE NINE

Free Will and Determinism

It has been already sufficiently proved that the soul is nothing more than the body considered relatively to some of its functions more concealed than others. . . . Consequently, it is subjected to the influence of those material and physical causes which give impulse to the body. . . . Thus man is a being purely physical; in whatever manner he is considered, he is connected to universal nature, and submitted to the necessary and immutable laws that she imposes on all the beings she contains. . . . Man's life is a line that nature commands him to describe upon the surface of the earth, without his ever being able to swerve from it, even for an instant. He is born without his own consent; his organization does in nowise depend upon himself; his ideas come to him involuntarily; his habits are in the power of those who cause him to contract them; he is unceasingly modified by causes, whether visible or concealed, over which he has no control. . . . Nevertheless, in despite of the shackles by which he is bound, it is pretended he is a free agent, or that independent of the causes by which he is moved, he determines his own will, and regulates his own condition.
—Baron Paul Henri Thiry d'Holbach (1723–1789 CE),
The System of Nature

The Philosopher

As can be judged from his name, Baron d'Holbach was a baron. He was rich. Filthy rich. D'Holbach was born in Landau, on the border between France and Germany. His mother was the daughter of the local tax collector. His father grew grapes for wine. However, his parents didn't raise him. Rather, d'Holbach's uncle raised him in Paris. His uncle was a millionaire who gained his wealth by speculating in the stock exchange.

Here's a timeline of d'Holbach's life from 1749 to 1755:

1749: D'Holbach marries his second cousin.

1753: D'Holbach's father-in-law and uncle die. He inherits lots of money.

1754: D'Holbach's wife dies.

1755: With special dispensation from the Pope, d'Holbach marries the younger sister of his deceased wife.

In Paris' high society, d'Holbach gained a reputation, but not for his questionable marital decisions. He became famous for the parties he threw. The food was magnificent. The wine was the best. When you're filthy rich, you can afford it.

D'Holbach also formed a *salon,* a gathering of like-minded people for the purpose of discussing philosophy, politics, or other intellectual topics. He invited only the smartest people in France to join. Among them were Denis Diderot and Jean le Rond d'Alembert (1713–1784 CE and 1717–1783 CE, respectively, editors and contributors to the *Encyclopédie,* a forerunner to our encyclopedias), Étienne Bonnot de Condillac and Jean Jacques Rousseau (1715–1780 CE and 1712–1778 CE, respectively, two of the leading philosophers in France), and the Marquis de Condorcet (1743–1794 CE, an important mathematician and political scientist). D'Holbach would also support these thinkers with generous, anonymous gifts. Philosophers outside of France also made their ways to d'Holbach's parties. Among them were David Hume (1711–1776 CE, a Scottish philosopher), Adam Smith (1723–1790 CE, economist and author of *The Wealth of Nations*), and Edward Gibbon (1737–1794 CE, historian and author of *The History of the Decline and Fall of the Roman Empire*).

The lesson to be learned here is that great thinkers never decline good food and good wine when another person is paying.

One peculiar fact about d'Holbach is that his reputation as a great and generous man never declined. However, he published books that endorsed atheism, determinism, and materialism. He denied God exists, he thought that we are governed by immutable natural laws and have no free will, and he argued that there is no spiritual, immaterial realm of being. Had the people of France known this, d'Holbach surely would have come under heavy criticism. He would have been ostracized from high society. Also, it's unlikely the Pope would have given him a special dispensation to marry to his dead wife's younger sister.

Fortunately for d'Holbach, no one did know these things. He published all of his highly contentious books anonymously. As a result, he was able to preserve his standing among Paris' elite and even in the Catholic Church. Moreover, his secret was carefully guarded. Not until the early eighteen hundreds did it become widely known that he was the author of these books.

D'Holbach died in 1789, just before the French Revolution. Ironically, he was buried at the Church of Saint Roch, Paris. However, the exact location of his grave is no longer known.

The Puzzle

What is d'Holbach's puzzling argument? It's as follows:

(1) Humans are wholly part of nature.

(2) Every event in nature is necessitated—or determined—by prior events, conditions, and the laws of nature.

(3) If humans are wholly part of nature and every natural event is determined, then all of our actions are determined.

(4) If all of our actions are determined, then none of our actions is done freely.

(5) Therefore, none of our actions is done freely; we have no free will.

Once again, this is a deductively valid argument. If we accept the premises, then we must accept the conclusion. There are no two ways about it. If the premises are true, then we have to admit that free will is just an illusion. Our actions are not freely chosen; we *had* to do them.

Above, I noted that d'Holbach was an atheist, determinist, and materialism. Here, we see his commitments to determinism and materialism come to the fore. Premise (1) expresses his commitment to materialism. We're wholly material beings. We don't have immaterial souls. We're not spiritual beings. We're physical beings who are wholly part of the natural order.

Premise (2) expresses d'Holbach's commitment to the view that regular and immutable laws govern all of nature. This view is often called *determinism*, the theory that prior events, conditions, and the laws of nature necessitate every event in the universe. Those events could not have been otherwise; they were necessary.

We can hardly deny that the conclusion of d'Holbach's argument is surprising. After all, it certainly seems as though we act freely. Indeed, if I don't have a free will, what explains the fact that I deliberate? Why would I weigh the pros and cons of various options if I couldn't freely choose among them? For example, just this morning I was trying to decide whether or not I should kick my downstairs neighbor's yappy dog. I thought of all the pros it would bring: great pleasure and a quieter home life. I also thought of all the cons it would bring: a lawsuit and a visit from the police. Ultimately, I decided not to do it. But why weigh the options at all if I have no free choice in the matter?

Another reason to think we have a free will is that we are morally responsible for our actions. But can we really be held morally responsible for our actions if we ultimately have no free choice in the matter, if we have no free will? For example, people who commit crimes while sleepwalking are not freely choosing to commit those crimes. Hence, sleepwalking has been used as a successful defense in murder trials. Murdering sleepwalkers don't freely choose to commit murder. They have no control over their actions, and so they're not guilty. Wouldn't the same be true for all our actions if we admit that they are necessitated, that they *had* to happen?

These—deliberation and moral responsibility—are two reasons to reject the conclusion of d'Holbach's argument. However, we can't reject an argument just because we disagree with the conclusion. That's because with valid arguments the premises *require* us to accept the conclusion. So, if we reject the conclusion, we must also reject one of the premises. But which one shall we reject? Before addressing that question, let's look at what can be said in favor of the premises themselves.

The Premises

Premise (1)

Humans are wholly part of nature. We don't have immaterial souls. Our mental lives—what we think, what we feel, and what we decide to do—depend on our brains, not on an immaterial soul really distinct from our brains.

Why think that's true? One reason is that if a neurosurgeon opens up our heads and starts poking around in our brains, we'll start to have different sorts of mental experiences. The same is true if we suffer a stroke or other brain trauma. What best explains this fact? The fact that our mental lives depend on our brains, not on an immaterial soul.

Another reason to think premise (1) is true is that drugs affect our brains chemically. Yet, whether its LSD, alcohol, or antidepressants, drugs also affect our moods, our thoughts, and our experiences. What's the best way to explain this correlation of chemical interaction to mental experience? Our mental lives depend on our bodies. All of our experiences, all of our thoughts, all of our beliefs, attitudes, and emotions depend on the white and grey matter that sloshes around in our skulls.

A third reason to endorse (1) is the development of humans themselves. When we're young, our bodies are growing and developing. Corresponding with that physical growth and development is mental growth and development. Yet when we're old, our bodies are weakening and declining. Corresponding with that weakening and declining is mental decline and, sometimes, senility. What best explains this parallelism? The fact that our mental lives are really a result of, depend on, our bodies.

That last argument isn't simply supported by observations of the ways bodies look and people behave. It's supported by studies of the way the brain develops. When we're young, our brains are highly plastic. That is, our brains form new neural connections quickly and easily. When we're old, those neural connections do not form so quickly and easily. So, there's a scientific basis for the saying that you can't teach an old dog new tricks. It's true of dogs and it's true of humans. And what explains this best? The fact that our mental lives depend on our brains, not immaterial souls separate from our brains. In short, we're physical beings through and through.

Premise (2)

In our first puzzle I mentioned Isaac Newton's (1643–1727 CE) discoveries of the laws of motion and gravity. Newton's law of gravity is able to explain the orbit of the earth around the sun, the tides, and the fact that objects fall when dropped. That's quite impressive.

Also, Newton's formulae enable us to predict what will happen. We can foresee where the sun will be, when the tides will ebb and flow, and how quickly objects accelerate when dropped. Moreover, nature never really veers from these laws. They are regular. They don't change.

D'Holbach was very impressed with Newton's discoveries. If what Newton discovered is true of the motions of the planets and oceans, why isn't it true of the whole of nature? Isn't it plausible to suppose that such immutable laws govern all of nature, not merely the planets and oceans? For millennia, humans trod the earth observing instances of gravitational attraction: the sun rising and setting, the tides rising, apples falling, etc. Newton showed that all of these occurrences are explained by, and are governed by, natural laws. Similarly, maybe all of the activities we observe today—handsome young men helping old ladies across the street, kittens yawning while watching tennis, courageous soldiers stabbing their mortal enemies to death, lovers gazing deeply into each other's eyes, and my kicking the neighbor's yappy dog—can be explained naturally. Maybe they, too, are governed by natural laws and necessitated by those natural laws in conjunction with the current state of the universe.

Such a view is what premise (2) endorses: every event in nature is necessitated by prior events, conditions, and the laws of nature. Consider, for example, a dropped pencil falling. The event of the pencil falling had to happen. Prior events (me letting go of the pencil), prior conditions (there is not, for example, a sudden gust of wind that might blow the pencil upward), and the laws of nature (most notably, the law of gravity) necessitate that the dropped pencil will fall. That's what *had* to happen.

In Puzzle One, I already mentioned two possible responses to this claim. First, the natural laws might change, so they're not immutable. Second, the natural laws admit a degree of indeterminacy such that they're not perfectly regularly. I'll take these up in the "Possible Responses" section below. As we shall see then, even if these claims are true it does not imperil d'Holbach's argument.

Premise (3)

Premise (3) follows directly from premises (1) and (2). First, premise (1) states that we're wholly part of nature. So, all of our actions occur in nature. There is nothing outside of the natural order that could cause our actions. Second, premise (2) states that every natural event is necessitated by prior events, conditions, and the laws of nature. Since our actions occur in nature and as part of the natural order of things, it follows that our actions must also be necessitated by prior events, conditions, and the laws of nature. In other words, if we're wholly part of nature and determinism is true then even our actions must be the necessary result of prior events, conditions, and the laws of nature.

Similar considerations apply to our supposedly free actions. When I kick my neighbor's yappy dog (I haven't done it, but *when* I do) it will be necessitated by prior events (hearing the yappy dog when I'm trying to sleep), conditions (no police officer being in the vicinity, since I would otherwise fear being arrested), and the laws of nature (the psychological laws that govern my hatred of yappy dogs, the laws that govern motion, etc.).

Premise (4)

Plausibly, when a person acts freely, when a person acts on the basis of her free will, she could have done otherwise. For example, if I leave a party of my own free will, it implies that I could have stayed. I wasn't required to leave. Rather, I opted to leave. I freely chose to leave. An action is free only if the agent could have done otherwise, only if there were some alternative possibilities open to the agent.

In contrast, if I leave a party under police escort I could not do otherwise than leave the party. I am forced to leave the party. Had

I tried to stay, I would have been pepper-sprayed, tased, cuffed, and carried out the front door. Thus, I do not leave the party freely.

In like manner, if our actions are necessitated then we could not do otherwise. It would be like leaving a party by police escort. The prior events, conditions, and laws of nature make it such that we cannot do otherwise. That's why premise (4) is plausible. If all of our actions are necessitated by prior events, conditions, and the laws of nature, then we could never act otherwise than we do. If we could never act otherwise than we do, then we have no free will, no action is done freely. Therefore, if all of our actions are necessitated by prior events, conditions, and the laws of nature, then none of our actions are free.

That's an argument for premise (4), but it's not the only one. Perhaps the most famous defense of (4) is Peter van Inwagen's (b. 1942 CE). He presents us with an argument called the *consequence argument*. To understand the argument, the first things we need to get a handle on are the phrases "necessary that" and "necessary in a way opposed to free will that." The first phrase refers to what must be the case logically or metaphysically. The second phrase refers to things that must be the case not because they are logically or metaphysically necessary but because no person has control over them. We might call this *unactionable necessity* (as opposed to logical or metaphysical necessity) because we are unable to undertake any action to change it.

To illustrate the difference, two examples are useful. First, it is *necessary that* squares have four sides. It is also *necessary in a way opposed to free will that* squares have four sides, for there is no action I could undertake to change it. Second, although it is *not necessary that* the Andromeda galaxy be at least 400 light years away from the Milky Way galaxy, it is *necessary in a way opposed to free will*. We have no choice over the matter.

The next things we need to understand van Inwagen's argument are two logical principles. The first principle is called the *alpha principle*. The alpha principle says that if something is *necessary* then we can also conclude that *it is necessary in a way opposed to free will*. To state it in an argument form, where S is a sentence, the alpha principle states:

It is necessary that: S.

Therefore, it is necessary in a way opposed to free will that: S.

To use our first example, it is necessary that squares have four sides. So, we can conclude that it is necessary in a way opposed to free will that squares have four sides. There is nothing we can do to change that fact.

The second principle is the *beta principle*. The beta principle is a lot like modus ponens, discussed in our first and third puzzles. Modus ponens, recall, has this form, where S and S′ are sentences:

> If S, then S′.
>
> S.
>
> Therefore, S′.

All the beta principle does is put "It is necessary in a way opposed to free will that:" in front of those premises. The beta principle in argument form is this:

> It is necessary in a way opposed to free will that: If S, then S′.
>
> It is necessary in a way opposed to free will that: S.
>
> Therefore, it is necessary in a way opposed to free will that: S′.

For example, it is necessary in a way opposed to free will that: if Pluto orbits the sun, then Pluto moves. Moreover, it is necessary in a way opposed to free that: Pluto orbits the sun. Therefore, it is necessary in a way opposed to free will that: Pluto moves.

With these two principles in place we can show that the theory of determinism entails that we have no free will. In other words, we can show that (4) is true. How so? First, we need to define two variables:

> Let U = The state of the universe 1 million years ago *and* the laws of nature.
>
> Let K = I kick my neighbor's yappy dog.

Now we move on to the argument. Determinism says that every event (for example, kicking my neighbor's yappy dog, K) is necessitated by prior events and conditions—even the state of the universe 1 million years ago—and the laws of nature (U). In other words, it affirms:

> (6) It is necessary that: If U, then K.

Using the alpha principle, we can now conclude that:

> (7) It is necessary in a way opposed to free will that: If U, then K.

It is also true, however, that the state of the universe 1 million years ago and the laws of the universe are necessary in a way opposed to free will. After all, I have no control over them and, as far as I can tell, no other person does. They are unactionably necessary. Hence, we can affirm:

> (8) It is necessary in a way opposed to free will that: U.

Now, using the beta principle on (7) and (8), we can conclude:

> (9) It is necessary in a way opposed to free will that: K.

But what does the argument from (6)–(9) show? Since we merely *assumed* that (6) was true, it shows that *if* (6) is true, *then* (9) is true. That is to say, it shows that:

> (10) If (6) it is necessary that: if U, then K, then (9) it is necessary in a way opposed to free will that: K.

Now recall that (6) is just the theory of determinism. Also, K could stand for any action whatsoever: kicking my neighbor's yappy dog; leaving a party; punching a stranger. So, all (10) is really saying is that:

> (4) If all of our actions are determined, then none of our actions is done freely.

And here we have a second argument for premise (4). If we accept both determinism and the alpha and beta principles, then we have to deny that we have free will.

I should note here that the consequence argument is still vigorously debated. Practically all of the debate centers around the beta principle, since the alpha principle is extremely plausible. Many philosophers now think that the beta principle, as originally stated by van Inwagen, is false. However, some philosophers also believe that it can be suitably altered to salvage the argument. The jury remains out.

Possible Responses

Whenever we encounter a philosophical puzzle we have just two options. The first is to reject one of the premises. The second is to accept the conclusion. (As stated earlier in the book, all of our puzzles are valid, so we cannot reject an argument on the grounds that the premises do not really entail the conclusion.)

I've already stated that premise (3) follows directly from premises (1) and (2), assuming that human actions are events. That assumption is uncontroversial. So, we're not really in a position to reject (3). Thus, our only viable options are to accept the conclusion, reject premise (1), reject premise (2), or reject premise (4).

Philosophers who accept the conclusion are called *hard determinists*. They claim that determinism and free will are incompatible and settle for determinism.

Philosophers who reject either premise (1) or premise (2) are called *libertarians*. Like determinists, libertarians think that determinism and free will are incompatible. Unlike hard determinists, libertarians settle for freedom of the will.

Philosophers who reject (4) are called *compatibilists* or, sometimes, *soft determinists*. As might be guessed, they get their name because they think that determinism and free will are compatible, unlike hard determinists and libertarians.

Accept the Conclusion

Maybe d'Holbach is correct. Perhaps we have no free will. What would that mean for us today? Probably it means nothing at all. We would keep doing what we do. We would still punish criminals. We would still hold each other morally responsible. We would still act and talk as though we have some free choice in what we decide to do.

Accepting the conclusion of d'Holbach's argument probably won't cause mass upheaval (at any rate, if it did, the mass upheaval would have been determined), but it can be quite disillusioning. We like to think we have some power over our lives. We like to think we can control our futures to some degree. But if d'Holbach's argument is sound, it turns out that what we like to think isn't what is true. And that's disappointing.

Yet disappointment and disillusionment have nothing to do with the soundness of d'Holbach's argument. We can't *philosophically* reject his argument just because it's disappointing and disillusioning. What we need is a good philosophical reason to reject one of the premises. Can we come up with one? Let's start with the two libertarian options: to reject premise (1) or to reject premise (2).

Reject Premise (1)

We might deny that we are wholly part of nature. Perhaps we have souls, souls that are really distinct from our bodies and so not subject to the laws of nature.

One reason to think this is true—that we have souls really distinct from our bodies and not subject to the laws of nature—is that many religions claim it is true. Those religions claim, for example, that when we die we go to heaven (or hell). We leave our bodies and exist in an immaterial world. The thing that survives, that continues to exist in an immaterial world, is our soul. Oftentimes, it has been thought that the afterlife is one of disembodiment. Rather than a material, embodied existence, in the afterlife our souls enjoy a disembodied, immaterial existence. So, if we're religious, we might deny (1) based on our beliefs.

Unfortunately, this view faces some very serious problems. First, how is it possible for an immaterial soul to interact with a material body? If we try to preserve freedom of the will by claiming that we have an immaterial soul that causes our bodies to act in certain ways, *how* does this happen? After all, immaterial souls don't have any *material*. They can't cause a body to move in the way that I cause my pen to move as I write. Immaterial souls don't even have a spatial location. Because they're immaterial, they are literally nowhere. But if they're *nowhere*, how do they cause motion *somewhere*?

A second problem with this strategy is that the religious texts of the major monotheistic religions (Judaism, Christianity, and Islam) do *not* claim we have a disembodied existence after death. Much to the contrary, all of those texts describe the afterlife as bodily. True, some of them say we have spiritual bodies. But a spiritual body is still a body. Yet, if we are bodily, physical beings, then we are part of nature. In fact, our word "physical" is derived from the Greek word *physis* (pronounced *foo-sis*), which means *nature*. So, the afterlife described in religious texts is not a disembodied and immaterial existence.

This raises a question: Why do some religious people teach that we have immaterial souls that go to heaven (or hell) after our deaths? Mainly its because at some point in their existence those religions incorporated the ideas and arguments of early Greek philosophers like Plato into their theology. In his "Phaedo," Plato (429–347 BCE) presents several arguments showing that humans have immaterial souls that are separate from their bodies. None of his arguments is very good, so I won't rehearse them here. Nonetheless, as religious thinkers began incorporating those ideas and arguments into their views, they concluded that we have immaterial souls that go to heaven after we die.

I should point out here that later religious thinkers (I dare say better ones)—for example, al-Ghazali (1058–1111 CE), mentioned in our sixth puzzle, and Thomas Aquinas (1225–1274 CE), mentioned in our first puzzle—deny that we have disembodied afterlives.

A third problem is that this view is not supported by our best science, as indicated in our discussion of premise (1) above. Our very best science affirms that our mental lives depend on our brains. Moreover, as we saw in Puzzle Six, it's generally not a good idea to endorse a position that runs contrary to our very best science. So, rejecting premise (1) on religious grounds is probably not the best strategy for responding to d'Holbach's argument.

If we cannot reject (1) on religious grounds, perhaps we can reject it on philosophical grounds. To be sure, many philosophers have offered arguments for the conclusion that the soul and body are separable. As I just mentioned, Plato is one such philosopher. Another philosopher is René Descartes (1596–1650 CE). However, none of the arguments for this view has much going for it. So, without further ado, let's turn to our next line of response.

Reject Premise (2)

Another line of response is to deny that every event in nature is necessitated by prior events, conditions, and the laws of nature. Someone who opts for this line of response might try one of two different strategies. The first one is hopeless. The second is promising.

Strategy One: Indeterminism: First is the hopeless strategy. It is widely admitted nowadays that nature is not entirely governed by necessary, regular, and immutable laws. D'Holbach and Newton knew nothing of quantum physics. But quantum physics tells us that there is a degree of randomness in nature, as discussed in Puzzle One. If that's true, not everything is determined. Nature is, to some degree, indeterminate, random.

The reason that this strategy is hopeless is that indeterminacy still does not make room for freedom of the will. An action that is random is no freer than an action that is necessitated. Suppose, for example, that I suffer from a neurological condition that *randomly* causes me to kick yappy dogs. Sure, I might end up kicking my neighbor's yappy dog. But would we say that I have freely chosen to kick his yappy dog? When the cause of my action *really is* my neurological condition, when my yappy-dog kicking really is *random*, I do not act freely.

The upshot of this is that d'Holbach's argument can be modified slightly so as to accommodate the insights of quantum physics. We can do so as follows:

(1a) Humans are wholly part of nature.

(2a) Every event in nature is either (i) determined or (ii) random.

(3a) If humans are wholly part of nature and every event in nature is either (i) determined or (ii) random, then all of our actions are either (i') determined or (ii') random.

(4a) If (i') our actions are determined, then our actions are not freely done, and if (ii') our actions are random, then they are not freely done.

(5a) Therefore, none of our actions is freely done; we have no free will.

In short, admitting that nature is to some degree indeterminate, random, doesn't help us respond to d'Holbach's puzzle. One last note on this: I also previously mentioned (in Puzzle One) the possibility that the laws of nature are not immutable. Perhaps they are changing. However, we have no control over the laws of nature. So, even if they are changing, all of our actions remain necessitated by prior events, conditions, and the *laws of nature as they stand at the time of the action.*

Strategy Two: Agent Causation: It should be noted that all the libertarian has to do in order to deny premise (2) is to show that there is just one action in each of our lives that is not necessitated by prior events, conditions, and the laws of nature. Libertarianism makes no claim as to *how many* of our actions are free.

Now suppose that you are playing roulette. You are trying to decide whether you will put your chips on red or black. Which should you choose? (Assume that you really want to play, so you do have to choose.) There is simply no reason to favor red over black or vice versa. On any spin of the wheel the ball is as likely to land on red as it is on black. So, you decide on black.

Notice that here it is up to *you*, the agent, to decide. You recognize that there are reasons to choose red. You recognize that there are reasons to choose black. However, neither of those reasons determines that you should choose one over the other. And yet, since you want to play, you must choose one over the other. It is now up to you, the agent, to make a decision. You are free to choose one or the other.

Your freedom in this case stems from the fact that there is nothing to determine you choosing one over the other but you are determined to choose. What is more, situations like this arise when the probability is not objective (see Puzzle One for a discussion of objective and subjective probability). For example, suppose you are deciding whether or not to call up John and ask him on a date. Obviously, you will either call him or not. You have some good reasons to call him. For example, you've seen him staring at you in class and you really think he is dreamy and his lips are so full and. . . . Well, you get the picture. Also, you have some good reasons not to call him. For example, you would be so embarrassed if he said no, and you might get flustered if his mom answers the phone, and you heard a rumor that he wasn't a good kisser anyway.

Now, it is possible that both sets of reasons are equally strong. It is not implausible to suppose that those reasons, while not quantifiable as objective probabilities, do not decisively favor one action over the other. Nevertheless, *you*, the agent, have to decide. You will either call him or not.

It is here that we begin to glimpse the agent causation view of free will, a view given recent development by Timothy O'Connor (b. 1965 CE) but originated by Thomas Reid (1710–1796 CE). On this view, it is true that humans are the result of a variety of causes. For example, your parents made sweet, sweet love. You were nourished and grew into the person you are. You had a variety of experiences—being teased, being turned down for dates, being hit on by strange men—that have informed your beliefs and desires.

Even though we are the result of a variety of causes, we are also agents. We decide on certain courses of actions. Sometimes those decisions are determined by our beliefs and desires. We want to play roulette. We want to eat a bowl of ice cream. We want to go swimming.

Yet at other times those decisions are not determined by our beliefs and desires. We are torn. We have equally strong reasons for different courses of action. We want to play roulette, but we must decide between red and black. We want to eat ice cream, but we must decide between mint chocolate chip and rocky road. We want to go swimming, but we must decide between the pool and the ocean. In this case, it is up to us, the agents, to make a choice. And when we do so, we choose freely.

Reject Premise (4)

Premise (4) states that if all of our actions are necessitated by prior events, conditions, and the laws of nature, then we have no free will. That may sound right to you: How could we freely do an action if it was necessitated by what came before it, if we could not have done otherwise? After all, the view that an action is free only if one could have done otherwise has significant appeal.

Moreover, we commonly suppose that having a free will means not being determined to act by something else. We take *acting freely* and *being determined* to be opposites. But is this the right way to think of free will? Perhaps it's not. In what follows, we'll look at two other ways of thinking about freedom of the will.

Strategy One: Classic Compatibilism: David Hume (1711–1776 CE) argues that free will and determinism are not opposites. Rather, the opposite of free will is constraint. The opposite of determinism is randomness or indeterminacy. Thus, on Hume's view, an action is free just because (i) we desire to do it and (ii) we are not constrained from doing it. Because we desire to do it, the action is still determined. It is determined by our desires. Yet because we are not constrained in doing it, our action is free.

Consider, for example, these three scenarios:

> *Scenario One:* I kick a yappy dog because I want to and no one stops me.
>
> *Scenario Two:* I kick a yappy dog just because a mad scientist has hooked me up to a yappy-dog-kicking machine.
>
> *Scenario Three:* I don't kick a yappy dog, even though I want to, because the police hold me back.

Notice, first, that in all three cases what happens is determined. In the first case, it is determined by my desire to kick the dog. In the second case, it is determined by the yappy-dog-kicking machine. In the third case, it is determined by the police restraining me.

Notice also, however, that in the first scenario my action is free whereas in the second and third scenarios I do not act freely. In the second, I do not desire to kick the yappy dog. Rather, I kick the yappy dog just because I am hooked up to a yappy-dog-kicking machine. In the third, because I am constrained, I do not refrain from kicking the dog freely.

This sounds like a pretty good position to take. It allows us to have our cake and eat it too. On the one hand, we get to endorse determinism because our actions are necessitated by prior events, conditions, and the laws of nature. On the other hand, we also get to endorse the claim that we have a free will. That's because all it means to act freely is to desire to do it and not be constrained from doing it.

Unfortunately, there are two problems with this view. The first problem is that the position implies that animals have free wills too. Animals, after all, desire to do the actions they do. Also, they are not externally constrained in doing them. However, it seems strange to claim that animals have free wills. For example, when I see a snail slithering toward blades of grass, I do not think it is acting freely. It is just doing what snails do.

The second problem is that if classic compatibilism is true it follows that no one can do otherwise. However, we tend to think that free will requires that we be able to do otherwise. The classic compatibilist has not addressed this issue.

Strategy Two: Real-Self Compatibilism: As just indicated in the discussion of animals, something is missing in the story of classic compatibilism. But what is it? In answering that question, it is helpful to begin with the other objection, the one about being able to do otherwise.

Harry Frankfurt (b. 1929 CE) has called into question the claim that an action is free only if we can do otherwise. To see how, let's extend the second scenario above, the one about me being hooked up to a yappy-dog-kicking machine. Imagine that a mad scientist really wants me to kick my neighbor's yappy dog. He would much prefer that I do it myself. Nonetheless, he wants to be sure that I really will do it. After all, I have been known to waver when it comes to kicking yappy dogs.

To make sure I kick my neighbor's yappy dog, the mad scientist has (unknown to me) hooked me up to a yappy-dog-kicking machine. The machine is such that *if I show no signs of wavering* in kicking my neighbor's yappy dog it does nothing. However, *if I do show signs of wavering* in kicking my neighbor's yappy dog the machine will trigger and cause me to kick it. Notice that no matter what happens there is only one possibility: I will kick my neighbor's yappy dog.

Now suppose further that I kick my neighbor's dog and *do not waver.* In that case, I have acted freely. I have done what I planned to do all along. Also, the machine did not trigger.

So, here is a case where I do act freely. However, there were no other possibilities. I was going to kick the dog no matter what. Acting freely does not require that we be able to do otherwise than we do.

Moreover, if we change things in this story just a little bit, we can begin to see what Frankfurt thinks is missing from classic compatibilism. For now suppose that I did waver but that the yappy-dog-kicking machine triggered. In that case, my action would not have been consistent with what *I really* wanted to do, with what my real self wants to do.

Here we finally get to Frankfurt's view. When I kick my neighbor's yappy dog and do *not* waver, I have a *first-order desire* (to kick the yappy dog) and a *second-order volition* (to follow through). In this case, my first-order desire and my second-order volition *mesh*. So, I act freely.

In contrast, when I kick my neighbor's yappy dog because of the machine, I still have a first-order desire to do so but I lack a second-order volition. It is because I lack the second-order volition that I begin to waver. In this case, even though I kick the yappy dog, my first-order desire and my second-order volition *do not mesh*. So, I do not act freely.

Notice, nonetheless, that in both cases my action is determined. In the first case, it is determined by my first-order desire and second-order volition. In the second case, it is determined by the yappy-dog-kicking machine. Thus, on Frankfurt's view free will is compatible with determinism.

To make Frankfurt's position clearer, it is helpful to have recourse to his own example. Imagine the following two drug addicts:

> *The Unwilling Addict:* The unwilling addict has a first-order desire to do drugs and a second-order volition not to do drugs. However, because of the strength of his first-order desire, he takes the drugs.

> *The Willing Addict:* The willing addict has a first-order desire to do drugs and a second-order volition to continue doing drugs. He takes the drugs.

Which addict acts freely? According to Frankfurt, it is the willing addict. That is because the willing addict's first-order desire meshes with his second-order volition. In contrast, the unwilling addict does not act freely. His first-order desire and second-order volition do not mesh.

Moreover, we are now in a position to see how Frankfurt's version of compatibilism can explain why animals do not have free wills. Animals lack second-order volitions. They merely act on their first-order desires. As such, action on their first-order desires cannot mesh (or fail to mesh) with their second-order volitions.

Unfortunately, there is a problem with Frankfurt's position. It is that the meshing of my first-order desires and second-order volitions might itself be a consequence of outside manipulation. Imagine, for example, that the yappy-dog-kicking machine works by causing me to have a second-order volition. In that case, my first-order desire and second-order volition *do* mesh. Frankfurt must then admit that I act freely even though my action was caused by the yappy-dog-kicking machine. However, that is implausible.

In conclusion, if we want to have our cake and eat it too, if we want to retain a commitment to determinism and yet make room for free will, Hume and Frankfurt have surely brought us some way in showing how it may be done. However, it is not clear that they have brought us far enough.

References

Al-Ghazali. *Incoherence of the Philosophers*. Trans. Sabih Ahmad Kamali. Lahore: Pakistan Philosophical Congress, 1958.

Descartes, René. *Meditations on First Philosophy*. In *The Philosophical Writings of Decartes*. Vol. 2. Trans. John Cottingham, Robert Stoothoff, and Dugald Murdoch. Cambridge: Cambridge UP, 1984.

D'Holbach, Baron Paul Henri Thiry. *The System of Nature*. Trans. H. D. Robinson. J.P. Mendum, 1889.

Frankfurt, Harry. "Alternate Possibilities and Moral Responsibility." *Journal of Philosophy*. 66: 829–39, 1969.

Frankfurt, Harry. "Freedom of the Will and the Concept of a Person." *Journal of Philosophy*. 68: 5–20, 1971.

Hume, David. *An Enquiry Concerning Human Understanding*. 2nd ed. Ed. Eric Steinberg. Indianapolis: Hackett, 1993.

Newton, Isaac. *The Principia: Mathematical Principles of Natural Philosophy*. Trans. I. Bernard Cohen and Anne Whitman. Berkeley: University of California Press, 1999.

O'Connor, Timothy. *Persons and Causes: The Metaphysics of Free Will*. New York: Oxford UP, 2000.

Plato. "Phaedo." In *Complete Works*. Trans. G. M. A. Grube. Eds. John M. Cooper and D. S. Hutchinson. Indianapolis: Hackett, 1997.

Reid, Thomas. *Essays on the Active Powers of Man*. Edinburgh: Bell and Robinson, 1788.

Thomas Aquinas. *Summa Theologiae*. Vol. 11. Trans. Timothy Suttor. London: Eyre and Spottiswoode Limited, 1970.

Van Inwagen, Peter. *An Essay on Free Will*. Oxford: Clarendon Press, 1983.

Contemporary Philosophy

Perception and Justification

Selfhood and Computers

Curry's Paradox

PUZZLE TEN

Perception and Justification

It will promote matters at this point to review very hastily some of the reasons for abandoning the search for a basis for knowledge outside the scope of our beliefs. By "basis" here I mean specifically an epistemological basis, a source of justification.

... The relation between a sensation and a belief cannot be logical, since sensations are not beliefs or other propositional attitudes. What then is the relation? The answer is, I think, obvious: the relation is causal. Sensations cause some beliefs and in this sense are the basis or ground of those beliefs. But a causal explanation of a belief does not show how or why the belief is justified.

—Donald Davidson (1917–2003 CE), "A Coherence Theory of Truth and Knowledge"

The Philosopher

Widely regarded as one of the most influential contemporary philosophers, Donald Davidson taught at some of the most prestigious universities in the United States, including Stanford, the University of Chicago, Princeton, and the University of California, Berkeley. He attended Harvard University, where he had begun studying English and comparative literature before switching to philosophy.

Aside from being a great philosopher, Davidson was also a proficient piano player. He wrote radio scripts for the show *Big Town*. In World War II, he served in the navy. He participated in the invasions of Sicily, Salerno, and Anzio. In his free time, he built radios, surfed, and flew planes.

The Puzzle

In order to understand our current puzzle, we need to cover some conceptual terrain regarding: belief, propositional structure, and concepts; justification; and perception and perception-that. After that, we'll move on to the puzzle.

Some Conceptual Terrain

Belief, Propositional Structure, and Concepts: First, a belief is a mental state that has for its content a sentence or proposition. For example, I can believe that the chair is red, that the sum of the squares of the sides of a right triangle is equal to the square of the hypotenuse, or that caterpillars are fuzzy aliens. "The chair is red," "The sum of the squares of the sides of a right triangle is equal to the square of the hypotenuse," and "Caterpillars are fuzzy aliens" are sentences. They can all be believed. The first two (supposing for the first I am referring to a red chair) are true beliefs. The third is a false belief because caterpillars are not aliens.

Note that "red chair," "the Pythagorean theorem," and "fuzzy caterpillars" are not beliefs. That's because they're not sentences or propositions. They don't have the right form or structure to be a sentence. A sentence has a subject and a predicate. In "the chair is red," "the chair" is the subject and "is red" is the predicate. The predicate (is red) tells us something about the subject (the chair).

I do *not* believe that the red chair. That's ungrammatical. I *do* believe that the chair is red. "Red chair" does not have a subject and a predicate. It has a noun—"chair"—and an adjective—"red." In order to turn it into a sentence and so make it something that could be believed, we have to give those words a different form or structure: "The chair is red."

This point may seem trivial but it's important. Sentences can stand in logical relationships to each other. In contrast, strings of words that have not been formed into sentences cannot stand in a logical relationship to other strings of words. For example, we can make the following argument:

(1) The chair is red.

(2) Red is a color.

(3) Therefore, the chair is colored.

However, the following is not an argument:

(4) Red chair

(5) The color red

(6) The colored chair

The series (4)–(6) is not an argument because the words cannot stand in a logical relationship to each other. Nothing about (4) and (5) can compel us to believe (6). In fact, we can't believe (6) because (6) isn't even a sentence! Sentences themselves are but particular linguistic expressions of propositions. Whether I say, "The chair is red," "La silla es roja," "La chaise est rouge," or "Der Stuhl ist rot," I express the same proposition. Even though the sentences are different they mean the same thing, and that is what makes them all expressions of the same proposition. Thus, propositions have structure just like sentences do.

Sentences and propositions are made out of concepts. Concepts are general terms that can be said of many different objects or attributes of those objects. For example, 'chair' is a concept. There are many things that are chairs (e.g. lounge chairs, desk chairs, patio chairs, etc.). Also, 'red' is a concept. Many things are red, such as blood, pomegranates, and sweaters. There are also many different shades of red, such as scarlet, burgundy, and vermillion. By putting concepts together, we can get sentences and propositions: "The chair is red," "La silla es roja," "La chaise est rouge," which are all just ways of expressing the same proposition that the chair is red.

Justification: This brings us to our second topic, justification. When we make an argument—for example, in (1)–(3) or any of the other puzzles in this book—we are offering a justification for a claim, the conclusion. Justification is a logical relationship. When a belief is justified, it is well supported by the evidence. Justification gives us an epistemic reason to adopt a belief.

We can have either pragmatic (that is, practical) or epistemic (*epistēmē* is Greek for *knowledge*) reasons to adopt beliefs. Suppose I am more likely to win a race if I believe that I am the best runner on the track. I now have a pragmatic reason to believe that I am the best runner on the track. It is useful for me to believe it. However, suppose further that a review of past races shows that I am actually the slowest runner on the track. The review of past races gives me an epistemic reason to believe I am not the best runner on the track. Justification—as we shall be concerned with it—is about epistemic reasons to adopt beliefs, not pragmatic ones.

It should be clear that not every belief is justified. If I hear two strangers conversing on the street and one of them says, "Cornstalks have only one ear of corn each," that person speaks truly. However, I am not justified in believing that claim if my only source of evidence is the word of a stranger on the street. For all I know he's a bumbling idiot who has never seen a cornstalk in his life.

Nevertheless, some beliefs are justified. If I happen to know a farmer in Iowa and he tells me that cornstalks have only one ear of corn each, then my belief is justified. I know the man is a farmer from Iowa (where they grow lots of corn), I have no reason to believe he is deceiving me, and he knows how to use the English language. I can take him at his word since he is an authority on corn. That suffices to justify my belief that cornstalks have only one ear of corn each.

A similar point can be made about my belief in the Pythagorean theorem. When taking geometry, I learned a proof of the Pythagorean theorem. As a result, I have a justified belief in the theorem. (Note that I can believe *in* the Pythagorean theorem but I don't believe *that* the Pythagorean theorem. In both cases, though, the content of my belief is the proposition that the sum of the squares of the sides of a right triangle is equal to the square of the hypotenuse.)

Importantly, merely having *some* reason to hold a belief is not sufficient for justification. Suppose a casual but friendly acquaintance has told you that your good friend is plotting to empty your bank account. You now have some reason to believe your good friend is plotting to empty your bank account. However, you are not justified in believing it. After all, it was but a casual acquaintance who told you so. Perhaps your acquaintance has personal reasons to spread malicious lies. Moreover, your good friend is, well, a *good* friend. Such a scheme is not consistent with what you know about your friend. So, while you have a reason to believe your good friend is hatching a scheme to empty your bank account, you're not justified in believing your friend plans to do so. You have *a* reason to believe it, just not a *good* epistemic reason. As a result, you're not justified in believing it.

Perception and Perception-That: Finally, let's consider perception. Perception is generally understood to be some sort of experiential intake from the world using one's sense capacities. For example, I see the red chair. I smell the cinnamon. I taste the lemon. I feel a poke. I hear the barking dog.

Now, consider this sentence:

I see that the chair is red.

The words to the left of the word "that"—"I see"—indicate perception is involved. The words to the right of the word "that" are a proposition—"the chair is red." This is known as perception-that. Perceptions-that are perceptions that involve propositions.

Many philosophers think perception-that involves two capacities, or mental powers. The first capacity is the capacity for perception. This, as noted above, involves seeing, hearing, smelling, etc. That's what is indicated on the left side of the "that" in the sentence above. It's the raw experiential intake to which we attach concepts.

The second capacity is the capacity for thought or conception. This is a capacity that attaches concepts—such as 'red' and 'chair'—to the experiential intake of perception. Doing so enables us to form a belief or judgment about what we see. What we see is *the red chair*. What we judge is *that the chair is red*. Recall that "the red chair" does not have propositional structure and so cannot stand in a logical relationship with other beliefs. "The chair is red," in contrast, can.

On the view that perception-that involves two capacities or mental powers, we have a three-step process that results in a perception-that:

> *First*, we receive some experiential intake by way of our sense organs. This is perception. For example, I see *the red chair*.

> *Second*, we apply concepts we already possess to that experiential intake. For example, I see the chair *to be red* and *to be a chair*.

> *Third*, we form a judgment about what we see, resulting in a perception-that. For example, I see that *the chair is red*.

In short, perceptions-that are just perceptions with something added on to them. What is added on to them? Concepts formed into propositions. And here we get to the heart of our puzzle: How are the experiential intake (our perception) and the concepts we possess supposed to link up so as to form *justified* beliefs about the world? Can they link up in a way that makes it *rational* to hold beliefs on the basis of perceptions?

The Puzzle Itself

We're now in a position to state our tenth puzzle:

(7) The only thing that can justify a belief is something with the appropriate propositional structure.

(8) Perceptions do not have propositional structure.

(9) Therefore, perceptions cannot justify beliefs.

The puzzle is worrisome because you take yourself to be justified in the belief that (for example) the words in this book are printed with black ink *just because* you *see* the words. But if this argument is sound, then you are not justified in your belief just because you see the black words. In fact, you might not be justified in your belief at all!

The worry that is lurking in the background here is a worry about skepticism. Skepticism is the theory that we cannot know anything at all or cannot know anything about the external world.

The question the argument raises is: What guarantees that our beliefs and our concepts track the world as it really is? If we know anything about the external world, then the world and our minds must link up in such a way that our experiences of the world justify our beliefs about the world. But the current argument, if sound, shows that our perceptions of the world cannot justify our beliefs about the world. And that is worrisome. The only access we have to the world is by way of our perceptions. Yet if our perceptions cannot justify our beliefs about the world, what epistemic reasons do we have to think the world really is the way we believe it to be?

One last comment: it should be clear that we have plenty of pragmatic reasons to think that the world is the way we believe it to be. If I perceive a quickly moving car heading directly toward me, I'll be much better off believing that the quickly moving car will strike me than disbelieving that it will strike me. The issue here is not whether our perceptions afford us pragmatic reasons to adopt beliefs. It is whether they can provide us with epistemic reasons to adopt beliefs.

The Premises

Premise (7)

The only thing that can justify a belief is something with the appropriate propositional structure. The reason for this should be fairly evident from our previous comments on belief, propositional structure, and justification. Justification is a logical relationship. For something to stand in a logical relationship to something else, it needs to have a logical form. Sentences have the right sort of logical form to stand in justificatory relationships. Words not formed into sentences do not have the right sort of logical form to stand in a relation of justification. Neither do pictures, nor images, nor experiences, etc., have the right form to stand in a logical relationship.

You might wonder: If I see a picture of myself from 2010 and I am wearing a red shirt, doesn't that justify my belief that I wore a red shirt in 2010? And doesn't that mean images (in this case, a picture) can justify beliefs (in this case, the belief that I wore a red shirt in 2010)?

This line of thought only reinstates our puzzle. To be sure, your knowledge of how cameras work and of the unlikelihood that the picture has been doctored in Photoshop justifies your belief that the picture preserves how you looked on some day in 2010. But now that you see your red-shirted self in the picture, how does seeing *your red-shirted self* justify you in the belief that *you wore a red shirt*? Note, again, that the former is not a sentence whereas the latter is. Yet that's the very question at stake in our puzzle: How is it that a perception, an experiential intake, can justify a belief?

Premise (8)

Premise (8) claims that perceptions do not have propositional structure. Two considerations support such a claim. First, infants and animals perceive. However, they lack concepts and so their perceptions do not involve concepts. Nonetheless, infant and animal perceptions must be very much like ours. After all, we were once infants. Also, our perceptual systems evolved from those of other animals, animals that lack concepts. So, our perceptions lack concepts and beliefs too. Perception-that *adds* concepts to our perceptions; the concepts are not already in or parts of our perceptions. Perceptions themselves do not have conceptual content. We "impose" them on our perceptions, so to speak. That is what makes perception-that possible.

A second consideration is that our perceptions are highly determinate whereas propositions are not. If I believe that the chair is red, the sentence tells me nothing about the shade of red or the kind of chair. Is it scarlet, burgundy, or vermillion? Is it a desk chair, a patio chair, or a lounge chair? My belief does not state exactly how the chair is. It is not determinate. In contrast, if I *see* a red chair, it is a highly determinate shade of red and it is a very specific shape. So, perceptions must not have propositional structure, for perceptions are highly determinate whereas propositions are not.

Possible Responses

As our current puzzle is a valid argument with plausible premises, we have but three options: we can accept the conclusion, we can reject premise (7), or we can reject premise (8). Let's consider each in turn.

Accept the Conclusion

Davidson's own solution to the puzzle is to accept the conclusion. He agrees that perceptions cannot justify beliefs. However, he's not very worried about it. He argues that although perceptions cannot *justify* beliefs they can still *cause* beliefs.

Justification and causation are not the same thing. For example, suppose I have just taken LSD (as part of a carefully controlled and legitimate psychological experiment, of course) and it is causing me to believe that a horse is right now standing on a man's head. Even though that might be true, I am not justified in believing that a horse is right now standing on a man's head. After all, I was just caused to believe it by consuming LSD and I know so. I don't have a good epistemic reason to believe it. Keeping this distinction between justification and causation in mind, Davidson does think that our perceptions cause our beliefs. However, our perceptions do not justify our beliefs, just as our puzzling argument proves.

Yet this raises a question: If Davidson is correct, then how do any of our beliefs about the perceived world get justified? If my perceptions merely cause me to believe, say, that the chair is red, then how can I also be justified in my belief that the chair is red?

Davidson's answer to this question is that our beliefs are justified by the beliefs we already hold. If those beliefs cohere with each other, if the belief I am caused to hold by virtue of my perception coheres with my other beliefs, then my caused belief is also justified. In short, our beliefs about the external world are *caused* by our perceptions. Our beliefs about the external world are *justified* by the other beliefs we already hold.

Unfortunately, there is a problem with Davidson's position. It's that his view does not relieve our skeptical worries. We might be caused to form beliefs about the perceived world and those beliefs might be justified by other beliefs, but our beliefs may nevertheless be *false*. Our minds may still fail to connect up with the world.

If that's hard to understand, then it can be helpful to think of a man who is paranoid that government agents are tracking him. Every time a person glances at him from behind a newspaper, he thinks that the person glancing at him is a government agent. Every time his phone rings and the caller hangs up, he thinks that it's a government agent tapping his phone. He thinks that every purchase he makes is recorded by a government agent. This person has a perfectly coherent set of beliefs. His beliefs are also caused by his experiences. However, he is flat-out wrong about government agents tracking him (hopefully!).

The same might be true of us. Perhaps we are caused to believe that (for example) the chair is red, and perhaps that belief coheres with all of our other beliefs. But maybe we're just wrong. Thus, our skeptical worries remain.

Reject Premise (7)

Another option is to reject premise (7). We need to show that justification doesn't require something with the appropriate propositional structure. Those who reject premise (7) endorse some version of a theory involving *the Given*. There are at least three different ways to understand the Given, so let's consider each.

Strategy One: Perceptions as Givens: One way to understand the Given is just as a perception, the bare seeing (or perceiving) of something. In this case, my mere seeing of a red chair justifies my belief that the chair is red.

One major question—indeed, our very puzzle—is how a perception can justify a belief when it is not the sort of thing that can stand in a logical relationship to a belief. That's what we said above in defense of premise (7).

Yet there is another problem with this solution, a problem pointed out by John McDowell (b. 1946 CE), whose views will be discussed below. It's that on this view no matter how our perceptions stand in relationship to our beliefs, when it comes down to giving a *reason* for believing that the chair is red, we can do no more than *point* at the red chair. If someone should say, "Why do you believe that the chair is red?" we will ultimately end up just pointing at the chair and exclaiming, "Look!"

The problem with this act of pointing is that it does not amount to a *justification*. It is really just *exculpation*. It's like saying: "I can't help but believe the chair is red! Every time I look at *that thing* [pointing to the red chair] I judge, 'The chair is red.' I can't be blamed for my belief." That's exculpation, blamelessness.

Exculpation, however, is not the same as justification. Being blameless for holding your belief is not the same as being justified. To see why, imagine that a tyrant holds you at gunpoint and says he will kill you if you don't believe that cows are the best astronauts. We won't blame you for believing that cows are the best astronauts. After all, you're trying to save your own life. However, neither are you justified in your belief. You're blameless but not justified. In like manner, if your perceptions hold you hostage (so to speak) and demand that you believe that the chair is red, you won't be blamed for believing it. Unfortunately, neither are you justified in your belief.

It bears mentioning at this point that we have now distinguished having a justified belief from (i) having a belief based merely on pragmatic reasons, (ii) having a belief based just on any old reason, (iii) having a belief merely because it is caused, and (iv) having a belief but being exculpated in holding it.

Strategy Two: Reports of Looks or Seemings as Givens: A second way to understand the Given is as a basic report about the way things *seem* to you. Your perception, even if it does not justify your belief that the chair *is* red, certainly does entitle you to the belief that the chair *looks* red. After all, that sort of looks-talk (or seemings-talk) makes no claim about the way the world *is*. It is only a claim about the way things *seem* to be to you. And you can't really be wrong about the way things seem to yourself.

At this point it's important to note that reports about seemings do have propositional structure. If I say, "The chair looks red to me," that is certainly a proposition. The problem is that they do not by themselves have the *appropriate* propositional structure to justify my belief that the chair is red. You can't infer *straightforwardly* from the fact the chair *looks* red to the conclusion that it *is* red.

Thus, the next step in this account is to claim that the way things seem to you *plus* your other beliefs (for example, that you're not suffering an illusion) *justify* you in the belief that the chair *is* red. From reports about the way things seem and your other beliefs, you are permitted to make an inference to the way things actually are.

One philosopher who adopts such a view is René Descartes (1596–1650 CE). As explained in Puzzle Seven, Descartes realizes that we cannot be certain that the way things appear to us is the way things are. So, how can we possibly be justified in concluding that just because things *appear* thus-and-so they *are* thus-and-so? Descartes claims we need the existence of an all-good, non-deceiving God to guarantee the connection between our minds and the world. We have that guarantee because God is not a deceiver and has made us in such a way that we can figure out the answer to any question. Therefore, we can be confident that the way things appear to us is, in fact, the way things are—or, if things are not the way they appear, we can at least figure out how things in fact are.

There are two problems with the idea of the Given as a report about how things seem. The first problem is that the inference to the way things are already assumes that perception does show us the way things are. As Wilfrid Sellars (1912–1989 CE) points out, claiming that we can infer from the way things appear to the way things are assumes that the way things appear is a reliable indicator of the way things are. However, our belief about the way things appear being a reliable indicator of the way things are comes about only *after* a number of occasions on which we have taken the way things appear to be the way things are. To put it another way, is-talk is prior to looks-talk. Granted this, what really does the work is not our judgment about the way things seem but the coherence of our judgment with other beliefs we hold. In short, this view threatens to collapse into something like Davidson's view.

The second problem with this view is that it involves an unacceptable understanding of perception. The person who adopts this position must claim that when we perceive we are not really being put into contact with the way things *are*. Rather, we are being put into contact with the way things *appear*. Thus, perception on this view does not reveal the world to us but acts as a veil between the world and us. But that is false. Perception really does put us in contact with the world. Perception does not veil the world but reveals the world.

Strategy Three: Logical Form as a Given: A third way to understand the Given is on analogy with valid inference forms. Valid inference forms are logical forms that justify us in accepting a conclusion if the premises are true or at least plausible. In Puzzle One, we discussed the logical argument form of modus ponens. Modus ponens, recall, has the following form, where S and S′ stand for sentences:

If S, then S′.

S.

Therefore, S′.

Perhaps the Given is like a valid inference form. This is the view of Anil Gupta (b. 1946 CE). Gupta argues that the Given is to be understood on analogy with modus ponens, only it has the form:

Such-and-such is the perceiver's view.

Such-and-such is the perceiver's experience.

Therefore, S, where S is a perceptual judgment that follows from a perceiver's view and experience.

Here, a view is a perceiver's beliefs and concepts. An experience is seeing something, hearing something, smelling something, etc. A perceptual judgment is the logical result of a view and an experience combined. Moreover, the view plus the experience generate a *justification* for the conclusion, the perceptual judgment. For example, when I am looking at a tomato, I am justified in the following perceptual judgment (12):

(10) My view is such that I believe I am not under the influence of a drug or an illusion, I am a competent user of the English language, I am familiar with different vegetables and fruits, I am knowledgeable about colors, etc.

(11) I see a smooth, bright red, round object with a green stem on my kitchen counter.

(12) Therefore, the tomato on my kitchen counter is red.

Unfortunately, this account faces a problem. The problem with Gupta's conception of the Given is that it is one thing to be justified in concluding that S *whenever we have such-and-such a view and such-and-such an experience* and quite a different thing to be justified in believing that S *full stop*. For example, from the premises:

(13) If squares are four-sided, then squares are circles.

(14) Squares are four-sided.

I can conclude:

(15) Squares are circles.

Moreover, I am perfectly justified in concluding (15) whenever I have (13) and (14). The problem is that (15) is false and everyone knows it is. It is true that squares are four-sided but false that squares are circles. So, even though I am justified in inferring (15) from (13) and (14), I am not justified in believing (15).

The same is true when it comes to Gupta's view of the Given. Even if I am justified in some perceptual judgment *granted my view and experience*, it does not follow that I am justified in my perceptual judgment *full stop*. After all, my view might be quite bad (if, for example, my concepts are confused) and so might my experience (if, for example, I try to perceive colors in the dark).

In sum, Gupta's conception of the Given isn't sufficient to respond to our present puzzle. It still does not justify my belief that the chair is red. To the contrary, it shows only that I am justified in believing that the chair is red *granted* my view and experience. If we are going to get Gupta's theory to work, we will need to give a separate account of how our views and experiences are "good" or "acceptable" enough to justify the conclusion (the perceptual judgment), much in the same way that we would need to give an account of how (13) and (14) are true or acceptable enough to justify (15). (Though clearly, in this case, (15) is neither true nor acceptable.) Gupta's position as roughly stated here might be a step in the right direction, but we need to take a few more steps to get to where we need to go.

Reject Premise (8)

Our final option is to reject premise (8). We can argue that, at least as far as normal adult human perception goes, perceptions stripped of all propositional structure and concepts are a fiction. Rather, normal adult human perception always and already implicates concepts and propositions. For normal adult humans, there is no such thing as perception without conception. That is, our perceptions have concepts, the building blocks of beliefs, already built into them. Perceptions are *concept-implicating*.

This is the position of John McDowell, mentioned above. He argues that neither Davidson's position nor the theory of a Given is acceptable. Instead, he claims that in our experiences, perception and conception are already united as a single unit. In other words, McDowell thinks that the account of perception-that given in "The Puzzle" section above (numbered *First, Second, Third*) is mistaken if we understand the parts as steps in a process. On his view, those features or elements of perception-that are not separable parts of a process even if they can be distinguished. (If that sounds odd, consider that concavity and convexity are not separable parts of a curve though they can be distinguished.) Normal adult human perception is already perception of a thing as being thus-and-so. Propositional structure is built into our perceptions themselves.

McDowell is aware that there are two significant objections to this view. We already saw them above, in defense of premise (8). The first is that animals and infants perceive but their perceptions do not involve concepts. The second is that perceptions are wholly determinate whereas our concepts are not.

He responds to these two objections. To the first objection, McDowell claims that human perception and animal perception are not alike. We cannot strip away what is unique to human perception to find some common element between it and animal perception. As for infant perception, he notes that infants at least have the capacity to develop perceptions that are like normal adult human perceptions. Through language acquisition and education, the perceptions of infants are radically transformed in such a way that there is no longer a common denominator between infant perception and normal human adult perception.

To the second objection, McDowell argues that we do have concepts that track the highly determinate nature of our perceptions. These are demonstrative concepts. For example, we can use the concept "that shade of red" to pick out the specific shade of red that the chair has. The "that" in "that shade of red" is what makes the concept demonstrative. It picks out the specific red shade of our perceptions.

McDowell's replies to these objections, however, are rather flat-footed. Why isn't there a common denominator for human and animal perception, especially since human perceptual systems evolved from animal perceptual systems? Also, it is not clear why acquiring language and education should so radically transform perception or even that it does. Finally, even if we can form demonstrative concepts, those demonstrative concepts are not obviously implicated in our perceptions. When we see the red chair, we do not judge that the chair is *that* shade of red. Rather, we judge that the chair is red.

References

Davidson, Donald. "A Coherence Theory of Truth and Knowledge." In *Subjective, Intersubjective, Objective*. Oxford: Oxford UP, 2001.

Descartes, René. *Meditations on First Philosophy*. In *The Philosophical Writings of Decartes*. Vol. 2. Trans. John Cottingham, Robert

Stoothoff, and Dugald Murdoch. Cambridge: Cambridge UP, 1984.

Gupta, Anil. *Empiricism and Experience.* New York: Oxford UP, 2006.

McDowell, John. *Mind and World.* Cambridge: Harvard UP, 1996.

Sellars, Wilfrid. *Empiricism and the Philosophy of Mind.* Cambridge: Harvard UP, 1997.

PUZZLE ELEVEN

Selfhood and Computers

[Daniel Dennett is giving a speech. He tells the audience a story according to which: (i) all of his thoughts have been uploaded to a computer named Hubert; (ii) his brain, called Yorick, has been removed from his body, called Hamlet; (iii) Yorick is kept alive in a vat of gelatinous goo and fed experiences by way of electrodes; (iv) Hamlet has died; but (v) Hubert and Yorick have been made to share a new body— via radio transmitters—called Fortinbras. Hubert and Yorick are supposed to be perfectly synched so that everything Yorick experiences Hubert does and vice versa. There is a switch on Fortinbras such that if Yorick is using Fortinbras and flips the switch, then it will transition to Hubert using Fortinbras. Hubert, too, can flip the switch to transition back to Yorick using Fortinbras. Dennett (whether using Yorick or Hubert we don't know) says:]

"By the way, the two positions on the switch are intentionally unmarked, so I never have the faintest idea whether I am switching from Hubert to Yorick or vice versa. . . .

"In any case, every time I've flipped the switch so far, nothing has happened. So let's give it a try. . . .

"THANK GOD! I THOUGHT YOU'D NEVER FLIP THAT SWITCH! You can't imagine how horrible it's been these last two weeks—but now you know, it's your turn in purgatory. How I've longed for this moment! You see, about two weeks ago . . . our two brains drifted just a bit out of synch. I don't know whether my brain is now Hubert or Yorick, any more than you do, but in any case, the two brains drifted apart, and of course once the process started, it snowballed."

—Daniel C. Dennett (b. 1942), "Where Am I?"

206

The Philosopher

Daniel C. Dennett was born in Boston, Massachusetts. He spent part of his childhood in Lebanon, where his father was a covert counter-intelligence agent for the US government. Unfortunately, his father died in a plane crash. Dennett and his mother returned to Boston. He attended Harvard University and received his doctorate from Oxford. He currently teaches at Tufts University in Massachusetts.

The Puzzle

What is it that makes you *yourself*? Obviously, you are someone, a self. But what about you makes you distinctively yourself?

One very plausible answer to that question is that it is your thoughts that make you the person that you are. It's your beliefs, your desires, your memories, etc. To be sure, it's not all of your thoughts. If that were true, then you would be a different self every time you changed your mind or gained a new memory. But presumably it is some group of your thoughts, some set of them and their relationships to each other, that makes you the self you are.

Suppose that is true. Two recent developments put a wrinkle into such an account. First, advancements in neuroscience suggest that mental states—beliefs, desires, memories, etc.—are nothing more than the functions or operations of our brains. Second, advancements in computer technology suggest computers could perform the same functions or operations as our brains.

These advancements are what motivate our eleventh puzzle, which may be expressed as follows:

(1) Your thoughts—your beliefs, your desires, your memories, etc.—are what make you your*self*.

(2) A computer could be programmed to have the very same beliefs, desires, memories, etc.

(3) So, a computer could be a self just as you are.

Once again, this is a valid argument. If you accept the premises, then you must accept the conclusion: a computer could be a self just as you are a self. But is that correct? After all, if a computer could be just like you, then it would be deserving of the same rights and privileges that you are. It should be able to get married. It should be able to vote. Turning it off would be tantamount to murder. A further complication is this: If a computer could be a self with the same thoughts as you, why shouldn't it *simply be you*? If you're married, why shouldn't your spouse also be married to the computer? Why shouldn't the computer be able to withdraw money from your bank account? Why shouldn't it go to work in place of you? What would be the relevant difference between you and it? After all, we know from cases of multiple-personality disorder that two different personalities can inhabit the same body. Is it any stranger to suggest that one's very self could inhabit two different "bodies," a human one and a computer? It is even conceivable that a brain and a computer could utilize the same body, as in Dennett's story of Hubert and Yorick utilizing the same body, Fortinbras. In that case, the computer might just be an extension of your selfhood.

One comment before proceeding: the current puzzle is different from the question of personal identity. One issue, our puzzle, is whether a computer could be a self just as you are a self. A second issue, the problem of personal identity, is what explains the fact that you are the same person from one moment to the next.

The second question is a question that is not uniquely about selves or persons. One example that is used to get into the issue of personal identity is to imagine that a ship—the ship of Theseus—has had every part and plank replaced over the last fifty years of use. What, then, explains the fact that the ship as it was originally made and the ship as it is now, with all of its parts and planks replaced, is the same ship, if it is at all? The matter is even more complicated if we suppose that all of the removed parts and planks have themselves been reassembled into a ship. Why should that reassembled ship not be the ship of Theseus?

Note, however, that our puzzle is uniquely about selves, not about ships or other kinds of things. Why can't a computer be a self just as you and I are? Perhaps it can be. If so, we should have to grant it all the rights and privileges that we have. Moreover—and here is where our puzzle does have some bearing on the question of personal identity—we might wonder why a computer uploaded with your very same thoughts would not be the very same self you are.

The Premises

Premise (1)

Premise (1) is highly plausible. The English philosopher John Locke (1632–1704 CE) gives us a thought experiment to support it. In fact, his thought experiment is familiar to nearly everyone since it is used in many different movies, books, and television shows.

What Locke asks us to imagine is that a prince and a cobbler (that is, a shoemaker) have their thoughts switched in the middle of the night. Maybe their thoughts switch because of an evil witch's spell. Maybe their thoughts switch because lightning strikes as they each make a wish on a star. Maybe it happens because of a magic amulet. Whatever the cause may be, the basic idea is the same: the cobbler's thoughts—his beliefs, desires, memories, etc.—are now in the body of the prince *and* the prince's thoughts are in the body of the cobbler.

Ask yourself: Which one is the prince *now*? Is the prince the one with the prince's body but the cobbler's thoughts? Or is the prince the one with the cobbler's body but the prince's thoughts?

Most people think the self follows the thoughts, not the body. So, the prince is now the cobbler's body with the prince's thoughts. Sure, the prince now looks different, but he is still the prince. He's just in a different body. What makes the prince the prince is his thoughts, not the way he looks. If you agree, then it surely follows that what makes *you* yourself are your thoughts too.

Premise (2)

A computer could be programmed to have your very same thoughts. Admittedly, given the *current* state of artificial intelligence research, a computer cannot *right now* be programmed to have your very same thoughts. But it's not far off. Consider, after all, how awesome computers already are. We can talk with them, and they respond to us conversationally. We can ask computers questions, and they can correctly answer them. They are able to translate one language into another. They are able to guide us, to help us navigate streets, oceans, and airspace. In 2011, an artificially intelligent computer named Watson competed on *Jeopardy!* and trounced two of the game's best players ever. So, although we cannot right now program a computer to have your very same thoughts, it's not too far off.

Possible Responses

Accept the Conclusion

Let's consider some responses to our current puzzle. Our first option is to accept the conclusion. We can admit that computers can be selves just like us. That's not so hard to accept. We can deny that computers right now are selves just as we are. We don't have to grant today's computers rights and privileges. We don't have to refrain from turning them off. But if a computer were made that were a self just as we are selves—an android like Data from *Star Trek: The Next Generation* or like HAL 9000 from *2001: A Space Odyssey*—we should grant it rights and privileges. Perhaps that means giving it the right to vote. Perhaps it means granting it a trial by jury. Whatever the case may be, we should grant rights and privileges to suitably intelligent creatures, whether they be humans, aliens, or androids. There is nothing peculiar about that.

Second, we can deny the plausibility of the claim that the computer would in fact be us. Even if all of our thoughts, even if all of our beliefs, desires, memories, etc., were uploaded to a computer, our own mental lives and that of the computer's would immediately diverge. We would have different experiences. We would end up having different memories, different beliefs, and different desires. That alone would suffice to distinguish us from the computer.

We might wonder, however, whether this is correct. First, even if the thoughts of you and the computer would immediately diverge, why shouldn't your selfhood have gone with the computer? If at time one you and the computer have the exact same thoughts, why at time two, if you and the computer now have different thoughts, has your selfhood stayed with your body rather than gone with the computer's processor? What determines that your selfhood didn't transfer to the computer just as your thoughts did? Plausibly, it's because your *brain* didn't transfer over to the computer, even though your thoughts did. You have your thoughts because of your brain;

the computer has its thoughts because of its processor. However, that suggests premise (1) is false. It's your brain that makes you the self you are, not your thoughts.

Second, if a computer could be made to be a self just as we are selves, why hasn't one been made? After all, funding has not been lacking. Tons of money and enormous resources have been spent on developing computers that are just like us. Certainly, there have been significant advancements. But is the prospect of creating a computer that is a self like us truly any more promising today than it was in 1960? Plausibly it is not. So, we might wonder if the conclusion really is correct, if a computer really can be made to be a self just like we are selves. Perhaps there is some important difference between computers and us that we have failed to take into account.

Reject Premise (1)

Premise (1) is that your thoughts are what make you yourself. To reject (1), we need to show that your thoughts alone are not what make you yourself. Let's look at three strategies for doing so.

Strategy One: Aristotelian Hylomorphism: Our first strategy for rejecting premise (1) comes about from ideas developed long before computers were even a twinkle in a programmer's eye. Thinking back to our second puzzle, recall that Aristotle (384–322 BCE) endorsed a theory called hylomorphism. According to that theory substances like you and I are composites of form and matter. We are formed (-*morph*) matter (*hylo*-).

A consequence of this view is that the definitions of natural things do not refer to the form alone but to the matter as well. This is a point that Thomas Aquinas (1225–1274 CE) makes. In discussing whether a man is his soul, Thomas points out that this could be taken in two senses. In the first sense, the question might be whether to belong to the human species is just to have a human—that is, a rational—soul. Thomas responds in the negative. It's not enough to be a human that you have a human soul. Your matter also has to be formed in the human way. Consider that we do not regard fictional, rational aliens as humans even though they exhibit humanlike thought.

In the second sense, whether you are your soul might be taken as meaning whether you, a particular individual (not the species), are your soul. Again, Thomas answers in the negative. You are not your soul alone because you also perceive. Consider, for example, that we do not say, "Socrates' body sees" but "Socrates sees." Yet perception depends on the body. For you are able to see only because you have eyes, and eyes are parts of your body. So, if you were your soul alone, then it would not be proper to say that you see. Rather, we would have to say that your body sees.

Thomas, then, rejects premise (1). You are a human. Yet it does not suffice to be a member of the human species that you have a human soul. You also have to have matter formed in the human way. Moreover, individual humans have bodies. Thus, humans are their souls plus their bodies, not their souls alone. Take away your body and it's no longer you. So, your thoughts are not what make you yourself. Rather, your thoughts—that is, your soul—*plus* your body are what make you yourself.

Of course, the success of Thomas' reply depends on whether we accept hylomorphism. In Puzzle Two, I presented two reasons to doubt it. Nonetheless, a number of philosophers still endorse the theory.

Strategy Two: Your Brain Makes You Yourself: A second strategy points to the fact that our thoughts depend on our brains. Because our thoughts depend on our brains, what makes us ourselves is not our thoughts but our brains.

Consider again John Locke's story of the prince and the cobbler. One feature of the story that Locke leaves out is what happens to the brains of the prince and the cobbler. Are they switched too? Or are their thoughts switched by hypnotism, for example? That— what happens to the brains—might matter for how we answer the question of whether or not the cobbler's body with the prince's thoughts really is the prince.

To see why the brain matters, imagine (following a proposal of Sydney Shoemaker [b. 1931 CE]) that an evil scientist has switched the brains of the prince and the cobbler. Once again, we will likely claim that the prince-body-with-cobbler-brain is not the prince *but* the cobbler-body-with-the-prince-brain is.

Now Shoemaker thinks that this shows that the prince follows his thoughts. However, that is far from clear. Bernard Gert (1934–2011 CE) asks us to suppose that instead of receiving the prince's brain in a transplant, the cobbler had only been hypnotized in such a way that he now has all of the same thoughts as the prince. In that case, we would be inclined to claim that the cobbler-body-with-cobbler-brain-hypnotized-to-be-like-the-prince is *not* the prince even though it has the prince's thoughts.

Yet what is the relevant difference between the cobbler-body-with-prince-brain and the cobbler-body-with-cobbler-brain-hypnotized-to-be-like-the-prince? It is not the thoughts. Rather, it is the brain. And so, contrary to Locke's story, the prince's thoughts are not what make the prince the prince. Rather, what makes the prince the prince is his brain. It just so happens that his thoughts depend on his brain.

We might wonder, however, whether this thought experiment succeeds. Its success depends on there being a significant difference between the cobbler's hypnotized brain and the prince's brain. Yet if the cobbler really does have the same thoughts as the prince and is not simply deluded *and* if our thoughts really do depend on our brains, then it would follow that the cobbler's hypnotized brain must have been transformed in such a way that it is identical—operationally or functionally—to the prince's brain. But if that is correct it suggests that what makes the prince the prince is *not* his brain but his brain's operations or functions. Yet, plausibly, our thoughts just are the operations or functions of our brains. So, the thoughts really are what make the prince the prince.

Strategy Three: The No-Self Doctrine: A third way of rejecting premise (1) is to claim that your thoughts are not what make you yourself just because there is no such thing as your self. There is no self. The self is just an illusion. This is sometimes referred to as the No-Self Doctrine.

The No-Self Doctrine does not require us to deny that there are conscious experiences and feelings. There is a stream of consciousness. What the No-Self Doctrine denies is that there is some thing, some self, which remains permanent in the stream of consciousness. There is not a singular thing that is your self. There is not something—a self—underlying and in addition to the stream of consciousness.

The No-Self Doctrine is a key tenet of certain strands of Buddhist thought. David Hume (1711–1776 CE) also doubts that there is a self. Hume argues that all of our abstract ideas—such as selfhood—must be traced back to our impressions, to our actual experiences. However, when we examine our impressions, we do not find a self. All we find is a bundle of ideas and impressions. Recently, Thomas Metzinger (b. 1958 CE) has argued that the self is no more than a theoretical postulate and a dispensable one at that. We are biological organisms—complexes of atoms, molecules, cells, etc., arranged in a particular way. As such a thing we obviously enjoy a stream of conscious experience. However, there is no need to identify something about the complex of cells and atoms and the stream of consciousness that makes you *yourself* anymore than there is a need to identify something about a bunch of atoms formed into a table that makes the table *the table*.

The plausibility of this position hinges on whether there truly is nothing in our actual experience that is the self and on whether the self really plays no important theoretical role. Below, I'll be discussing enactive, externalist accounts of consciousness. Two defenders of such a view—Shaun Gallagher (b. 1948 CE) and Dan Zahavi (b. 1967 CE)—have argued that proprioceptive awareness in infants is a sort of pre-reflective self-awareness. Proprioceptive awareness is the awareness we have of the positioning of our own bodies. I am, for example, proprioceptively aware of the position of my ankles right now as I type this. Infants are also proprioceptively aware. If you touch an infant's chin, it will begin to suckle. This is known as the rooting instinct. However, infants are able to distinguish between being touched by external stimuli and touching their own faces, for when they touch their own faces they are less likely to root. This suggests a sense of self that is present in our impressions—our proprioceptive impressions—and that the self does have some explanatory role to play. In particular, the self explains our awareness of being embodied organisms in an environment.

Reject Premise (2)

A second option for responding to our puzzle is to reject premise (2) that a computer could be programmed to have our very same thoughts. In order to do so, we need to show that a computer cannot be programmed to have our very same thoughts.

Strategy One: The Chinese Room: In order to show that a computer cannot be programmed to have our very same thoughts, we might claim that there is something unique about human consciousness that will always be left out of a computer program. Even if a computer has the same inputs as us and gives us the right outputs, there will be something unique about the experiences we humans have.

John Searle (b. 1932 CE) has argued that what would be missing from a computer program is intentionality. Intentionality is that feature of human thought that is directed to or about the world itself. A computer, Searle argues, would lack intentionality. It is not capable of having mental states directed toward the world. A brain, in contrast, can.

Searle supports his claim with a thought experiment called The Chinese Room. He asks us to imagine that scientists have designed a computer program capable of carrying on a written conversation in Chinese. The computer program is thoroughly convincing. If you were to feed a sentence in Chinese into the computer you would receive an intelligent response and be unable to tell it was a program. You might think that you were conversing with a native Chinese speaker by email, for example.

Next, Searle asks us to imagine that he, a person who knows no Chinese but does know English, has been put into a room. He has been given a set of instructions in English. The instructions tell him how to convert Chinese-symbol inputs into Chinese-symbol outputs. We can imagine that Searle becomes so good at converting Chinese-symbol inputs into Chinese-symbol outputs that he is able to dupe people who feed him inputs into thinking he is fluent in Chinese. However, Searle has no clue what the inputs say. He has no clue what the outputs say. Clearly, Searle does not understand the conversation in the least.

But what is the difference between the computer program and Searle in The Chinese Room? Just like Searle, the computer program merely manipulates symbols according to a set of instructions (the program). It does not understand Chinese any more than Searle does.

Moving to our puzzle, it follows that a computer program cannot be uploaded with our thoughts. It can manipulate symbols. It might be able to provide the exact same responses to questions that we would. But it cannot think as we think. It cannot have mental states about the world. It cannot intend nor represent or think about the world at all. That is unlike our brains, which can.

Strategy Two: Enactivist, Externalist Accounts of Consciousness: The plausibility of premise (2) rests on the claim that consciousness is something that arises in the brain. On this view, the brain is like a super-complicated computer processor. Because the brain, a super-complicated computer processor, gives rise to consciousness, it is only reasonable to suppose an actual computer could be conscious, too.

The claim that the brain is like a computer processor, however, has recently been called into doubt. Among the most notable detractors is Alva Noë (b. 1964 CE). Noë argues that the error in (2) arises from thinking of the brain as something that thinks. He contends that the brain does not think. It is true that the world appears for us, in part, thanks to our brains. Something like a brain is necessary to be conscious. However, the brain itself is not what presents the world to us. Rather, what fills out our thoughts, what gives them content, is our active, bodily engagement with the world. The brain does not think. Rather, *we*, embodied organisms, think. Consciousness is a product of our active bodily engagement with the world. That is the thesis of enactive, externalist accounts of consciousness.

One way to get a handle on Noë's position is by way of vision. When we're in grade school we learn that the images on our retinas are flipped upside down because of the lenses in our eyes. Moreover, many of us have two eyes. So, how is it that we see just one image right side up? After all, it seems as though we should see two images upside down. In answer to that question, we're told that our brains flip and combine the images.

While this may be a helpful explanation for grade-school kids, Noë points out that it is fundamentally wrongheaded. There simply are no images on our retinas for our brains to flip and combine. Moreover, it is not as though we have an additional set of eyes in our heads that see the inverted image. Even if there is, in some sense, an image (or, better, a projection) on our retinas, it makes no sense to say it *appears* upside down. It doesn't appear to be anyway at all. We simply do not see it.

The error of the grade-school account is that it treats visual experiences as arising in the brain. It presupposes that the brain is an additional observer in our heads. But it is not. To be sure, the brain makes possible our experiences. It facilitates them. But it does not follow from the fact we would not have consciousness without brains that consciousness simply is something in the brain. And here we see the relevant difference between computers and us. Computers are not embodied organisms engaged with the world. They are mere tools that we use. They receive inputs and give us outputs, as Searle notes. But a mere symbol manipulator cannot give rise to conscious experiences anymore than our brains can. Consciousness arises from an active bodily engagement with the world, not from symbol manipulation.

One argument against Noë's position is that it is possible we are nothing more than brains in vats and that all of our experiences are fed to us by way of scientists, much as Dennett's story above imagines. However, Noë rejects this view. First, while it is true that we can produce some experiences by activating parts of the brain, it does not follow that we can produce all of them. Second, it is important to this story that there is some scientist manipulating the brain. Hence, our brains are still in some sense engaged with the world. We do not imagine the brain giving rise to conscious experiences all by itself. Third, bodily movements also affect our brains. So, the brain would have to be provided with a body in order for a scientist to simulate our interaction with the environment. But that means consciousness would arise from an active, bodily engagement with the world, just as Noë claims.

Two final comments: First, Noë's position does not prove that (1) is false, that your self is not your thoughts. What it does prove is that if your thoughts are what make you yourself and even if your thoughts depend on your brain, it still does not follow that your brain alone is what makes you yourself. Rather, if you are your thoughts, what makes you yourself is your active, bodily engagement with the world and not just your brain. Hence, strategy two for rejecting premise (1) must be mistaken.

Second, if Noë is correct, then Searle is also correct that a computer cannot have the same thoughts that we do. Where Searle goes wrong, however, is in thinking that our brains are capable of intentionality. Alone, they are not. Rather, our ability to represent the world, to intend it, is a feature of our bodily engagement with the world, not merely a feat of neural activity.

Bonus Puzzle

I noted above that our present puzzle has some bearing on questions of personal identity. Moreover, some of the promising solutions to our present puzzle suggest that you are not your thoughts alone but your thoughts plus your body or that your thoughts themselves arise from your embodiment. On the question of personal identity, Derek Parfit (b. 1942 CE) asks us to consider teletransporters from *Star Trek*. Imagine that a teletransporter works by taking apart your body atom by atom but reconstructing your body out of those very same atoms at a different location. Are you the same person even though your atoms were taken apart and put back together? Why or why not?

Now suppose that instead of reconstructing you out of the very same atoms, the teletransporter works by making an exact replica of you out of different atoms. Are you the same person as the exactly replicated you? Why or why not?

References

Dennett, Daniel. "Where Am I?" In *Brainstorms*. Cambridge: Bradford Books, 1978.

Gallagher, Shaun and Dan Zahavi. *The Phenomenological Mind*. 2nd ed. New York: Routledge, 2012.

Gert, Bernard. "Personal Identity and the Body." *Dialogue*. X(3): 458–78, 1971.

Hume, David. *A Treatise of Human Nature*. Ed. David Fate Norton and Mary J. Norton. New York: Oxford UP, 2001.

Locke, John. *An Essay Concerning Human Understanding*. Ed. Peter H. Nidditch. Oxford: Oxford UP, 1975

Metzinger, Thomas. *Being No One*. Cambridge: MIT Press, 2003.

Noë, Alva. *Out of Our Heads*. New York: Hill and Wang, 2009.

Parfit, Derek. "Divided Minds and the Nature of Persons." In *Mindwaves*. Ed. Colin Blackmore and Susan A Greenwood. Oxford: Blackwell, 1987.

Searle, John. "Minds, Brains and Programs." *Behavioral and Brain Sciences*. 3(3): 417–57, 1980.

Shoemaker, Sydney. *Self-Knowledge and Self-Identity*. Ithaca: Cornell UP, 1963.

Thomas Aquinas. *Summa Theologiae*. Vol. 11. Trans. Timothy Suttor. London: Eyre and Spottiswoode Limited, 1970.

PUZZLE TWELVE

Curry's Paradox

A proof that certain systems of formal logic are inconsistent, in the sense that every formula expressible in them is provable, was published by Kleene and Rosser . . . in 1935. . . . The object of the present paper is to show that, if we use other paradoxes, an inconsistency will result from a very much simpler argument and on much less restrictive hypotheses.

—Haskell B. Curry (1900–1982 CE), "The Inconsistency of Certain Formal Logics"

The Philosopher

Curry's Paradox is named for the American logician and mathematician Haskell B. Curry. Curry was born in Mills, Massachusetts. He lectured at Princeton and studied at the University of Göttingen in Germany. After finishing his dissertation he took a teaching position at Penn State University where he taught for the next 37 years. Curry also worked on ENIAC, the first general-purpose electronic computer. Designed and constructed during World War II, ENIAC's initial purpose was to compute trajectories for projectiles.

The Puzzle and Its Premises

Contrary to prevailing opinion, *Puzzled?!* is the greatest book ever written. In fact, I can prove it is. I'll do it right now.

The Premises (Our Logical Commitments)

For Curry's Paradox, like the Liar Paradox, we need to begin with the premises, which are really a group of extremely plausible logical commitments. Also like the Liar Paradox, this is dense reading. So, take it slow and make sure that every step is clear to you. For Curry's Paradox, we need only three commitments. Here they are:

Modus Ponens (MP): Our first logical commitment is to the validity of modus ponens. By now you should be amply familiar with modus ponens. It states that if you have two premises of the following form:

> If S, then S′.
>
> S.

Then you can infer:

> Therefore, S′.

Again, this is a valid argument form. If you accept the premises, then you must also accept the conclusion.

Conditional Proof (CP): Our second commitment is that conditional proof is a valid argument form. Conditional proof basically works in this way: Make some assumption A. If from assumption A you can prove S, then A implies S (in other words, we can conclude: if A, then S). We already used conditional proof in Puzzle Nine. Although I didn't make a big deal out of it then, Peter van Inwagen's consequence argument takes the form of a conditional proof.

Conditional proof isn't all that complicated. In order to see it in action, we'll do well to consider an argument form called hypothetical syllogism. Hypothetical syllogism is sometimes called chain argument because its basic form is like a chain. Here is the form:

> If S, then S′.
>
> If S′, then S″.
>
> Therefore, if S, then S″.

Hopefully you can see that this argument is like a chain. S′ is the link in the chain holding S and S″ together in the conclusion.

Hypothetical syllogism is obviously valid. What's more, we can prove it's valid using modus ponens and conditional proof. We begin with our premises:

(1) If S, then S'.

(2) If S', then S''.

Next, we make an assumption, (A). That assumption will be the *if* . . . part of the conclusion, S. We'll indent (A) so that it is clear (A) is just an assumption:

(1) If S, then S'.

(2) If S', then S''.

   (A) S.

The question we now want to ask ourselves is: Can we get S'' from (1), (2), and (A)? The answer is that we can by using MP twice:

(1) If S, then S'.

(2) If S', then S''.

   (A) S.   Assumption

   (B) S'.   MP using (1) and (A)

   (C) S''.   MP using (2) and (B)

At this stage, we have shown that *if* we accept (1) and (2) and *assume* S, then we can prove S''. But that is just to show that if we accept (1) and (2), then (3) if S, then S''. In other words, we can now "discharge" or "release" what our assumption entails:

(1) If S, then S'.

(2) If S', then S''.

   (A) S.   Assumption

   (B) S'.   MP using (1) and (A)

   (C) S''.   MP using (2) and (B)

(3) If S, then S''.   Conditional proof

This is a conditional proof because we have proven a conditional sentence (an *if . . . then . . .* sentence) by showing that on the condition you assume S you can logically prove S″.

One cool thing about conditional proof is that you can prove some sentences are true even if you have no premises. For example, it should be pretty clear that the following sentence is true:

> (4) If horses are animals and cats are furry, then horses are animals.

Premise (4) is obviously true because the *if . . .* part already contains the *then . . .* part.

We can use conditional proof to prove that (4) is true. To prove (4) we want to begin with our assumption, the *if . . .* part of (4):

> (D) Horses are animals and cats are furry.
>
> Assumption

Next, "and" statements—conjunctions—are true just in case both conjuncts are true. That means that our assumption is really assuming two different sentences: first, that horses are animals; second, that cats are furry. Therefore, we can *simplify* "and" statements into their constituent claims, as follows:

> (D) Horses are animals and cats are furry.
>
> Assumption
>
> (E) Horses are animals.
>
> Simplification
>
> (F) Cats are furry.
>
> Simplification

Yet here (F) does not really matter. What we had wanted to show is that from our assumption:

> (D) Horses are animals and cats are furry.
>
> Assumption

We could prove:

> (E) Horses are animals.
>
> Simplification

And we did show that, using simplification. Hence, we can discharge (or release) our conclusion (4):

> (D) Horses are animals and cats are furry.
>
> Assumption
>
> (E) Horses are animals.
>
> Simplification
>
> (4) Therefore, if horses are animals and cats are furry, then horses are animals.
>
> Conditional proof

I might note that we could just as easily have proven that if horses are animals and cats are furry, then cats are furry.

Restatement (RES): The last logical commitment we need is a commitment to restatement. Restatement is really two related commitments about how and when we're permitted to restate previous claims. For our first commitment we allow that from the statement that some sentence is true we can just restate the sentence itself. For example, if we have:

> (5) Sentence (4) is true.

We can restate (4) itself:

> (6) If horses are animals and cats are furry, then horses are animals.

Let's call that Restatement$_1$ (RES$_1$).

The second commitment is that if we have *proven* that a sentence is true, then we are permitted to restate the claim by saying that the sentence itself is true. For example, since we have *proven*:

> (4) If horses are animals and cats are furry, then horses are animals.

We can restate (4) as:

> (7) Sentence (4) is true.

Let's call that Restatement$_2$ (RES$_2$).

The Puzzle

And now to the puzzle! My aim is to prove that *Puzzled?!* is the best book ever written. To begin, I'll state this sentence:

> (8) If sentence (8) is true, then *Puzzled?!* is the best book ever written.

Note that in asserting (8) I am not claiming that *Puzzled?!* really is the best book ever written. I am only claiming that *if* (8) is true, then *Puzzled?!* is the best book ever written. Also, notice that we haven't yet shown (8) is true.

But is (8) true? Let's try to use conditional proof to prove (8). To do so, we begin by assuming the "if" part of (8), just as we did to prove (4). Here goes:

> (G) Sentence (8) is true.
>
> Assumption

It's important to stress that we are not here committing ourselves to the truth of (8). We're only making an *assumption* and seeing what logically follows from it.

Now you'll notice that sentence (8) is identical to "If sentence (8) is true, then *Puzzled?!* is the best book ever written." That means we can use Restatement$_1$, as follows:

> (G) Sentence (8) is true.
>
> Assumption

(H) If sentence (8) is true, then *Puzzled?!* is the best book ever written.

RES$_1$ of (G)

Hopefully, you'll also now notice that (G) and (H) have the right sort of form to use MP. That means we can use (G) and (H) as follows:

(G) Sentence (8) is true.

Assumption

(H) If sentence (8) is true, then *Puzzled?!* is the best book ever written.

RES$_1$ of (G)

(I)   *Puzzled?!* is the best book ever written.

MP (G)–(H)

You'll notice that we began with the assumption that sentence (8) is true. From that it follows that *Puzzled?!* is the best book ever written. So, using conditional proof, we can discharge, or release, if (G), then (I). That is:

(G) Sentence (8) is true.

Assumption

(H) If sentence (8) is true, then *Puzzled?!* is the best book ever written.

RES$_1$ of (G)

(I)   *Puzzled?!* is the best book ever written.

MP (G)–(H)

(8)   Therefore, if sentence (8) is true, then *Puzzled?!* is the best book ever written.

CP (G)–(I)

Here, I must stress that we have proven (8) in just the same way we proved the truth of (4) above. That is to say, you have to believe

(8). If sentence (8) is true, then it really does follow that *Puzzled?!* is the best book ever written. The conclusion (8) is perfectly validly deduced, even though we proved it using no premises. We proved it just as we proved (4) without using premises.

This is where things get interesting. Because we now have proven that (8) is in fact true, just like we proved (4) is in fact true, we can use Restatement$_2$, as follows:

> (G) Sentence (8) is true.
>
> Assumption
>
>> (H) If sentence (8) is true, then *Puzzled?!* is the best book ever written.
>>
>> RES$_1$ of (G)
>>
>> (I) *Puzzled?!* is the best book ever written.
>>
>> MP (G)–(H)
>
> (8) If sentence (8) is true, then *Puzzled?!* is the best book ever written. CP (G)–(I)
>
> (9) Sentence (8) is true.
>
> RES$_2$ of (8)

We can do this because we proved sentence (8) in (G)–(8). Hence, we know (8) is true, which is what (9) states.

With all of this in place, the last thing we need to do is to employ MP to prove that *Puzzled?!* is the best book ever written. Here's the whole proof:

> (G) Sentence (8) is true.
>
> Assumption
>
>> (H) If sentence (8) is true, then *Puzzled?!* is the best book ever written.
>>
>> RES$_1$ of (G)
>>
>> (I) *Puzzled?!* is the best book ever written.
>>
>> MP (G)–(H)

(8) If sentence (8) is true, then *Puzzled?!* is the best book ever written.

CP (G)–(I)

(9) Sentence (8) is true.

RES$_2$ of (8)

(10) *Puzzled?!* is the best book ever written.

MP (8)–(9)

There it is: I've proven that *Puzzled?!* is the best book ever written. But that's false! There are better books than *Puzzled?!* (though for the life of me I can't remember any of their titles). Hence, something must be wrong with the above argument.

Possible Responses

I hope it is clear that you could use Curry's Paradox to prove anything: that *Puzzled?!* is the best book ever written; that *Puzzled?!* is the worst book ever written; that cats are aliens from the planet Catatonia plotting to destroy human civilization; that goats that live on sunshine are our only defense against the wicked plans of cats; that God exists; that God does not exist; etc. That's a pretty surprising, and puzzling, result.

What, then, are we to say in response to Curry's Paradox? Unfortunately, philosophers have reached no consensus on the issue whatsoever. Hardly anyone is willing to reject conditional proof. After all, it amounts to a statement of what an *if . . . then . . .* sentence means. Modus ponens is at the very heart of human reasoning. That means our best shot is to reject Restatement. The problem lies in giving a good reason to reject it.

Perhaps, then, the right solution is to claim that there is something wrong with (8) itself, much as some people claim there is something wrong with the liar sentence, as discussed in Puzzle Three. The problem, though, is in identifying *what* is wrong with it. Good luck with that!

References

Curry, Haskell. "The Inconsistency of Certain Formal Logics." *The Journal of Symbolic Logic.* 7(3): 115–17, 1942.

Index of Names